THE HR BOOK

Human resources management for business

THE HR BOOK

Human resources management for business

Lin Grensing-Pophal

Self-Counsel Press
(a division of)
International Self-Counsel Press Ltd.
USA   Canada

Printed in Canada.

First edition: September 1999

Canadian Cataloguing in Publication Data
Grensing-Pophal, Lin, 1959-
   The HR book

   (Self-counsel business series)
   ISBN 1-55180-241-4

   1. Personnel management. 2. Small business—Personnel management. I. Title. II. Series.
HF5549.G73 1999   658.3'03   C99-910551-5

Self-Counsel Press
(a division of)
International Self-Counsel Press Ltd.

1704 N. State Street	1481 Charlotte Road
Bellingham, WA 98225	North Vancouver, BC V7J 1H1
USA	Canada

Contents

Tables

Introduction

In an economic environment where it has become increasingly difficult to assemble a capable, well-functioning work force and even harder to maintain one, businesses are quite cognizant of the value of their investment in human resources. Finding, hiring, motivating, coaching, disciplining, and developing employees has become the number one priority for most businesses.

While establishing a well-functioning staff may not appear straightforward, it is a linear process. From hiring, and through orientation and development, you have the ability to select and nurture employees to closely fit your company's culture and performance requirements. Of course, at any given time you have employees who are at different stages along this linear process — from the yet-to-be-hired unknown candidate to the seasoned, high-performing veteran, and every stage in between. This process is complex, as you must rely upon the skills and intuition of hiring managers — each of whom have their own management challenges and varying positions along the developmental continuum.

Inevitably, though, human resources management is a process — a process that can be effectively and productively managed. *The HR Book* provides both forms and philosophy for effectively managing your investment in human resources. It contains practical information (human resources forms, completed sample forms, useful checklists, tables, and discussion of important legal issues) to help guide you through every stage of the employee development cycle. Anyone who manages people will find this book to be an invaluable and comprehensive resource, whether they manage 1, 100, or 1000 employees.

1

Do You Really Need a New Employee?

There comes a point in every business life cycle when the amount of work seems to surpass the number of hours that existing employees have to do the work. Employees will approach supervisors and say, "I have too much to do." Supervisors will approach management and say, "We have too much to do. We need to hire more people." Management will ponder and, far too often, respond, "Okay. Let's hire some more people."

a. Why Hiring Isn't Always the Answer

The next time an employee or manager comes to you and says, "We're too busy," remember these three words: "Busy is good."

Busy *is* good. Busy means that you are obtaining value from your investment in human resources. When employees are not busy, it means that you are paying for time that is not being fully utilized. Certainly there is a gray area between not being busy enough and legitimately being so busy that the quality of output begins to suffer. Adding additional staff at the proper time is somewhat of a science. It pays, though, to err on the side of caution — for a couple of reasons:

(a) *Human resources are a substantial investment for most companies.* They represent a significant portion of your overhead costs. More overhead means less profit. Small companies sometimes have a tendency to view human capital as a measure of their success. The more employees the company employs, the more successful the company must be, right? Not necessarily. Using growth in employee numbers to represent growth in your business success is a dangerous exercise. Employees add cost. If revenue is not surpassing the added cost of additional employees, your business is not growing. Growth is only measured through profit.

Busy is good. Remember that work tends to expand to fill the time allotted for it. Before adding additional staff, take the time to examine your processes to determine if tasks can be eliminated or made more efficient.

1

(b) *Human resources represent a significant potential liability to your company.* It is no secret that labor laws have become increasingly stringent and that employers frequently feel themselves stymied by restrictions that apply to their hiring, promotion, disciplinary, and dismissal procedures. Make the wrong move and you could pay for it — dearly.

(c) *Unless your need for additional human resources is real, you may find yourself facing an uncomfortable downsizing or layoff situation.* Being overstaffed could mean that you will be in a position where you have to cut costs to maintain the margin you need to survive as a business. Cutting costs frequently means cutting employees. There is no more difficult task for any businessperson than letting valuable people go.

b. Alternatives to Hiring

Let's assume that one of your company's supervisors has come forward with a request for additional staff. Your company takes a reasoned and cautious approach to the addition of new employees, so you decide to explore other alternatives to adding a full-time staff person. What might those alternatives be?

1. Reviewing work processes

First make certain that the work that is being done is critical to the production of your company's end product or service. Frequently, as companies grow, jobs begin to take on a life of their own, with the jobholder determining what needs to be done. That individual's belief may or may not reflect what the business owners believe needs to be done. Continual review of work processes and close contact with supervisors and managers to ensure that employees are using their time most effectively and efficiently to contribute to the goals of the organization are the best ways to maintain a smoothly running operation. (See chapters 9 and 15.)

In addition, whenever a request is made for a new hire, you are presented with an opportunity to critically assess the nature of the position and the work that is being done. Even if there is currently a person in the position and the request is simply for a replacement, it is wise to take the time to evaluate the need for the position as well as the need for each of the individual tasks and assignments that make up the position.

Reviewing work processes is an exercise that should involve employees, supervisors, management — anybody in your organization with an awareness of the position and how it is currently performed, as well as people who have a close understanding of the company's overall business goals and objectives. Some questions to consider during this process:

➤ Does this task need to be done to meet the company's goals and objectives?

➤ Does this task need to be done by this position?

➤ Could the task be more efficiently accomplished in some other part of the company?

➤ Could the task be streamlined through technology or job restructuring?

➤ Is this a long- or a short-term need?

2. Hiring temporary workers

Temporary workers have assumed an important place in the ongoing personnel strategies of many companies, large and small. The cost savings of staffing with temporary employees can be attractive to many businesses, especially in an atmosphere of downsizing, restructuring, and cost cutting. Hiring temporary staff should not be done casually, however. Many companies simply call a temporary agency and say something like, "Send me someone who knows Windows." They may not realize that they have the option of interviewing temporary candidates just as they do when hiring an employee, and they should certainly take advantage of this option to ensure a good fit (see chapter 2).

The human resources department plays a critical role in defining the relationship between the temporary worker and the organization. In addition to selecting the most appropriate candidate, a key to establishing a successful temporary work relationship is setting clear expectations. Too often temporary workers seem to become "part of the woodwork." They work at a company by the temporary agency, yet they feel a close affinity with the company they physically operate from each day. This can lead to frustration both for the temporary worker and for other employees, who wonder, "Why don't we just hire this person full time and provide them with benefits and proper pay?" The perception can be that the company is taking advantage of the temporary worker. It is critical to make clear at the outset exactly what is expected of the temporary employee and what the length of the relationship will be. Having done this, companies must also ensure that they communicate any changes in expectations as time goes by. This is an ongoing activity, not something that can be done once, at the beginning of a relationship, and then ignored.

It is important that companies be able to explain — to managers and employees, as well as to the temporary employee — the basis behind the decision to make the position a temporary one.

One reason you should carefully manage the relationship between your company and any temporary employee is the possibility of *co-employment*. Co-employment occurs when two or more companies (typically your company and a temporary agency) jointly administer responsibilities, salary and benefit

Be as selective when hiring staff from temporary agencies as you are when hiring your own employees.

reviews, counseling, and selection or termination of an assignment employee. If co-employment is found to exist, each company is liable for the employment decisions made by the other. If an assignment employee files a legal complaint and wins, both the agency and the client company could be responsible for any damages awarded.

To avoid problems with co-employment in your temporary employee work arrangements —

➤ report any absences, tardiness, or unacceptable behavior to the agency;

➤ refer all questions relative to pay, benefits, duration of position, or opportunity for employment to the agency;

➤ inform the agency about any changes in an employee's work schedule; and

➤ assist the agency in evaluating employees by completing quarterly or annual surveys.

Do not —

➤ inform any temporary employee that he or she is terminated or suspended — notification must come through the temporary agency;

➤ discuss pay rates, increases, incentives, or bonuses;

➤ discuss opportunities for full-time employment;

➤ extend an offer for employment; or

➤ request that an assignment employee complete timecards/forms with your company's name on them.

3. Working with freelancers

More and more small businesses are relying on freelancers to provide services ranging from copywriting to strategic planning. It makes good sense. You hire the help you need, when you need it, and you are not faced with the burden of paying a full-time salary. One of the best referral sources for freelance assistance is other small businesses. Ask your colleagues who they have used and what results were obtained. Were they horrified, dissatisfied, satisfied, or elated with the results? Were deadlines met? Would they use the same person or company again?

The best freelancers to hire are those who have already worked for other companies in the same business as you. They will already have knowledge they can draw from, and you will save time in briefing them and feel more confident that the finished work product will be acceptable.

Just as when you are hiring temporary employees through an agency, the more precisely you can indicate what you are looking for, the more likely you

More and more people are choosing to work from home. Most communities have a ready supply of freelance talent. Other businesses in your area can be a good source of referrals.

are to get what you want. This seems to make perfect sense, but many employers get lazy at this point and provide sparse instructions.

Know what you want when you make your initial assignment. Put your requirements, payment agreements, and any other important elements of the relationship in writing so that both you and your freelancer have guidelines to follow and are clear about what is expected.

Assign someone in your company to be the person through whom communication can be channeled from the off-site employee to others in your company — and vice versa. This individual will need to keep up-to-date on what projects the employee is working on, what his or her schedule looks like for the future, when he or she will be in the office, etc.

Regardless of how good the person you are working with is, if you are not able to communicate effectively with your freelance help, your projects are destined for disaster. You need to be open, honest, and thorough when explaining a project and reviewing completed work. Here are some tips for working effectively with outside help:

➤ Talk about price up front. Get a written estimate that spells out what is to be done, when it is due, when money will be paid, what circumstances would result in additional charges, and what happens if you are not satisfied with the work.

➤ Provide ample informational material. The more information you can provide, the happier you will be with the completed project.

➤ Be available to answer questions, review work, etc.

➤ Be open to new ideas. Don't interfere. Don't tell your freelancers how to do their job. That is what you are paying them for. But...

➤ Don't be afraid to speak up if they are way off base. Be constructive in your criticism.

Working with temporary employees and freelancers can be a good alternative to hiring permanent staff members. Sometimes, though, these temporary solutions just are not appropriate. When that's the case, you need to begin preparing for hiring.

2
Preparing for Hiring

You have carefully considered your need for additional staff and have determined that you do, indeed, need to hire an employee. This decision is typically made for one of two reasons:

(a) Your ability to produce products or provide services is hindered because you do not have adequate staff to cover production needs.

(b) You have a need for a specific skill that is not present in your existing work force.

When you hire, you need to do it right. Doing it right means doing it in the most cost-effective and time-efficient manner possible. Hiring a new employee may seem like a fairly straightforward endeavor upon first examination, but don't act before carefully preparing.

While there are never any guarantees that the person you hire will work out, there are some steps you can take to attract the best candidates and precautions you can take to improve your chances of making an informed decision.

a. Determining What You Need

Before you start the process of hiring somebody for a new or existing position, you have to know what you are looking for. The more completely you understand the position for which you will be interviewing, the better you will be able to evaluate applications and choose the best ones for consideration.

Job descriptions and specifications are two tools that will greatly help you evaluate potential candidates.

1. Job description

A job description is a written record of the responsibilities of a particular job.

There are many jobs that are similar from one company to another. To get a head start in developing job descriptions, gather examples from other companies, associations, or from the Internet.

7

It indicates the qualifications required for the position and outlines how the job relates to others in the company. In a clear, concise manner, the job description should indicate:

- Position title
- Salary or pay grade
- Department
- To whom the position is accountable (the supervisor/manager)
- Hours required
- A summary of the job
- Major responsibilities or tasks
- Qualifications
- Relation of the position to others in the company

The job description should be organized in such a way that it indicates not only the responsibilities involved, but also the relative importance of these responsibilities. Within the broad categories mentioned above, you will want to include such information as the following examples:

- Extent of authority exercised over the position
- Level of complexity of the duties performed
- Amount of internal and external contact
- Amount of access to confidential information
- Amount of independent judgment required
- Amount of pressure involved in the job
- Type of machinery or equipment used
- Working conditions
- Terms of employment

If the position you are filling is new, preparing the job description will help you clarify what the position entails and its necessary qualifications. If you are filling a position that is being vacated, and if it is possible to do so, ask the departing employee to update the job description. It is common for a job description to become quickly outdated. Sample 1 contains a form you can use to create or update a job description.

A departing employee may also help you review the job description to determine if activities being performed are still critical to the functioning of your company and still add value to the organization. This may also be an opportunity to redistribute workload among other employees.

SAMPLE 1
JOB DESCRIPTION

Position **Marketing Assistant** Department **Marketing**

Accountable to **Marketing Director** Salary/pay grade **$25,000/yr Grade: J**

☑ 35 - 40 hrs/wk ◯ 20 - 35 hrs/wk ◯ less than 20 hrs/wk

Job summary

To assist the marketing director in helping to meet the department's goals of communicating with targeted audiences thorugh the coordination and implementation of various marketing communication activities.

Responsibilities/daily tasks

- General clerical duties including word processing, spreadsheet development, development of slide show presentations
- Responsible for gathering information, tracking and reporting on community relations activities
- Coordination of Speaker's Bureau activities
- In cooperation with department director coordinate the development of print communica tion materials

Qualifications

- Bachelor's degree in communications, journalism, marketing, business or related field.
- Minimum three years experience in communications position.
- Excellent, demonstrated, written and verbal communication skills.
- Excellent, demonstrated, computer skills; proficiency with Microsoft Word, Microsoft Excel and Microsoft Power Point programs

Relation of the position to others in the company

- Reports directly to marketing director
- Will work cooperatively with other members of the marketing department and may be called upon to provide assistance as needed
- Will interact with all departments in the organization in developing and distributing communication materials

2. Job specifications

Job specifications fill the same purpose as specifications for bridges, buildings, and other structures. They indicate the materials needed to get the job done. Job specifications describe the personal qualifications that are required for a job and include any special conditions of employment such as hazardous environmental conditions.

As you review the job description you will want to ask yourself the following questions as a guide to determining the specifications for the position:

➤ What is the purpose of the job?

➤ What day-to-day duties are performed?

➤ What other duties are performed?

➤ How is the position supervised?

➤ What other positions receive supervision from this position?

➤ How much, or how little, control is exercised over this position?

➤ What machines or equipment must be operated?

➤ What types of records need to be kept by this position?

➤ To what extent is this position involved in analysis and planning?

➤ What internal and external contacts are required of this position?

➤ What verbal, numerical, or mechanical aptitudes are required?

➤ You can use the form in Sample 2 as a guide when you are listing job specifications.

b. Determining the Requirements of a Position

When you are determining hiring criteria, you will need to examine experience, education, intelligence, and personality requirements. By establishing these requirements objectively through the use of job analysis, job descriptions, and job specifications, you will eliminate bias that might be caused by personal values and will be able to look objectively at traits tied directly to performance of the job.

As you define selection criteria, you will need to look at the recent job performance of the former employee and isolate two or three characteristics that have had the most impact on his or her successful job performance. Before you begin your search for qualified applicants, consider the following:

➤ *Education.* What level of education is necessary to perform effectively in the position? High school? College? Special training? Will job performance require any type of special certificate or license? Be careful

SAMPLE 2
JOB SPECIFICATION

Job Title: Administrative Assistant   **Date**   3/17

Department or Division: Public Relations

Accountable to: Vice President, Public Relations

Status: Excempt

1. Diploma in secretarial/business field

2. Minimum two years' experience in an advanced secretarial position

3. Excellent typing ability — 80 wpm accurately.

4. Excellent machine transcription skills.

5. Pleasant telephone voice.

6. Ability to handle highly confidential business information.

7. Ability to deal effectively with time pressures, stress and changing demands of job on a regular basis.

here. What you need to do is identify the minimum qualifications required, not what would be nice to have. While you may think it would be great to hire someone with a master's degree to head your bookkeeping staff, requiring a bachelor's degree — perhaps even an associate's degree — might be most appropriate.

➤ *Experience.* How much previous, related experience should a new employee have? Will training be offered on the job? Experience and education requirements are often tied together: i.e., "Bachelor's degree plus a minimum of three years' experience in the field."

➤ *Physical requirements.* What specific physical skills will be necessary? Manual dexterity? The ability to lift ___ pounds?

➤ *Personality requirements.* Is this a position that requires close adherence to tight deadlines? Overtime? Ability to work with a variety of personality types? Ability to negotiate?

Be careful that each requirement you identify is specifically job related. This can help you avoid potential problems later. For example, a job-related requirement for a typing position might be the ability to type at least 60 words per minute. Requiring that the candidate be female or have a master's degree might not be job related.

Don't make these job determinations in a vacuum. Ask other members of the organization for their perspectives. If appropriate, talk to the person who is leaving the position. Ask colleagues at other organizations for their insights and experience.

Once you have taken these steps in identifying and defining specific requirements of the position, you are ready to move on to the next step — recruitment.

c. Where Do You Look for Help?

Whether you are staffing up in anticipation of increased human resources needs, replacing an employee who is leaving, or just thinking about the possibility of future hiring needs, your first question will be, "Where do I find the person I need?"

The job market has become increasingly competitive in recent years, with qualified candidates being in high demand and, consequently, less available. Because of this, many companies are looking to new and more creative ways of staffing.

There are several options available to you — each offering unique advantages and disadvantages and each requiring slightly different approaches.

1. In-house

The most qualified applicant for a position may well be a person you already have on staff. Most companies have procedures established for hiring from within. The reasons for this are many:

➤ The morale of employees improves when they may be considered for internal promotions or new opportunities.

➤ Management can identify those employees who are interested in career advancement.

➤ Management already knows the job history and capability of internal job candidates.

➤ Less time is needed for employee orientation and training.

➤ Turnover is reduced, as employees look for career progression within their company.

➤ The company is able to make better use of its human resources.

There are also disadvantages created by hiring from within.

➤ The number of potential job candidates is limited to qualified personnel in the company.

➤ It limits the introduction of new blood, which sometimes results in internal stagnation.

➤ Internal recruitment produces a "ripple effect" in terms of hiring. As one person leaves a position to take another, a new vacancy is created. This effect continues down to the lowest-level jobs, which must then be filled through other means.

It is important for a company considering an internal job-posting system to establish a formal process for using the system and to communicate that process to all employees. Most commonly, when there is a job opening, all employees are notified of the position and given specific information on the job title, salary, department, supervisor's name and title, responsibilities of the job, qualifications, and skills required. The posting remains displayed in a prominent place for a specified number of days. The supervisor or manager doing the hiring reviews internal applications before going outside the company. Generally, employees are required to notify their current supervisor or manager when applying for an internal position.

Even if you have an internal process for posting available jobs, there may be times when you decide not to follow this process. For instance, a position may have been created especially for a particular employee, or a job can be

Giving your employees opportunities to take on new responsibilities or be promoted into more challenging positions can boost morale and provide incentive for all staff members.

best filled through a predetermined and logical career path. Keep in mind, though, that straying from this process can create ill will, and employees will wonder why you are not following the process that has been communicated.

The most important consideration when using a job-posting system is to be fair and consistent. Morale will be reduced dramatically if employees begin to feel that the system is administered in a biased or inconsistent manner.

2. Recruiting services

"Recruiting services" is a broad term that refers to personnel agencies, executive recruiters, headhunters, and any other agencies that perform the function of finding, screening, and recommending candidates for a position.

There are some obvious advantages to using recruiting services:

➤ You are able to take advantage of the agency's knowledge and contacts for finding qualified job candidates.

➤ You save the time (and expense) of advertising, screening resumes, and conducting preliminary interviews.

➤ You are able to keep the name of your company and the fact that you are hiring confidential until you actually begin the interviews.

➤ You are assured that the people you eventually interview are qualified for the position.

With these important benefits, why don't more people use recruiting services?

➤ Unfamiliarity with the use of recruiting services or fear of the unknown.

➤ Expense — fees can range from 10 to 25 percent of the candidate's starting salary.

➤ Personal experience or knowledge of others' experiences with disreputable agencies.

➤ Feeling that nobody else could know the type of candidate you are looking for as well as you could.

These drawbacks are very real. Disreputable agencies do exist and fees can be high. If you do decide to use a recruiting agency, follow these guidelines to make the experience as positive as possible:

➤ Seek recommendations for these service providers. Don't hesitate to ask the agency itself for references.

➤ Ask what the costs will be. Be sure to ask about possible hidden fees like telephone or travel expenses.

➤ Consider working with more than one agency until you become comfortable with one.

➤ Establish a relationship and build loyalty with a particular recruiter, not necessarily the agency.

➤ Be clear and specific about job requirements and candidate specifications.

➤ Be firm and clear about your expectations of the agency and its services.

3. Newspaper and trade journal ads

Advertising in the newspaper or in trade journals is a common recruiting method for many positions, one that is familiar to most job seekers. Advertising for job candidates follows the same principles as any other type of advertising — you need to identify your target audience, write an ad that will attract its attention, and provide information that will help audience members determine whether they are qualified for, and interested in, the position you have available.

The function of recruitment advertising is to attract qualified applicants. If your ads are not on target, you are going to fail in your initial efforts at recruitment. You need to know specifically what kind of person you are looking for and be thoroughly familiar with the job requirements and specifications before you develop your ad.

You are most likely to get a large response if you run employment ads in your weekend newspaper, but there are some exceptions. The *Wall Street Journal*, for instance, runs a special section on Tuesdays devoted to employment advertising. Other papers may also have special days that you should be aware of. You can bet that the job hunters know about them.

Most employment ads are run in the employment section of the classified ads. However, you might also consider running a display ad in another section of the paper. For instance, if you are looking for a manager or supervisor, you might want to run a display ad in the business section. If you are looking for someone for real estate sales, you might advertise in the real estate section of the paper. Some papers have separate career listings in business sections or other sections of the paper for professional and managerial career opportunities.

Be innovative. And remember, there is no reason why you can't advertise in two or more sections of the same paper, using a combination of approaches.

Another popular means of attracting potential employees is through the use of trade publications that are geared specifically to a certain trade or profession. The one drawback here is that most of these publications are monthly and have long lead times for advertising. You might need to have your ad ready three months in advance before it will even appear in one of these publications.

4. Campus recruiting

On-campus recruiting is provided as a service to students by colleges, universities, and technical schools. Many companies are taking advantage of these opportunities to interview prescreened, qualified individuals.

Campus recruiting is an effective way to fill entry-level positions. To find out more about campus recruiting in your area, call the placement offices of the colleges, universities, and technical schools near you.

5. Job fairs

Job fairs are becoming an increasingly popular source of job candidates. Generally organized by industry, job fairs are like trade shows that provide employers with the opportunity to meet interested job searchers in a particular field. For instance, a community might sponsor a "small manufacturing" job fair where area manufacturers would be present to provide information on their company and their personnel needs. The job fair would be advertised in the community, drawing those individuals interested in the type of position being represented at the fair.

6. Recruitment open houses

While job fairs generally provide a number of employers with the opportunity to meet potential job candidates, holding an open house for your own company provides you with the opportunity to present your job opportunities exclusively to a group of interested job candidates. Recruitment open houses can be a good way to attract a large number of candidates, particularly if you are adding a large number of new positions or are opening a new facility. Advertise your open house through area newspapers and through notices at local universities and technical colleges.

7. Recommendations and referrals

At any company there is a proliferation of recommendations and referrals from existing employees. This is certainly a way of adding applicants to your files and, particularly in today's competitive environment, can be an excellent way to obtain qualified leads.

Many employers view referrals from existing employees as a great source of potential job candidates. Why? They feel that if an employee is willing to go out on a limb to offer the name of someone for employment, that employee is going to have a vested interest in seeing that this person performs well. It is unlikely that an employee will recommend someone who will not be successful on the job.

8. Walk-ins and unsolicited resumes

Walk-in applicants should not be dismissed out of hand. It's not at all unlikely for a qualified person to make the rounds in person rather than submitting an application.

Similarly, you should give due consideration to all resumes received when you are making hiring decisions. Give the same consideration to all applicants regardless of their source.

9. Job hot lines

If you frequently have positions open, it might be a good idea to set up a job hot line where potential applicants can call in to check on job openings. Establishing a hot line is simple and requires a minimal investment in terms of time and money. All you need is a telephone line tied to a recording of available positions. Beyond this you need only advertise the existence of the job hot line and make sure that you keep advertised positions up-to-date.

10. The Internet

The growing popularity of the Internet is changing the way we communicate both inside and outside our organizations. Human resources professionals are beginning to embrace the Internet and its online opportunities to recruit employees from a much broader market, often at lower costs and with quicker turnaround than was possible with more traditional channels.

Employers can post job openings where they will be viewed by a much broader market, at a much lower cost, than ever before. Conversely, they have access to resumes that job seekers have posted online. These changes are exciting, but they require a shift in the traditional thinking about recruitment and require flexibility, creativity, and the willingness to consider new methods of interacting with potential employees.

Review the various services that are available online, keeping in mind that you want to find one that is most advantageous for you. This may not necessarily mean one of the major commercial sites like the *Monster Board*. Smaller, more specialized services may be more appropriate for your needs depending on the type of position you are attempting to fill.

If you're recruiting online you need to have the same familiarity with these services as you would with any technical or professional journal you were advertising in. Who are the users of the site? What are their characteristics? How frequently is the site accessed? How widely do they advertise? Is the profession you are recruiting for well represented?

The use of key words — the search words that online job seekers will enter to pull up your listing — is a critical and often overlooked skill. You need to tie the appropriate key words to your ads. And you need to probe to make sure that your ads are being coded properly. If you have posted ads and wonder why you are not receiving any inquiries, the coding process may be the culprit. Each search engine is different and you need to take the time to learn how each one functions and what sort of patterns there are in putting the key words together. You don't want to code too restrictively or too broadly. Knowledge of how terminology is used in the field you're recruiting from is a must.

A good way to become familiar with the technology is to practice with your own resume or advertisement. This will give you insights into how easy or difficult it is to access the online resumes of qualified candidates — or how easy it is for candidates to find your ad. If you post your resume or ad to a service and it is not pulled up when you enter the key words that you feel are most relevant, something is wrong.

d. Developing Your Recruitment Ad

Your employment ad should cover four areas: the type of person you are looking for, pay, benefits, and where and how to apply. You also need to be aware of equal opportunity requirements (in the United States) or human rights legislation (in Canada).

A common question when developing recruitment ads is whether or not to include your company name in the advertisement. While blind ads (those where the name of the company is not revealed) are commonly used, the consensus is that open ads draw more, and better, candidates for job openings. There are a few reasons for this:

➤ Blind ads rarely draw responses from people who are currently employed.

➤ Many people will not answer blind ads, so your response is dramatically decreased.

➤ Your company misses out on some public relations opportunities when you choose to use a blind ad, particularly if new positions are being created. You will help yourself in the long run by letting people know who you are.

If blind ads are so bad, why are they used so frequently? One reason is that the company is looking outside for employees and does not want its current employees to know. Another (hopefully not one you have to worry about) is that the company does not have a good reputation and potential applicants would be scared off if its name were used.

A common mistake that is made when running recruitment ads is to over-sell the position. You are anxious to find someone to fill a position so you naturally want to make the job sound as attractive as possible. Misrepresenting the position will only create problems — and waste time — later. Candidates may resent finding out at an interview that the job is not quite as attractive as it sounded in the ad. Or after accepting the position they may become disillusioned and leave, putting you right back in the same position again.

To avoid turnover and dissatisfied employees, don't misrepresent the positions you advertise. Share information about the potentially negative aspects of a position as well as the benefits.

Include in the advertisement information about any specific requirements or idiosyncrasies of the position that might create concern. For instance, is evening or weekend work required? Is overtime required? Travel?

The more accurately you can present the job and its requirements, the more appropriate you will find the resumes you receive. Your job of filling the position will be made easier and you will avoid frustrating yourself and the job seekers you'll be dealing with.

1. The four elements of your recruitment ad

(a) The type of person you are looking for

If you are not clear and specific in your ad about the qualifications you expect applicants to have, you are going to be disappointed when resumes start coming in. Clearly stating the qualifications you're looking for minimizes the number of unsuitable resumes and applications and makes choosing interviewees much more manageable. Your ad should indicate:

➤ Specific job skills required

➤ Experience and background required

➤ Educational requirements

➤ Travel or relocation requirements

➤ Whether or not training will be provided

When stating these requirements, be particularly careful to avoid the excessive use of empty adjectives like "dynamic" or "creative." Be precise and realistic. Don't exaggerate the qualifications or responsibilities of the position.

(b) Pay

Whether you actually state the salary for the position is up to you. However, some mention of pay should be made. You might ask applicants to submit salary requirements or simply state "Competitive salary."

By stating the salary, you will decrease the number of responses if your salary is lower than that paid by other competitive businesses, but you won't have to worry about the possibility of losing applicants if the salary is not up to their expectations — and you won't waste everyone's valuable time.

On the other hand, by stating the salary you may not get the opportunity to convince applicants to start at a lower rate of pay than they had expected because of the other benefits your company has to offer.

(c) Benefits

While salary is still a top priority for job seekers, medical and other benefits are becoming increasingly important. Company benefits can attract good candidates. Challenger, Gray & Christmas, an employment consulting firm, reported that in a recent survey of job seekers, 57 percent considered salary their primary concern — compared to about 90 percent a few years ago. Today, 42 percent of those seeking employment are just as interested in good benefits.

(d) Where and how to apply

Be specific here, and be careful that you don't omit the obvious. It is not uncommon to find an employment advertisement that says "Send resume" but neglects to say where.

If you are running an open ad, you will want to include your company's name, address, and phone number (if you are accepting call-ins). If you use a blind ad, you still need to indicate where resumes should be sent. Be specific about what applicants need to do to indicate their interest in the position. Should they send in a resume, phone in, or apply in person? Do you want to give them more than one option? Is there a deadline after which you will no longer accept applications? Spell out the details clearly to limit the chances for misunderstanding. Refer to Checklist 1 as a guide.

2. Equal opportunity requirements (United States) or human rights legislation (Canada)

If you are placing an ad in the United States, you must be careful that your ad does not contain any language that violates Equal Employment Opportunity Commission (EEOC) requirements. You cannot make statements such as "Recent college graduates please apply" or "No applicants over 40, please." You should also include a statement of your status as an equal opportunity employer.

Similarly in Canada, statements that unnecessarily restrict certain people (based on age or sex) are prohibited by federal and provincial human rights legislation that regulates discrimination.

CHECKLIST 1
CREATING RECRUITMENT ADVERTISEMENT

Position: _____ Date to be filled: _____

Job grade: _____ Salary range: _____

_____

1. Job description up to date?

2. Job specification up to date?

3. Use the following sources of applicants?

- ❑ Appliants on file
- ❑ Internal job posting
- ❑ Local newpaper
- ❑ Regional newspapers (list): _____
- ❑ National trade publications (list): _____
- ❑ On-line (list sites): _____
- ❑ Job fair
- ❑ Recruiter

4. Open/blind ad?

5. Ad contains:

- ❑ Specific job skills required
- ❑ Experience and background required
- ❑ Educational requirements
- ❑ Travel or relocation requirements
- ❑ Pay
- ❑ Benefits
- ❑ Where and how to apply
- ❑ EEOC or Human Rights Legislations copy
- ❑ Cut-off date for submission of applications

You should also be aware that Internet recruitment presents some challenges. One major question that continues to be debated is "What is an applicant?" If you receive an unsolicited resume when you have not posted a job, do you need to consider that resume when an appropriate job — or any job — opens up?

In certain cases, your company might be required to demonstrate it practiced fair hiring practices by defining the eligible population for your job search. This means you must determine the proportion of people of a certain sex or ethnic background in the general population and compare that to the number of applications you received from members of that sex or ethnic background. If the proportion of applications is similar to that group's representation in the general population, you can be confident your hiring process didn't inadvertently create barriers for that group. Defining the eligible population in your city is relatively easy. Defining that population online presents some unique challenges. One way to avoid problems if you are using the Internet for recruitment is to use other sources of candidates as well.

To avoid any problems with your recruitment practices, contact the EEOC (in the United States) or the federal and provincial human rights commissions (in Canada) to ensure that you are abiding by the law.

> The easiest way to avoid legal problems in the hiring process is to ensure that all requirements and selection decisions are directly related to legitimate job requirements.

The Law — What You Need to Know

3

Tami is 22 and has spent the past two months actively looking for a full-time job where she can put her recently acquired business degree to use. On two occasions she has been involved in a one-to-one interview with a potential employer who preceded the serious questioning with a request for some background information. For example:

➤ "Are you married?"

➤ "Do you plan to marry?"

➤ "What about children?"

Denise works for her local municipality as a light equipment operator. Recently a heavy equipment operator position was posted. As Denise was signing her name, a supervisor from the department with the job opening came up behind her. Chuckling, he patted her on the back. "What's a little thing like you thinking of a position like this for, honey? We need a big, brawny man to handle this job."

These two situations are fictitious, but this type of activity happens every day to thousands of people across the country. Aren't these actions illegal? You bet. And in your position as human resources manager or small business owner you had better be certain that your hiring practices don't include this type of blatant discriminatory practice — or even less blatant, but equally illegal, discrimination.

Today it may seem that when it comes to hiring and firing, it's the employees who have an edge. Not so. Business owners still have the right — and the responsibility — to hire the best person for the job. When someone doesn't work out, they have the right — and the responsibility — to terminate the relationship. But along the way there are certain rules, regulations, and restrictions that every business owner needs to be aware of.

a. The Best Person for the Job

Chris wanted to hire a new sales associate to sell power tools. He ran an advertisement for a salesman in the local paper, interviewed only male applicants, and when asked why he was discriminating against women, he seemed surprised. "I'm not discriminating against women — what do they know about power tools?"

Chris is not alone in his attitudes. These kinds of misconceptions and biases are prevalent, even in today's supposedly enlightened hiring environment. Unfortunately, some of these attitudes are so ingrained that many employers don't even realize that they are making biased decisions.

Your goal when filling any position is to find the best person for the job. By definition, the best person is the one who most closely meets the qualifications for the position. Qualifications refer to objective characteristics of the job applicant — not personal characteristics (like sex, age, and race).

To avoid falling victim to unintentional bias, you must carefully and consistently do two things:

(a) Specifically identify the knowledge, skills, and abilities needed to do the job.

(b) Measure all candidates objectively against the criteria you have established.

Keeping the goal of hiring the best person foremost in your mind as you select employees can help you avoid legal problems.

Employers tend to get into trouble when they let personal opinions and biases interfere with hiring decisions. "I don't feel comfortable working with women." "Older employees are stubborn and will be difficult to manage." At best, these stereotypes can lead you to overlook a qualified candidate. At worst, they can land you in court.

To avoid trouble, be objective and realistic about the qualifications needed for the job. Some of the questions you should ask yourself are:

➤ What is the primary reason for the job?

➤ What is difficult about the job?

➤ How much supervision is provided?

➤ What types of people must the new employee get along with?

➤ What technical knowledge or experience is required?

As you develop questions, or as you speak with job candidates, be careful that the questions you ask are all related directly to the qualifications required

> A good way to help minimize the potential for bias in employee selection is to involve a group of people in the selection process.

for the position. Even during small talk you should avoid any questions of a personal, non-job-related nature.

What are some examples of questions that are inappropriate (or illegal)? Any question that seeks an answer unrelated to the qualifications required to perform the job. For instance:

(a) *Are you married?* How does marital status affect a candidate's ability to perform? It doesn't. Therefore, any questioning along these lines is inappropriate — and illegal. An employer might argue that "a married employee will be more reliable." If your concern is about whether the employee will be at work regularly, ask about past attendance history. Focus on specific issues that you can relate directly to performance and avoid relying on misconceptions or prejudice.

(b) *Do you plan to have children?* Again, some employers defend questions about children, or plans to have children, by saying that they are concerned the employee may miss a lot of work. A better way to address this concern is to ask, more specifically, "Are there any reasons that you would not be able to meet the work hour requirements of this position?"

(c) *How old are you?* Why does age matter? Your questions should focus on skills, abilities, or experience — age is irrelevant.

Before interviewing any job candidate, ask yourself these questions:

➤ What are the requirements of the job?

➤ What are the requirements of the job?

➤ What are the requirements of the job?

Keep this thought foremost in your mind and you will be in a better position to avoid inappropriate lines of questioning — and potential legal problems.

b. Guidelines in the United States

It is important to remember that it is the *consequence* of employment practices and not the *intent* that determines whether discrimination exists. Any employment practice or policy, regardless of how innocuous in intent, which has a "disparate effect" on members of a "protected class" constitutes unlawful discrimination unless it can be proven that such a policy is required due to "business necessity."

The Supreme Court has ordered the removal of "artificial, arbitrary and unnecessary barriers to employment when the barriers operate invidiously to discriminate on the basis of racial or other impermissible classification." The practices and policies that create barriers may take place in the context of recruitment, selection, placement, testing, transfer, promotion, seniority, lines of progression, and many other of the basic terms and conditions of employment.

The removal of these barriers requires employers to practice affirmative action and provide new policies and practices. It also requires a firm knowledge of the rules and regulations surrounding equal employment opportunity and the affirmative action concept.

In the United States, affirmative action refers to equal opportunity in employment for all people regardless of physical handicap, race, nationality, age, sex, religion, or any other non-job-related means of determining eligibility for a position of employment. It is a term that encompasses various methods through which the concept of equal employment opportunity becomes a reality.

1. Legislation prohibiting discrimination in employment

The affirmative action concept became law in 1964 with the enactment of the Civil Rights Act. Title VII mandates equal employment opportunity by —

(a) prohibiting job discrimination on the basis of race, color, religion, sex, or national origin, and

(b) establishing an Equal Employment Opportunity Commission (EEOC) to administer the law.

The EEOC is a five-member independent executive agency that is authorized to receive and investigate discrimination complaints filed by individuals and EEOC commissioners, and to remedy any discriminatory practices encountered. If mediation and conciliation fail, the EEOC can file suit against private employers on behalf of the charging party. The Justice Department may file suit against public sector employers.

There are three ways in which allegations of discrimination may come to the EEOC:

(a) Individuals may file complaints.

(b) EEOC Commissioners may file on behalf of an individual.

(c) Class action suits may be filed against both the public and the private sectors.

Penalties that may be imposed include the following:

(a) Cease and desist orders to stop all hiring.

(b) Reimbursement of back pay.

(c) Reinstatement of employees who have been terminated due to discrimination.

Specific regulations and case law may vary from state to state and province to province. Become familiar with the requirements in your area and rely on the advice and counsel of qualified legal professionals.

    (d) Institutional change in personnel systems.

    (e) Establishment of quota hiring systems.

    (f) Development of affirmative action plans.

    (g) Elimination of artificial barriers to employment that tend to screen out groups protected by Title VII of the Civil Rights Act of 1964.

For employers, recognizing the possibility of bias in selection is the first step toward correcting the problem. Decision makers should make efforts to quantitatively specify the work-related criteria that will be used in the selection process and then make their judgments based solely on these criteria.

2. Improving recruiting efforts

The EEOC has listed six major guidelines for employers to follow in establishing fair recruitment practices:

    (a) Analyzing current recruitment procedures to eliminate such discriminatory barriers as word-of-mouth or walk-in sources of employees.

    (b) Establishing objective measures to monitor the applicant pool in the recruitment process (e.g., enabling the employer to identify how many candidates were females and/or minorities).

    (c) Training recruiters so that they use only fair objectives and job-related criteria.

    (d) Maintaining files on minority and women applicants not hired for one job who may be contacted in future recruiting, and making full use of women and minorities who are already on the staff as recruiters, sources of information, and interviewers.

    (e) Publicizing vacancies by means of advertising directed toward recruiting as many minorities and women as possible, including the use of the suggested phrase, "Equal Opportunity Employer M/F." (Avoid references to age, sex, race, national origin, and marital status. Minimum qualifications needed to perform the job should be stated.).

    (f) Making full use of community resources, including educational institutions, women's and minorities' organizations, employment services, and public training programs, and placing ads in newspapers that are likely to be read by minority groups.

3. Fine-tuning the selection process

Discrimination in hiring practices does occur — as many discover to their dismay and frustration. The EEOC has found that the selection process itself contains more possibility for discrimination than any other area of hiring practice.

In an effort to deal with these problems, the EEOC has set up guidelines that employers are expected to follow.

(a) Selection procedures must be based on job-related standards. Criteria used to select employees must be demonstrably related to job performance. Only when sex is a "bona fide occupational qualification" can it be used as a determinant in hiring.

(b) If discrimination in hiring is indicated, employers must be able to prove that they have, indeed, used valid hiring standards.

(c) Jobs cannot be classified by sex or any other discriminatory means. Nor can there be separate sex-based lines of progression or seniority lists.

(d) Job opportunities must be advertised without indicating preference, limitation, specification, or discrimination because of sex or any other discriminatory measure unless there is a bona fide occupational qualification (BFOQ).

(e) In regard to preemployment inquiries, all personnel involved in employment decisions are prohibited from asking questions that express a limitation, specification, or discrimination as to sex. An applicant may be asked to indicate his or her sex, provided the question is put in good faith that the information will not be used for discriminatory purposes.

4. Avoiding nonessential inquiries

When interviewing candidates for a position, ask yourself these questions:

➤ Does this question result in the screening out of women and minorities?

➤ Is this question necessary to judge competence in job performance?

➤ Are there other nondiscriminatory ways to obtain this information?

Court decisions and the EEOC have found many common preemployment inquiries to disproportionately reject minorities and females. Some of these questions have been expressly prohibited by the courts. These include questions referring to the following areas.

(a) Race, religion, and national origin

Though employers are not expressly prohibited from recording this information in personnel files for affirmative action purposes, these inquiries are explicitly prohibited in many states. In the event of discrimination charges, information of this nature recorded in the personnel files will be examined carefully.

"Is this question necessary to judge competence in job performance?" Review your interview questions carefully to avoid straying into prohibited areas of questioning.

(b) Education

Requirements for education that are not specifically needed for the job in question may be placed under examination in discrimination suits. Inflated education requirements can result in higher turnover due to overqualified employees and can serve to eliminate women and other minorities from the job force.

(c) Arrest and conviction records

These questions are unlawful as the basis for employment unless the employer can demonstrate a "business necessity."

(d) Sex, marital, and family status

The Supreme Court has ruled that an employer may not have different hiring practices for men and women with preschool children. In addition, any questions related to marital or family status, if asked of female candidates, must also be asked of male candidates. This information is needed for Social Security and tax records, but it can be obtained after employment. Although many personnel officials may argue this point, the best approach is always to remain focused on the specific job-related skills necessary for the particular job.

(e) Physical requirements

Requirements related to such things as height and weight should be obtained when necessary for the performance of a particular job. An employer must be able to show that these requirements are reasonably related to job performance.

(f) Age

The Age Discrimination section in the Employment Act of 1967, amended in 1978, prohibits discrimination against workers between 40 and 70 years of age. Its stated purpose is "to promote the employment of older persons based on their ability rather than their age."

(g) Maintenance of records

Even if you can honestly say that your employment methods are fair and you have never had any problems with grievances, you must still maintain records of your employment practices. This is necessary both to satisfy federal laws and to protect yourself in the event of a future grievance.

Under federal law, all recruitment forms must be retained for at least one year after an employment decision has been made. Under the Age Discrimination Act, employers must retain job applications of successful applicants for at least three years after they are hired.

Job descriptions are another source of important information relative to fair hiring practices. Your job descriptions should be carefully reviewed to ensure that they are up-to-date and that they adequately reflect the requirements of the position being filled. Further, job descriptions can be an important source of information about the physical and mental requirements of a position, providing adequate documentation of job functions. For instance, if the job requires lifting of heavy materials, and the job description clearly states that the "job-holder must be able to lift and carry materials weighing up to 100 pounds," your decision not to hire a candidate confined to a wheelchair would be based on bona fide occupational qualifications.

(h) AIDS in the workplace

AIDS has become an issue that concerns us on both personal and professional levels, affecting the lives of millions of people — regardless of whether they currently suffer from the disease. Much of the fear surrounding AIDS is focused on its transmission. HIV cannot be transmitted through casual contact with HIV carriers. While virtually all researchers agree on this point, there is still a good deal of misconception and fear surrounding AIDS. There is so much fear, in fact, that it has been necessary to develop laws to protect those who suffer from the disease from being discriminated against in employment situations.

The Americans with Disabilities Act (ADA) has established AIDS as a protected disability under federal law. Employers can't legally allow the fact that a worker has AIDS to influence any facet of employment unless the employee cannot perform the "essential functions" of the job with or without "reasonable accommodation."

A number of states and municipalities have adopted AIDS antidiscrimination acts and ordinances. The common theme of these ordinances is that employees who are capable of performing their jobs without endangering themselves or others should be allowed to do so. However, many states and municipalities do allow preemployment inquiries and screenings for AIDS and HIV, primarily when dealing with employment in the areas of health care, personal service, and bond service. For employers dealing with employees in other categories, though, it is best to avoid this line of questioning.

(i) Reasonable accommodation

With AIDS, as with any other handicap, an employer cannot discriminate against an applicant on the basis of that person's disability unless the employer can demonstrate that the handicap would adversely affect the person's ability to perform the job.

The typical statute or ordinance requires that employers not take adverse action against the handicapped employee if "reasonable accommodation" can be made to allow the employee to perform his or her job. Such reasonable

Employers are expected to provide reasonable accommodation for disabled workers. Guidelines are somewhat subjective but generally designed to provide equal opportunity to this protected class of employee.

accommodation may include providing special equipment, modifying work hours, or allowing for work to be done at home.

The employer is not required to create a new job, substantially change the old one or the working conditions, or spend undue sums of money to accommodate the handicapped employee. Obviously these guidelines are extremely subjective as there has been (and will continue to be) a great deal of litigation surrounding this issue. The resultant case law will eventually provide more distinct guidelines for employers dealing with issues of disability in the workplace.

In terms of dealing with questions related to candidate's disabilities, a simple way to determine whether you can ask a question is to focus on issues that directly affect the candidate's ability to perform the job. Whether dealing with physical disability, AIDS, age, sex, or other protected areas, it is always permissible to ask applicants if they have any condition that would prevent them from performing the job. Keep in mind that these questions must be asked of all candidates. Further, these questions should be followed up with inquiries about what type of special accommodations would need to be made should this employee be hired.

Don't ask "Do you have AIDS?" or "Have you tested positive for the HIV antibody?" or "Do you have a disability?" Do ask "Do you have any impairment that would keep you from performing the requirements of this job?"

5. Drug testing

The issue of drug-use testing has reared its head in boardrooms and on loading docks throughout North America. Many states and municipalities have adopted measures restricting or regulating the use of drug testing by employers. In addition, certain other national regulations may apply depending on the industry you are in and the type of business you do. For instance, the Drug-Free Workplace Act, passed in October 1987, requires all government contractors to certify that they will maintain a drug-free environment to be eligible for contracts of $25,000 or more. Executive Order 12564, established in 1986, requires federal agencies to develop antidrug programs that include requirements for testing employees for drug use. The Department of Transportation rules require that employers test an employee for the presence of illicit drugs if the employee's performance may have contributed to an accident. And the Department of Defense rules specify that a contractor must establish a program for testing of employees in "sensitive positions."

Naturally employers want to protect themselves, their clientele, and other employees from the adverse effects of an employee who abuses illicit drugs. Employees are equally concerned about the preservation of their right to privacy, about the possibility of misread or botched tests, and about the effects of drug testing on their current and future earning capacity.

Drug use has been shown to increase industrial accidents, including property damage and personal injury. In addition, drug use can lower productivity and increase absenteeism and tardiness. Drug-use testing programs, on the other hand, can have a negative impact on morale and can have their own adverse effects of productivity.

If you are considering establishing a drug-free workplace program, make sure that you —

➤ are aware of federal, regional, and local requirements applying to drug testing;

➤ consider the possible application of general handicap discrimination laws that may apply to rehabilitated drug users;

➤ consider the issues of employee privacy, test accuracy, and confidentiality and how they may affect claims of abusive discharge; and

➤ consider the subjective impact of such a decision on your work force.

Drug use affects businesses to the tune of billions of dollars each year. Regardless of the existing state of the law, employers must consider the pros and cons of implementing programs to combat these costs. A proactive approach is needed to strike a balance between the needs and rights of employees and the needs of the company.

c. Guidelines in Canada

Every jurisdiction in Canada has legislation designed to ensure equality for its people. These statutes have their origin in the 1948 Universal Declaration of Human Rights (UDHR) of the United Nations. All jurisdictions express opposition to discrimination on the basis of race, nationality, ethnic origin or place of origin, color, religion or creed, marital status, or sex.

The authority to enact laws in Canada is divided between the provincial and the federal governments. The laws enacted by the federal government are contained in the Canada Labour Code and apply mainly to employees of federal Crown corporations and federally regulated areas, including the following:

(a) Works or undertakings in connecting a province with another province or country, such as railways, bus operations, trucking, pipelines, ferries, tunnels, bridges, canals, and telegraph and cable systems.

(b) All extra-provincial shipping and services connected with such shipping (e.g., longshoring and stevedoring).

(c) Air transport, aircraft, and airdromes.

(d) Radio and television broadcasting.

(e) Banks.

(f) Defined operations of specific works that have been declared to be for the general advantage of Canada or of two or more provinces, such as flour, feed and seed cleaning mills, feed warehouses, grain elevators, the British Columbia Telephone Company, and uranium mining and processing.

(g) Most federal Crown corporations (e.g., the Canadian Broadcasting Corporation and the St. Lawrence Seaway Authority).

Between August 1, 1994, and July 31, 1995, many significant changes were made in the different areas of labor legislation in Canada. With respect to labor standards, the most significant changes have been the adoption of a new Employment Standards Act in British Columbia, the proclamation of a new Labour Standards Act in Saskatchewan, and extensive amendments to the Yukon's Employment Standards Act. In addition, the minimum wage rates were increased in British Columbia, Manitoba, Ontario, Quebec, and the Yukon. Because laws and regulations vary by province, it is important to check the regulations that apply in your area. A useful resource available online is the Human Resources Development Canada home page: (http://labour-travail.hrdc-drhc.gc.ca/).

1. Canadian Human Rights Act

The Canadian Human Rights Act regulates discrimination against employees who come under federal jurisdiction. Other employees are covered by the human rights code of their specific province.

The Canadian Human Rights Act prohibits discrimination on the grounds of race, national or ethnic origin, color, religion, age, sex, marital status, family status, disability, and conviction for which a pardon has been granted. The act further states that if a complaint is based on pregnancy or childbirth, the discrimination shall be deemed to be based on the grounds of sex.

However, under the act it is not a discriminatory practice to —

(a) refuse, exclude, specify, or express a preference in relation to employment if based on a bona fide occupational requirement;

(b) refuse or terminate employment because an individual has not reached the minimum age for legal employment by law or under regulations;

(c) terminate an individual's employment because that person has reached normal retirement age for employees in similar positions;

(d) vest or lock in pension contributions if the terms and conditions of a pension fund or plan established by an employer provide for the compulsory vesting or locking in of pension contributions at a fixed or determinable age;

Laws related to employee selection are very similar in the United States and Canada and are clearly designed to help employers focus on bona fide job requirements.

(e) discriminate on a prohibited ground of discrimination in a manner that is proscribed by guidelines issued by the Commission; or

(f) grant a female employee maternity leave.

2. The Canadian Human Rights Commission

The Canadian Human Rights Commission consists of a chief commissioner and a deputy chief commissioner in addition to three to six members who may be either full or part time.

The Commission administers the Canadian Human Rights Act, the conduct of public information programs, the sponsorship of research projects, and the review of regulations and orders issued by parliament to determine whether they are consistent with the principles expressed in the Canadian Human Rights Act.

In addition to the Commission, a human rights tribunal panel has been established whose members are appointed by the Governor General.

3. Complaints

An individual or group of individuals may file a complaint with the Commission if there are reasonable grounds for believing that a person has engaged in or is engaging in a discriminatory practice. The discriminatory act or omission must have occurred —

(a) in Canada, and the aggrieved person must have been lawfully present in Canada or, if absent, must have been entitled to return;

(b) outside Canada, and the person discriminated against must have been a Canadian citizen or a person admitted for permanent residence; or

(c) in Canada, and must have been a discriminatory practice against a class of individuals rather than one person in particular (e.g., discriminatory advertisements, discriminatory employment policies, and hate literature).

After the complaint has been filed, the Commission may request the president of the human rights tribunal panel to appoint a human rights tribunal to look into the complaint. As a result of such an inquiry, a person may be ordered to —

(a) cease the discriminatory practice and take measures to prevent a similar practice from occurring in the future, including the adoption of an affirmative action plan;

(b) make available the rights, opportunities, or privileges that were denied the victim as a result of the discriminatory practice; or

(c) compensate the victim for lost wages and any expenses incurred as a result of the discriminatory practice.

In Canada, as in the United States, the emphasis is on fair and consistent treatment of all potential and current employees. Common sense and fair dealings should prevail in any of your recruitment, interviewing, and selection procedures.

Take steps now to prevent problems from occurring. Make sure that your hiring practices are fair, equitable, and consistent.

4

The Application Form and Resume

The application and the resume go hand in hand. They are two important tools in your recruiting efforts and you should rely on both when conducting your interviews. While the resume provides you with information that the applicant wants you to know, the application provides you with the information that you need to know — in a format that is easy for you and your company to view.

It is important that you have all applicants complete an application form, even if you have already received a resume. Having completed application forms for all job candidates clearly shows that you asked for the same information from all applicants and provides you with documentation of each candidate's background and reference information.

a. Application Forms

Your application form should be designed to provide you with the information you need to evaluate the ability, experience, skills, knowledge, and other job qualifications of people applying for employment with your company. The application form in Sample 3 is a good format for most businesses and can be modified to meet your specific needs. You may also wish to develop and use more than one form — the information you need before hiring a clerk is different from the information you need before hiring a manager. Your application forms should reflect these differences.

1. What to include and why

There are a lot of questions you could ask on your application form. Some of those questions are unnecessary, however, and provide information that you really don't need until after a hiring decision has been made.

Information you should request in your application form includes the following:

Maintaining complete and accurate records of job applicants is an important administrative task. The application form can serve as a consistent means of collecting this information.

SAMPLE 3
APPLICATION FOR EMPLOYMENT

Position applied for _____ Date available _____

_____
Last name   First name(s)

_____
Street address   City   State/Province   Zip/Postal code

_____
Telephone (include area code)   Fax   E-mail

Are you applying for: ○ Full-time   ○ Part-time   ○ Temporary

Hours available: Mon _____ Tue _____ Wed _____ Thur _____ Fri _____ Sat _____ Sun _____

Work experience (Please list most recent first)

1 Position _____ Date of employment _____
  Employer _____ Address _____
Supervisor _____ Telephone _____ E-mail _____
Beginning pay_____ Ending pay _____
Reasons for leaving _____ May we contact this employer? ○ Yes   ○ No
Responsibilities _____
_____

2 Position _____ Date of employment _____
  Employer _____ Address _____
Supervisor _____ Telephone _____ E-mail _____
Beginning pay_____ Ending pay _____
Reasons for leaving _____ May we contact this employer? ○ Yes   ○ No
Responsibilities _____
_____

3 Position _____ Date of employment _____
  Employer _____ Address _____
Supervisor _____ Telephone _____ E-mail _____
Beginning pay_____ Ending pay _____
Reasons for leaving _____ May we contact this employer? ○ Yes   ○ No
Responsibilities _____
_____

List other relevant work experience _____
_____
_____
_____

Sample 3 — Continued

Education/training
List secondary and post-secondary education including course of study, and degree or diploma received (highest level achieved first)

_____
_____
_____
_____

List other relevant training (most recent first)

_____
_____
_____
_____

Other activities
List volunteer work, leadership positions, or other activities that you feel may be relevant to this application

_____
_____
_____

Personal references
Please provide three reference contacts other than family members or people you have previously worked with

Name	Telephone	Occupation
Name	Telephone	Occupation
Name	Telephone	Occupation

Is there anything else you would like to tell us about yourself?

_____
_____
_____
_____
_____

I certify that all information provided in this application is accurate and complete to the best of my knowledge, and I understand that intentionally providing false information could result in refusal of employment or discharge. I also authorize the employers, schools, organizations, or persons named above to provide information regarding my employment, education, character, and qualifications.

_____   _____
Signature   Date

(a) Applicant's name

(b) Address and phone number where applicant can be reached during the day

(c) Position applicant is applying for

(d) Prior work experience

(e) Educational experience

(f) Training, skills, licenses, or certification

(g) Hours available to work

(h) Whether the applicant is seeking full-time, part-time, temporary, or seasonal employment

Let's look at the application form content in more detail.

(a) Contact information

Without information on where to contact prospective applicants, the application is not much use. Provide space for a home phone number, a business phone number, and an address. You may also want to ask for a number where the applicant can be reached during the day or where a message can be left. And in this electronic age it can also be helpful to ask for fax and e-mail information.

(b) Work experience

The applicant's employment history should provide you with a chronological summary of jobs held, starting with the most recent job. For each job, candidates should be asked to indicate the dates of employment, supervisor's name, responsibilities, and reason for leaving. In addition, you will want some indication of whether you may contact the former employer for a reference.

While job candidates can often skillfully hide gaps in employment history on their resumes, your application form should provide a clear indication of positions held and allow you to quickly spot such things as long periods of time between positions, short periods of time spent in a job, etc.

This is information that you want to review carefully and thoroughly, so make sure that you allow ample space for candidates to respond to these questions.

(c) Other relevant work experience

The application form shown here includes space for candidates to provide information on other relevant work experience. This could include such things as volunteer experience, freelance work, or contract positions.

Take the time to carefully examine the resume and application form. A lot can be learned from thorough analysis and careful attention to detail.

(d) Education/training

Your application form should provide you with information on schools the applicant attended and dates of attendance. You may also wish to ask for information on overall standing or grade point average and special achievements.

Include sufficient space on the application form to gather information about job-related skills and knowledge. Depending on the position being filled, you may want to know about typing ability, teaching experience, skill with certain computer programs, or supervisory skills.

(e) Other activities

Provide space on the form for applicants to provide any other information they feel might be pertinent to your hiring decision.

(f) Personal references

Personal references are people the candidate is not related to and has not worked with in the past. These people might be teachers, members of the community, or volunteers.

(g) Agreement clause

The agreement clause indicates that the candidate has provided accurate information and is authorizing you, as the potential employer, to contact all individuals and organizations named within the application form. A statement such as, "I certify that all information provided in this application is accurate and complete to the best of my knowledge and I understand that intentionally providing false information could result in refusal of employment or discharge. I also authorize the employers, schools, organizations, or persons named above to provide information regarding my employment, education, character, and qualifications" would be appropriate for most positions and companies.

Include a line for the applicant's signature and a line for the date that the application form was completed.

2. What not to include

For every question you come up with for your application form, ask yourself the following:

➤ Does this question need to be asked now, or could it be asked after the job is offered?

➤ Does the question refer specifically to a job-related responsibility?

If you answer no, delete the question from the application form.

None of the questions on your application form should touch on an applicant's race, color, religion, national origin, age, sex, marital status, or disability.

It is a good idea to have your application form reviewed by legal counsel before putting it to use to make sure that you have complied with all legal requirements and have avoided any prohibited areas of questioning.

3. Maintaining application files

Many applications get lost in the shuffle, and good applicants may never be retrieved from the personnel files. A walk-in candidate may fill out an application for a position that is not open at that time. The application is filed and two weeks or two months later, when the position opens up, the application isn't retrieved. This oversight has two potential negative outcomes:

➤ A good candidate for the job may be overlooked.

➤ The candidate may later claim that he or she has been a victim of discrimination by not being considered for a job for which he or she was qualified.

All applications that your company has on file are considered to be active unless you establish otherwise. The more applications you have on file, and the more outdated they become, the greater liability you expose yourself to. There are steps you can take, however, to protect yourself:

(a) Accept applications only when you are filling a position and only for that position.

(b) When applications are being accepted, limit the time period during which they will be taken and then close off all applications.

(c) Limit the time period that you will consider an application to be active and clearly indicate to all applicants this time period.

(d) Keep active and inactive applications in separate files.

4. Precautions

We have already seen one way in which applications can incur potential liability for employers. There are others, and you should consider including the following two statements on your application form to provide yourself with some protection:

"This company is an Equal Employment Opportunity Employer and does not discriminate on the basis of race, color, religion, national origin, age, sex, marital status, or handicap."

Directly above the signature line, print, "I understand that this employment application, by itself or together with other company documents or policy statements, does not create a contract of employment. I also understand that I may voluntarily leave or be terminated at any time and for any reason."

5. Reviewing the application form

A quick review of the completed application form can alert you to potential danger signs. You should check to see if the applicant —

(a) has had an erratic job history, with many periods of brief unemployment or job-hopping,

(b) has left major gaps in employment unaccounted for,

(c) has potential salary requirements that your company will be unable to meet,

(d) has changed residence frequently,

(e) has given past experience and educational information that is not related to the requirements of the position applied for,

(f) has given reasons for leaving previous jobs that suggest the employee may have been a problem, or

(g) has a physical disability or health problem that would prevent him or her from performing the duties of the job

b. Resumes

Applicants are relying on the same books, experts, and resume preparation services, so many resumes seem to have similar formats and buzzwords. As resumes start to look more and more alike, your task of screening them becomes increasingly difficult.

Remember also that resumes provide you with a one-sided look at an applicant — the positive side. Resumes, by their very nature, are devised to help the applicant put his or her best face forward.

There is general agreement among interviewers that there is no significant correlation between the quality of a resume and the likelihood that an applicant will prove to be a good employee. You need to do more than simply read the resumes you receive; you need to be able to read between the lines.

1. Key areas of the resume

There are four key areas in the resume, each providing specific information that you need to consider. These areas are career objectives, education, work experience, and personal data.

An erratic job history or gaps in employment can be a warning sign — but remember that people often take time off for various legitimate reasons: family issues, education, etc.

(a) Career objectives

Most applicants include a brief statement at the beginning of their resumes summarizing their career or employment objectives. If the resume has been sent in response to a specific position in your company, the title of that position most often appears under career objectives, unless the applicant is sending in a preprinted resume. In that case, the stated career objective may not be as specific.

This is a good place to begin your perusal of the resume. Has somebody with a stated career objective of "administrative assistant" applied for a position as sales manager? Is the statement vague and open-ended, leading you to believe that the applicant doesn't have a clear goal in mind — for example, a statement such as, "I'm interested in a challenging position with potential for personal growth."

Be cautious of wordy statements that include jargon and "fifty-dollar words." These statements may be intended to impress, but they do not clarify a candidate's goals.

(b) Educational history

The educational history section of the resume will contain information on the level of formal education the applicant has attained and may also include specific courses taken, specialized training programs or professional development workshops attended, and standing or grade point average.

It is interesting to note that the length and detail of the educational history section of the resume varies in inverse proportion to the length and detail of the experience section. When the educational section is long and detailed, the experience section is generally short or nonexistent. Where the experience section is long and detailed, the education section is generally brief.

Recent college graduates are usually the applicants lacking depth in experience. They tend to expand on the educational section and often provide information that is detailed but of little practical use to the interviewer. People who have been in the work force longer, on the other hand, put more emphasis on their work accomplishments.

When reviewing the educational history section of the resume, look for an educational background that clearly meets the requirements of the position. Look for supplemental education, too, especially where it indicates a clear progression and interest in the area of training that corresponds to the job opening.

(c) Work experience

This section of the resume is the one that should hold the most interest for you. Here is where you find specifics on the applicant's qualifications, experience, and career progression.

Education is important, but don't be unduly impressed by prestigious degrees. Make sure the candidate can demonstrate the ability to apply the things he or she has learned.

The most important things to be on guard for are unexplained gaps in employment or frequent job changes that do not indicate progression.

This is an area that lends itself to filler materials. You have to be particularly careful not to fall prey to colorful language and cleverly devised descriptions of job responsibilities that are vague and meaningless.

Look for areas of past performance that are applicable to the position you hope to fill. Does the applicant's experience seem on target or is it above or below the requirements for the job?

(d) Personal data

The personal section of the resume can often be a surprising treasure-trove of information. Participation in civic groups or volunteer activities indicates ambition and other-centeredness. Specific hobbies related to job responsibilities can indicate a particularly strong interest in the line of work being applied for.

It is a good idea to have somebody in your organization in charge of screening all applications that come into the company and cutting or blacking out information that is prohibited by EEOC or Human Rights guidelines. Such things as date of birth, marital status, height, and weight should be deleted from the resume. Photos submitted with resumes should also be removed.

2. What to look for

When reviewing the resumes you receive, you should be looking for more than facts. You should be looking for specific signs or indications of potential achievement, such as the following:

➤ *Profit-mindedness.* Does the applicant highlight areas in which duties or responsibilities in previous positions contributed to or affected the bottom line?

➤ *Stability and career direction.* Frequent job changes don't necessarily portend disaster. If a progression is evident through these job changes it may simply indicate that the applicant is aggressive and career-minded. Conversely, a long stint in one job is not necessarily good. If no progression is evident, this apparent stability may be an indicator of low motivation.

➤ *Use of specific descriptions.* Beware of generalities. The more general an applicant's description is, the more likely he or she is inflating job responsibilities and achievements. Look for specific, quantifiable examples of demonstrated success — both educational and work-related.

➤ *Ambition.* Look for evidence that the candidate is a hard worker, willing to do more than is required. Do the job responsibilities the candidate has listed for a previous position as a file clerk, for example, seem to extend beyond the scope of what is normally required of that type of position? This may be a sign of the candidate's ability to work hard and willingness to accept increased responsibility.

3. Danger signals

As you wade through resumes, also be aware of danger signals. First, be on guard for slick resumes. Don't be taken in by gloss. Look beyond the surface appearance of the resume to the information presented. Beware of lengthy descriptions of education that may hide a lack of experience. All you really need is an indication of skills attained and degrees earned.

Also, watch for gaps in background. Some resumes are prepared in functional rather than chronological form. This format makes it easier to hide or completely leave out gaps in education or experience.

Overuse of general terms such as "knowledge of," "experience with," or "exposure to" is another danger signal. You need to look for indications of hands-on experience.

Finally, if you sense any anger toward previous employers as you read the resume, beware. Chances are that if anger shows through in a resume, it will surface on the job.

c. Narrowing It Down

Now that you find yourself faced with a formidable pile of applicants and resumes, it is time to sift through the responses and identify those that show the most promise — the applicants you will eventually want to interview.

Your decision should be based on objective criteria related to the requirements of the position you are filling. Those requirements can be found directly in the job specifications and can be based on items found in the job description. For example: the job description might include responsibility for developing a newsletter, and the job specifications might state that the employee must have a "bachelor's degree in journalism or a related field"; candidates with this type of experience would have the appropriate skills you are looking for.

As you compare the qualifications of candidates to the criteria you have selected, you may find it helpful to use a selection grid. By making the process as objective as possible, you can avoid some of the bias that often creeps into selection decisions.

Table 1 provides an example of a selection grid. You can insert candidates' names down the left side of the chart; selection criteria can be indicated along the top. Certain criteria might be required — i.e., having a bachelor's degree in a certain field. In this case, you might only check that box on the grid to indicate the candidate qualifies. In other cases — newsletter experience, for example — you might score each criterion on a scale of one to five, with five being the optimal score. You may also wish to include space for comments and observations.

TABLE 1
Evaluating resumes on a selection grid

Candidate	BA/ Journalism	Newsletter experience	Desktop publishing	Budgeting experience	Supervisory experience	Total
Applicant A	X	3	3	1	2	X9
Applicant B		1	3	4	3	11
Applicant C	X	5	3	5	5	X18
Applicant D	X	2	4	3	3	X12
Applicant E		5	5	4	4	18

A selection grid is a good way to objectively compare the qualifications of various candidates. Base the grid on your selection criteria and have more than one person rate each candidate to help strengthen objectivity.

As Table 1 demonstrates, using a selection grid can help you to quickly, and objectively, review the applications you receive for a job. It may also point out areas of concern. For instance, while Applicant E has the same number of "points" as Applicant C, he or she does not have a degree, which is required in the job specifications. You may wish to reconsider whether this is a bona fide occupational qualification; what is it about having a degree that you feel lends additional credibility or reliability to job candidates? Is a degree critical for the functioning of the job? If it is, fine — Applicant E would not be a candidate for the position. But if you are unsure, you may wish to change the requirements to "Bachelor's degree or comparable experience." Requiring a degree for a position where it is not necessarily warranted may be viewed as having a disparate impact on certain segments of the population.

1. Using the selection grid to structure the interview

You can devise a selection grid, containing questions you will ask each applicant, to structure your job interviews. Based on the criteria set out in the job description and job specifications, you should develop questions that will help you determine which applicant most closely meets the requirements of

While you will use a standard set of questions when interviewing each applicant, you may want to add additional questions to help clarify points from the resume or explore unique aspects of the candidate's background.

the position. By determining ahead of time the responses you are looking for, questions can be arranged in the same grid format as shown above; this grid can then be used to rate each candidate's responses and, again, to ensure that your decision is based on objective information that is directly tied to the requirements of the position.

For example, based on the criteria you established for this position, you might develop a series of questions as follows:

➤ Tell me about your experience and role in developing newsletters.

➤ Do you have experience using XYZ design software?

➤ Tell me about your experience working with print production?

➤ What type of positions have you supervised in the past?

Scoring candidates on a one to five scale, your grid might look like the one in Table 2.

TABLE 2
Using the selection grid to structure the interview

Question/ desired response:	Applicant A	Applicant B	Applicant C	Applicant D	Applicant E
Role in developing newsletters. (at least two years' experience in a senior editor position, responsible for content, oversight of design and production)	3	5	4	2	5
XYZ software experience	3	4	5	3	4
Print production experience (at least two years' experience submitting print bids and working directly with printers)	2	4	4	4	4
Supervisory experience (at least three years' experience supervising both staff and freelance positions; experience working with writers and graphic designers)	3	5	4	4	5
Total	11	18	17	13	18

While there is always a certain amount of subjectivity involved in evaluating any job candidate, you can see how using a grid system based directly on job requirements can help you to maintain a focus on objective criteria that are clearly related to the position being filled. In addition, the grid also provides you with a quantifiable way of rating each applicant and making comparisons between applicants.

2. Probing

In addition to the standard questions that you will ask each applicant, there may be specific questions that crop up based on your review of each resume. As you analyze the resumes, jot down questions that arise and areas where you will need to ask applicants for clarification. Here are some examples:

➤ Why are there gaps in your educational (or employment) history? What did you do during these periods?

➤ Why is there a shift in your educational emphasis?

➤ Why is there a shift in your career emphasis?

➤ Why have you changed jobs so frequently?

➤ Why are you making a career change at this time?

➤ Why are your career ambitions so different from your educational achievements?

➤ As you consider your career progression to date, where do you see yourself heading?

3. Guarding against resume falsification

Unfortunately, some people lie on their resumes. As an employer, you need to be aware of this and know how you can protect yourself from being deceived.

One applicant may have attended three years of college but never graduated. He writes on his resume that he received a BA. Another candidate received a BA and always intended to go on for a Master's. She writes that she received an MA. Yet another candidate never received any formal education and considers it a sore spot — a blight in the midst of his otherwise excellent qualifications. He feels his experience has given him the equivalent (or better) of a formal education. His resume indicates not only that he received a BA, but that he graduated in the top 10 percent of his class.

The best way to protect yourself is to check the information given to you. Top universities get several calls a week from employers attempting to verify that applicants have attended their universities.

Applicants who lie are hoping that you, like many prospective employers, will not check their claims. Chapter 7 discusses ways you can check into educational and work backgrounds as well as personal and professional references.

4. How to use the application and resume during the interview

You can, and should, make extensive use of both the application and the resume before the actual interview. But once the interview begins, you should put them aside.

The application and resume are the basis of the interview, but the interview itself should be structured to delve into the gray areas that have not been fully addressed by either of these forms. Most job applicants find it insulting to be asked to reiterate points they have already covered in their resume or on the application form. Moreover, using these props during the interview prevents you from developing the conversational interview approach described in the next two chapters.

5

The Interview

While job interviews are often viewed with trepidation by both the interviewer and the interviewee, no one has yet developed a better way to facilitate the selection of candidates for a position. The purpose of a job interview is threefold:

(a) For the interviewee to describe job-related skills and qualifications.

(b) For the interviewer to provide the applicant with information about the job and the company.

(c) For both interviewee and interviewer to get to know each other and to assess some of the more qualitative aspects of the relationship.

As an interviewer, you want to determine if the applicant is qualified for the job, how well the applicant will fit in with the company, to what extent the applicant will be able to grow in the company, and if it would be a benefit to the company to hire the applicant.

Based on your analysis of the applications and resumes you have received and your comparison of each candidate's skills with regard to the position requirements, you should have developed a good list of people to interview.

While most interviews are done face-to-face, there are situations in which you might conduct interviews — at least initial interviews — over the phone. For instance, if you are hiring individuals who will be taking orders over the phone or serving in some other customer service capacity, an initial telephone interview will give you a good sense of their telephone skills, voice qualities, and phone presence. Also, as telecommuting becomes more prevalent — an option allowing employees to work from a site other than the home office — it is possible that you might be interviewing a candidate who lives in a different geographic area. While you may want to set up a face-to-face meeting at some point, your initial interview may well occur over the telephone.

Regardless of whether you meet in person or conduct the interview by phone, the basics remain the same. Interviewing is a skill — and an art. The

> The interview is the most critical element in making a hiring decision. Careful planning and execution are extremely important.

right selection choice can mean increased productivity and an improved reputation for your department or work group. The wrong choice can be devastating to you, to the candidate, to your department, and to your company. In this chapter we will look at kinds of interviews and questions, while in the next we will explore the skills needed to conduct a successful interview.

a. Types of Interviews

The type of interview you conduct will depend on the job you are interviewing for and on the interviewing procedures your company has established. There are certain standard types of interviews that cover the gamut of how these encounters take place in most companies. They are:

1. The "informal chat"

This type of interview is, unfortunately, what many interviewers end up conducting after they fail to prepare. It is an unplanned, haphazard discussion that progresses with no clear direction and leaves the interviewer still needing additional information to make a hiring choice.

While this type of interview approach is not recommended, there are situations in which a more conversational approach, at least initially, might be warranted. For instance, you might be conducting first interviews for salespeople. The informal chat format would allow you to assess the candidate's conversational style, ability to interact informally, and to think on his or her feet. In a situation like this, the conversational interview might serve as a prelude to a more structured interview.

2. The structured interview

The structured interview is an interview situation where questions are standard and predetermined — designed to help you assess how well each candidate meets the requirements of the position. This type of interview allows you to cover specific areas and identify personal strengths and weaknesses of each candidate. Since each applicant is asked the same series of questions, the structured interview can also help avoid charges of discriminatory hiring or favoritism.

3. The traditional interview

The traditional interview is a combination of the informal chat and the structured interview. In the traditional interview, the interviewer has a definite plan to follow but also allows for deviations from the plan so that important details can be explored further. Discussion is encouraged and respect is shown for each applicant.

While you should attempt to structure the interviews as much as possible and remain focused on a series of questions that you ask each applicant, you also need the flexibility to probe certain areas in more depth depending on the background and characteristics of each applicant. For this reason, a combination of the structured and informal interview is often the best choice.

4. The group interview

Increasingly popular, the group interview affords you the opportunity to get a variety of opinions about a candidate's qualifications. The big advantage, for you, is that you will have a number of perspectives to help you make a hiring decision. There are, however, two important disadvantages that you should consider:

> A group interview will automatically place the candidate under a certain amount of stress.

> When peers are involved, there may be a tendency for them to view applicants as competitors.

However, since hiring decisions are long-term and since the candidate will not be working in a vacuum, it can be helpful to gather opinions from other sources within the company.

b. Stages of the Interview

Each interview proceeds in stages, much like the scenes in a play. Each stage has its own purpose and is intended to accomplish certain goals. An awareness of the purpose of each stage and the goals you are to accomplish makes the entire process much smoother and trouble-free.

1. Opening

There are four objectives you need to accomplish during the opening of the interview. How well you accomplish these objectives will set the stage for how well the interview proceeds.

During the opening of the interview you want to put the applicant at ease, establish the objective of the interview, explain how the interview will proceed, and exchange enough information to allow you both to determine if the interview should continue.

Before you begin the interview, you want to make the applicant feel welcome and comfortable. As in any social situation, you want to exercise the usual amenities: shake hands, take the applicant's coat, offer the applicant a chair and coffee or something to drink, introduce yourself, and begin with some informal discussion.

Group interviews may be stressful for job applicants but offer many advantages to the employer. Involve people who will work with the new employee and whose opinions you value.

You should set the stage for what is to follow to provide both you and the applicant with a frame of reference for the interview. You may say something like "The objective of this interview is to determine how your interests and qualifications fit in with our company's needs."

Again, your purpose is to make the applicant comfortable by making this meeting seem a bit more familiar and a little less frightening. Tell the applicant what you intend to do during the meeting, approximately how long you think it will take, and what your expectations are.

If, for some reason, the candidate is not interested in this particular position or didn't understand exactly what was going to happen, you want to know that now before you both spend time going through the rest of the meeting.

You might say something like "To make sure we're both clear on what we intend to accomplish today, why don't you tell me what you know about ABC Company and what you understand this position entails." In this way you will get a better idea of the applicant's expectations and make sure that the applicant understands the way in which your discussion will proceed.

It is important during this more informal portion of the interview that you do not become so informal that you stray into areas of discussion that could be perceived as inappropriate. For instance, during a casual discussion it might seem perfectly natural to ask about the candidate's family. In an interview setting, however, this would be inappropriate and could suggest that you are attempting to assess non-job-related (and prohibited) areas of a candidate's background.

> The most likely time for employers to stray into prohibited areas is during the opening of the interview. Casual conversations can lead to inadvertent discussion of personal issues not related to the requirements of the job.

2. Data exchange

The data exchange is the core of the interview. This is the stage where you will gather the information you need to make an informed hiring selection. Obviously the way you conduct the data exchange is crucial. You need to ask the appropriate questions, solicit pertinent responses, and constantly evaluate the applicant's verbal and nonverbal expressions. During the data exchange you will gather information on work history, educational background, and professional goals.

In the area of work history there are several areas you may want to explore:

➤ Specific duties and responsibilities in prior positions.

➤ Accomplishments at previous jobs.

➤ Progress in terms of promotions, pay increases, or added responsibilities.

➤ Failures and how they were handled.

- What the applicant liked and disliked about each of the previous jobs held.

- The reasons for leaving each previous position.

When exploring educational background you may want to know:

- What education, beyond high school, the applicant has.

- When and where post-secondary degrees or diplomas (if any) were obtained.

- How successful the applicant was.

- What the applicant's best and worst subjects were.

- What extracurricular activities the applicant was involved in.

An important aspect of any interview is determining what the applicant's personal and professional goals are. You will want to know:

- What the applicant considers to be his or her outstanding achievements.

- What the applicant's long-range career goals are.

3. Closing

After you have solicited all the information you need to make an informed hiring choice, it is time to close the interview. At this time you want to tie up any loose ends, allow for questions from the applicant, and establish a system for follow-up.

The interview can be a stress-filled process for both the applicant and the interviewer. It is quite possible that you may have neglected to obtain some important information. Now is the time to get that information. Review your notes and take a few moments to recap the interview with the applicant to make sure you have covered all the pertinent information and gathered the responses you need to make a decision.

After the applicant has answered all of your questions, and you have had the opportunity to explain what the position involves and provide information about the company, you should solicit questions. Some things that the applicant feels are relevant may not have been covered. The applicant may often be able to provide you with important additional information that you failed to solicit.

Let the applicant know when you expect to make a decision and how he or she will be contacted. Will you be conducting second interviews? Contacting the applicant's references? Be clear about the steps you intend to take to set the applicant at ease about the waiting period that will follow the interview. Be

Interviewing is a skill — and an art. Your confidence and effectiveness will grow as you become more experienced. If you are new to interviewing, prepare carefully and rely on advice and assistance from others if this is possible and practical.

careful, though, not to say anything that could be construed as a job offer or a promise of employment.

c. Setting Up the Interview Framework

It is pure folly to go into an interview with no idea of the direction you want to take. If you have not mapped out a specific questioning strategy and determined the information you will need, you can't possibly expect to ask the right questions.

The kind of information you need to gather will depend on the position you are interviewing for. You should be familiar with the qualifications the position requires of a jobholder. You will also need to know how to solicit the responses that will help you determine if specific candidates have these qualifications.

Outline a plan of action and organize your questions in a logical sequence. If you haphazardly jump from one area of questioning to another, you will not only confuse the applicants, but will likely confuse yourself as well.

Follow a natural progression of data gathering. The most typical progression proceeds from work history to educational background to personal and professional goals. You may decide for various reasons to follow a different progression. The important thing is that the interview proceeds smoothly from one area to another and that the questions you ask are focused specifically on the qualifications for the job.

Don't waste time by asking unnecessary questions. It is not at all uncommon for interviewers to blithely embark on a line of questioning that covers virtually verbatim the information that has already been supplied in the resume or on the application form. While you may legitimately want to explore in more detail some of these points, avoid having the candidate reiterate information that has already been provided.

Carefully worded questions can help generate the maximum amount of information from job candidates. The majority of your questions should be open-ended.

At all times remember that you are in control. While you don't want to rush applicants in and out of your office in assembly line fashion, you also don't want to let them ramble on indefinitely. You don't have to be rude or abrupt to keep the interview on track. You are in the position of control and your applicants will expect you to indicate when they have answered a question to your satisfaction. Don't be too timid to intervene when an applicant strays off on a tangent.

1. Five types of questions

There are five broad categories of questions that you may use during an interview. Each type has specific advantages and disadvantages.

(a) Closed-ended questions

Closed-ended questions elicit yes/no answers or factual responses. An example of a closed-ended question is, "Do you like clerical work?" The job applicant can only respond with a simple yes or no. The interviewer, consequently, does not gain much from the exchange.

An example of a question eliciting a factual response would be, "How long did you work for ABC Company?" Again, since the applicant can only give a short, factual answer, the interviewer does not gain a great deal of information.

Questions that start with the words do, have, is, was, would, did, had, are, were, and could produce a closed-ended response.

The disadvantages of closed-ended questions are obvious. They provide little information and often force polar responses — since the applicant either agrees or disagrees, everything is black and white, and you don't get any shades of gray or variations of response.

Closed-ended questions are not all bad, however. They can allow you to get specific answers, they are easy to tabulate, and they require less effort for the respondent.

It is quite possible that, after asking an applicant a series of questions that require a great deal of thought and lengthy response, you might want to throw in a few closed-ended questions to provide a respite. In general, however, if you want to keep the conversation flowing during the interview, avoid closed-ended questions.

(b) Open-ended questions

An open-ended or broad question is one that expands the range of applicant responses and requires a thoughtful answer. They are good for exploring attitudes, philosophies, and areas in which it is difficult to be specific. Open-ended questions allow you to determine how well the applicant thinks, communicates, and is able to organize and structure responses.

By allowing the applicant to formulate responses in his or her own way, you create a nondefensive atmosphere. You also place the burden of responsibility for carrying the conversation on the applicant by asking questions that encourage free verbalization.

Questions that begin with the words who, what, where, when, why, and how solicit open responses. Open-ended questions might also start with a phrase such as, "Tell me..."

Closed-ended questions can easily be converted to open-ended questions. Here are some examples:

Closed: How long did you work for ABC Company?

Open: Tell me about your employment with ABC Company.

Closed: Have you had any sales experience?

Open: What type of sales experience have you had?

Closed: Do you mind working overtime?

Open: How do you feel about working overtime?

Closed: Are you good at handling stress?

Open: When you're under a lot of stress, what do you do?

When you use open-ended questions, an applicant may ask, "What exactly do you want to know?" Your response should be "I don't have anything specific in mind. Whatever you'd like to tell me would be fine," or "Just tell me anything that you think would be helpful."

Don't be put off by silence. Be patient and resist the impulse to fill the void.

The value of the open-ended question can be ruined if you interrupt the applicant's train of thought. The job applicant should do the majority of the talking during the interview and you should listen carefully, taking notes to help you remember specifics about the interview later. The only exception to the no-interruption rule is if the applicant goes off on a tangent unrelated to the question you asked; then you will want to gently guide the conversation back to the specific area you were exploring.

One disadvantage of open-ended questions is that you may not get the answer you need. This simply requires persistence on your part and you may need to rephrase the question or probe for more detail.

Some examples of probing questions are: "Could you explain what you meant by...?" or "Could you please tell me more about...?" or "How did you feel about that?"

(c) Leading questions

Many interviewers inadvertently give away the answers they are looking for by the way they phrase their questions. For example:

➤ "I'm sure you wouldn't mind working Saturdays, would you?"

➤ "What exactly do you like about working with numbers?" (when the applicant hasn't even indicated that he or she likes working with numbers).

Avoid leading questions. Review your questions in advance to make sure that they do not indicate to your applicants the response you are looking for.

You are not trying to spoon-feed answers; you're trying to solicit information.

(d) Sensitive questions

In every interview you will be asking some questions that an applicant might consider sensitive. Your ability to ask sensitive questions effectively presupposes that you have established a climate of rapport during the interview. Once you have developed an atmosphere of trust and mutual respect, you are ready to move into more delicate areas of questioning.

Suppose one of the applicants has been fired from his or her last job. You will want to know why. But you don't want to simply blurt out "Why were you fired?" You will want to lead into the question carefully in a nonthreatening manner.

You might broach this sensitive subject by beginning with a qualifying statement: "It isn't uncommon for employees to have a few things that they dislike about their managers. What were some of the things you found troubling about your last employer?" Or "I understand that you were released from your last job. I know there are any number of reasons that an employer decides to lay off an employee. Could you tell me what the circumstances were in your case?"

The important factor when asking sensitive questions is to maintain a climate of support and acceptance. What you reveal nonverbally is as important as what you say. Guard your reactions carefully so that you are not projecting an attitude of disapproval or censure.

Here are some additional tips for handling sensitive areas:

➤ Keep questions open-ended.

➤ Speak the applicant's language. For example, if you have a Ph.D., and you are interviewing applicants for a position in which only a high school diploma is required, pay careful attention to the type of language you use so you don't appear "snobbish." On the other hand, don't speak down to the applicant either.

➤ Don't be unnecessarily lofty or obviously condescending.

➤ Don't allow yourself to respond negatively to responses made by the applicant. Maintain a nonjudgmental posture throughout the interview.

➤ After asking a particularly threatening question, follow the question with a few easier questions before going on to another more difficult one.

Don't avoid sensitive areas of questioning. A little discomfort at this stage can help to avoid a lot of discomfort later.

You can soften direct questions by beginning with qualifying statements such as "Is it possible...?" or "How did it happen that...?" or "Why, in your opinion...?"

(e) Hypothetical questions

Hypothetical questions may be the best questions you can ask to get at the specific qualifications of the job you are hiring for. They are also the questions that require the most creativity and forethought to develop effectively.

When asking hypothetical questions, you are not necessarily looking for a specific answer but are trying to understand the process used by the applicant to arrive at an answer. Here is an example:

"A supervisor has been lenient in letting staff members come in after 8:00 a.m., satisfied that the work will be done and that the employees will stay later if necessary. Now this supervisor's manager is applying pressure to get these people to work on time. How would you evaluate this situation? What would you do if you were the supervisor?"

Hypothetical questions draw out a wide range of responses that are behavior-oriented. They are one of the best ways to explore an applicant's judgment and decision-making skills and have been shown to have high predictive value.

Two cautions about hypothetical questions:

➤ Be careful not to lead the applicant with your question.

➤ Be sure the question you ask addresses a specific aspect of the job that you feel will be a good indicator of job performance.

The interview questions contained in Sample 4 give you a good starting point for developing questions of your own. The questions correspond to those on the interview summary form, which is discussed later in this chapter.

2. Common errors when developing questions

Developing effective questions for the selection interview is a crucial aspect of effective hiring. Yet many interviewers are hampered by the following traps.

(a) *Using generic questions for all job openings.* While there are some standard questions that you can build your interview around, you should not simply pull a list of questions from a book and use them, verbatim, for your interview. While these questions can serve as a helpful starting point, each business is different and each position is different. One set of generic questions will not fit every need.

SAMPLE 4
INTERVIEW QUESTIONS

Educational background and work experience

1. In your post-secondary education, what was your main course of study? Why did you choose that field?

2. What skills, relevant to the position applied for, have you gained and developed from your educational experience and/or other training?

3. Describe your duties and responsibilities in each of the three most recent jobs you've held.

4. What were some of your major accomplishments in jobs previously (or currently) held? What were some disappointments and how did you overcome them?

5. How have you benefited from previous employment in terms of your skills and personal development?

6. What are your interests outside of work and why?

7. What accomplishments have you had in activities outside of work and school?

Personal qualities

1. Think about one of the jobs you've had recently that you feel has been significant in your life. What did you like and dislike about this job and why?

2. Why are you applying for this position? Why do you want to work for our company?

3. What are your strengths and weaknesses (list three or four of each)? How are you working to overcome your weaknesses?

4. (*Interviewer: take an opportunity to bring up something particular about your company and its business environment and give the interviewee the opportunity to comment and ask further questions.*)

Subject to discuss:

Interpersonal qualities and communication skills

1. Describe a situation in which you had difficulty with a coworker or supervisor, such as a personality conflict or misunderstanding. How did you handle it?

2. Consider a job in which you had contact with customers or clients and think of a time when a customer or client came to you with a complaint. Describe what happened, how upset the person was, and how you dealt with the situation.

Organizational skills

1. Thinking of a job in which you worked reasonably or completely independently, explain how you organized your workload.

2. Consider this hypothetical situation: If several people depend on you to do certain tasks for them and someone needs you to do something else on top of your regular workload, what would you do? If you've taken on the extra project and it's so time consuming that you know you'll have problems finishing either it or your regular work, how would you handle the situation and why?

3. Describe an instance when you've changed or attempted to change the way a certain task was done. What kinds of changes become more productive? What changes didn't?

Technical/mechanical skills

1. Do you have experience in (*name relevant computer applications*)? How much experience do you have with these applications and in what ways have you worked with them?

2. What experience do you have with other types of office and computer-related equipment? Specify exact machines and models if possible.

3. *Interviewer: Ask about the applicant's experience with equipment specific to your business. Also consider asking if the applicant knows how to handle technical problems, do repairs, or can perform certain jobs manually if necessary.*

List equipment to be discussed:

Closing the interview

Always give the applicant the opportunity to ask questions, request further clarification of job duties, or make additional comments about his or her experience, qualifications, or character. Finish the interview by explaining the next step in the job selection process (e.g., when he or she will hear about your decision, if you will have time to notify each applicant), arrange a time for further contact (a second interview perhaps), and thank the applicant for his or her interest and time.

(b) *Asking all candidates for one position the same questions.* While you should work from a list of questions that is consistent for all job candidates, you will occasionally want to stray beyond the list to explore unique aspects of each candidate's background.

(c) *Asking questions not related to job duties.* One of the best ways to avoid the possibility of legal problems when interviewing is never to ask any question that is not directly related to the performance of the job.

Consequently, if you are interviewing for a Sunday delivery person, it would be appropriate — and necessary — to ask applicants if they would be available to work on Sundays. If you are interviewing for a Monday to Friday, nine to five position, this question would not be appropriate. Be certain that you can directly tie each question you ask to some specific aspect of the position you are interviewing for.

(d) *Asking unnecessarily sensitive questions.* While it is sometimes necessary — even beneficial — to delve into sensitive areas, make sure that you are not doing this unnecessarily. The interviewer is in a position of power and authority. As in any other situation where power is involved, it can be tempting to misuse that power.

Avoid the temptation. You are not interviewing to intimidate the applicants and demonstrate your authority. You are interviewing to determine whether or not each applicant fits the specific requirements of the position being filled. Sensitive questions have their place and often must be asked. Be careful, however, to use them only where appropriate.

(e) *Not probing for depth.* Inexperienced interviewers, especially, fall into this trap. They ask a question and, whether or not the response really gives them the information they need, they move on to the next question.

Don't be too timid to probe for the answers you are looking for. If the responses you get are superficial, you will need to spend some time coaching and prompting the applicant to expand on the responses. But don't give up. This is your one chance to get the information you need.

d. Using the Past to Predict the Future

"What would you do if..." As any good interviewer knows, asking hypothetical questions about how an interviewee would react to a specific situation can

> If a candidate does not answer a question to your satisfaction, don't just move on to the next question. Ask again or probe for additional information.

yield valuable information about future job performance. But there is another technique that can yield even more valid information about future performance — asking a prospective employee about how he or she handled past situations that are likely to crop up in the new job can give you a good idea of what you can expect in the future.

Here is an example: "Have you ever encountered a situation where you had to make a choice between following or going against company procedure, when going against it made more sense to you? Tell me about the situation, how you handled it, and what the outcome was." This kind of specific information can be particularly telling about the future. Learning how to formulate, ask, and evaluate these types of questions can help you become a better interviewer and selector of good job candidates.

1. Formulating the questions

Just as when you are formulating general interview questions, you will want to identify behaviors that will lead to successful job performance and devise questions that let you determine if applicants fit the bill. Consider the people who have held the position in the past. What traits did they have that made them effective or ineffective? What traits would you like to see in the next job-holder?

Suppose you are looking for a housekeeper. From past experience you have determined that certain traits are necessary for success:

➤ The ability to take instruction from a number of different people.

➤ The ability to make decisions quickly and effectively.

➤ The ability to cheerfully perform mundane and/or unpleasant duties.

Here are some questions you might ask that would address each of these points:

➤ "As a housekeeper at XYZ Motel, you will need to take directions from a number of different people. Could you tell me about a situation in the past where you've dealt successfully with multiple supervisors?"

➤ "Could you tell me about a time when you had to make a decision immediately and what the consequences were?"

➤ "Have you ever had to _____? How did you feel about it? How successful were you?"

The questions you ask don't need to focus only on positive events. In fact, it can be useful to know about the times when the candidate has failed and how he or she has handled those failures. For instance, you might ask, "Tell me about a time when you made a decision you regretted. What was the situation and what happened after you made the decision?"

2. Asking the questions

When you ask questions during an interview, you want to gather as much information as possible and probe for meaningful responses. Your skill in questioning the applicants you interview will determine whether or not you gather all the pertinent information.

When you are probing into past experiences, the potential for bumping into areas the applicant feels are sensitive increases. The two problem responses you should be prepared for with this type of questioning are the silent response and the no-response response.

Most interviewees are taken off-guard when they are asked a hypothetical question — especially when it focuses on what they have done or done wrong in the past. When you ask, "Tell me about the biggest mistake you've made on a job and how you dealt with it," you can expect your question to be met with an initial silence. Don't let silence unnerve you. Fifteen seconds can seem like an eternity when you are facing a silent stranger across a quiet room, but wait it out. If the silence seems interminable, you can say, "Take your time. I realize this is a tough question." Let the candidate know that you are willing to wait.

Sometimes a candidate will respond with something like, "I really can't think of anything." Resist the impulse to simply move on to the next question. Don't let them off the hook that easily. If you have asked something like, "Tell me about a time when you made a decision you regret," and they respond, "I can't think of anything," you can be assured that there are instances in their past when they have made these decisions. It can be uncomfortable, but it is important that you persist in getting the best response possible to the questions you pose. After all, you are going to be making a hiring decision and you want to make the best choice possible.

Another variation of the no-response response is the political response. The candidate embarks on a lengthy discussion about something — but that something really has nothing to do with the question you asked. Instead of telling about a regretful decision he or she made, you hear about all the great things he or she accomplished in the last job. Don't just go on to the next question. Probe. You are in the driver's seat and you need to get an appropriate answer to your question.

3. Evaluating the responses

Applicants should be evaluated both in terms of how well they meet the job specifications and how they compare to other applicants. For this reason, it is

Employers have found that the best way to get good information at an interview is to ask candidates to give examples from past experience. These can be challenging lines of inquiry, so give candidates plenty of time to think of an appropriate example.

important to reserve a final decision until all interviews have been completed. Don't make a yes or no decision after each interview. It is better to wait until all interviews are completed and then rate interviewees on the basis of the criteria you have determined are the best predictors of future job performance.

While there are never any guarantees that the person you hire will work out, there are steps you can take to attract the best candidates, as well as precautions that will improve your chances of making an informed decision. By focusing on past instead of future behavior, you will find that the information you gather is more relevant and more predictive than the information you would gain from a more traditional interview.

The interview summary form in Sample 5 corresponds to the sample interview questions presented in Sample 4. Developing a summary form that corresponds to the questions you ask is a good way to evaluate candidate's responses and to ensure that you are viewing each applicant consistently. You, and each person involved in the interview, should fill out an interview summary for each candidate. As discussed in chapter 4, both the interview questions and the summary form can be devised in the same way as you develop a selection grid that is tied to the job description and job specifications.

SAMPLE 5
INTERVIEW SUMMARY

Name of applicant __Jane Smith__ Interviewer __Cris Jones__

Position applied for __Marketing Assistant__ Department __Marketing__

Interview date __7/17__ Hiring deadline __9/1__

Summary of relevant work experience and education

__B.A. Journalism__

__3 yrs. as marketing clerk__

__1 yr. as marketing intern__

Rating the applicant

Rate the applicant on a scale of one to five for the following qualities and skills, one meaning the applicant has little or no ability in this area and five meaning he or she has excellent abilities and qualities. The categories correspond to the grouping of the Interview Questions form so that this form can be done simultaneous to the interview. Evaluation of some qualities (e.g., writing ability) will most likely come from the Application for Employment form, but it's possible, depending on the position applied for and the natural development of the interview, that similar information can be learned through conversation. Add the marks for each category, and transcribe them to the second half of the Applicant Selection Summary.

Personal qualities

Appearance	5	4	3	2	1
Punctuality	5	4	3	2	1
Dependability	5	4	3	2	1
Enthusiasm	5	4	3	2	1
Integrity	5	4	3	2	1
TOTAL	19				

Interpersonal qualities

Confidence	5	4	3	2	1
Assertiveness	5	4	3	2	1
Amiableness	5	4	3	2	1
Flexibility	5	4	3	2	1
Teamwork	5	4	3	2	1
TOTAL	17				

Communication skills

Listening	5	4	3	2	1
Verbal expression	5	4	3	2	1
Writing ability	5	4	3	2	1
Understanding	5	4	3	2	1
Developing ideas	5	4	3	2	1
TOTAL	19				

Organizational skills

Prioritizing tasks	5	4	3	2	1
Time management	5	4	3	2	1
Multi-tasking	5	4	3	2	1
Efficiency	5	4	3	2	1
Accuracy	5	4	3	2	1
TOTAL	18				

Technical/mechanical skills

Office equipment	5	4	3	2	1
Computer literacy	5	4	3	2	1

Computer knowledge (list specific programs and applications)

Microsoft Office	5	4	3	2	1
Quark	5	4	3	2	1
TOTAL	19				

Other skills needed for the position (list)

Newsletter development	5 4 3 2 1
Working w/ print production	5 4 3 2 1
Meeting facilitation	5 4 3 2 1
	5 4 3 2 1
	5 4 3 2 1
	5 4 3 2 1
TOTAL	10

Checklist

- ☑ Permission to check employment and personal references
- ☑ Date available confirmed
- ☑ Meets educational requirements
- ☑ Meets work experience requirements
- ◯ Recommend for follow-up interviews
- ◯ Recommend for hiring

Other Comments

Not strong in several areas

Computer skills high

Interpersonal skills moderate

6

Questioning Skills

Since the body of a job interview involves data exchange, your effectiveness at questioning is extremely important. In a meeting that generally lasts no more than one hour, you are challenged to make a decision that will affect your work force and your organization's productivity. Based on the questions you ask, your interviewing skills, and your ability to accurately evaluate responses in comparison to qualifications, you will make the choice of whether to hire or not hire each candidate.

Questioning may seem like a simple skill. It is not. Interviewers who are able to keep an applicant talking have mastered a fine art. They are the interviewers who manage to dig out the hidden bits of information that can make or break the interview — and the hiring decision. They are also the interviewers who seem, time and again, to choose employees who are both effective and efficient in the positions for which they are hired.

a. Developing Rapport

The approach you take in an interview is determined, to a great degree, by your own personality. Your biggest challenge will be to develop rapport with the applicants you meet. When you develop good rapport with applicants, you establish a climate that allows them to reveal negative as well as positive information about themselves.

The first important consideration in establishing rapport is the setting for the interview. Make sure that you have chosen a place that is quiet, comfortable, and private. You should not be vulnerable to any interruptions during the interview, either from walk-in visitors or phone calls.

When applicants arrive, be prompt. Don't leave them cooling their heels in the reception area unless you are trying to gauge their behavior under pressure. In that case, you may have asked the receptionist to let you know how the applicant responded to a wait of five or ten minutes.

As you greet the applicant, be friendly and make eye contact. Introduce yourself, show the applicant to your office, and offer him or her a seat. Make sure the person is comfortable. If the candidate is not relaxed and at ease, you will not get an accurate portrait of his or her normal behavior.

Before you begin the interview, spend a few minutes in small talk to break the ice. Any topic will do as long as it involves a casual, neutral subject. Keep in mind that you will be most successful in building rapport if you can get the applicant to do most of the talking.

As you conduct the interview, you should take notes. Note-taking does not need to be a stressful experience for the applicant. Keep the notepad on your lap as you jot down key responses to your questions and impressions of the applicant. Be as unobtrusive as possible. If the applicant is discussing a sensitive matter, stop taking notes until after the topic changes. You can catch up later.

As the interviewer, it is your job to guide the interview and keep the applicant at ease. If you sense that the applicant's anxiety level is rising, you may want to change the course of your questioning. As you move into more sensitive areas you can assess how well the applicant is responding and proceed accordingly.

Many of the techniques that are traditionally used in psychological counseling situations can also be applied effectively to the interview setting. These techniques can be either behavioral or verbal.

1. Behavioral encouragement

Attentiveness is an important aspect of your behavior that the applicant will quickly pick up on. When you ask a question, do you listen carefully for the response and give the impression that you are sincerely interested in what is being said, or do you act impatient and preoccupied? Your animation and enthusiasm are important in soliciting responses from the applicants you interview.

Other behavioral cues that will encourage applicants to keep talking are smiles, nods, leaning forward slightly in your chair, and maintaining direct eye contact. Even silence can be an important behavioral cue. Make sure that you are giving applicants adequate time to answer your questions — don't jump in too quickly if there is a silent moment.

2. Verbal encouragement

Praise, encouragement, and supportive comments will help you maintain a continuing flow of information from the applicant. Words such as "I see," "I understand," or "yes," are all good encouragers. Nonwords like "mmm," "ahhh," or "uh huh" are also good.

Your own behavior during the interview will have an impact on the candidate's level of comfort. Be aware of your own behavioral and verbal cues.

In addition, you may want to use clarifying statements. When an applicant responds to a question, you may want to repeat the response and preface it with "You're saying that" or "As I understand it." Neutral phrases such as "Tell me more about it" or "Go on" are also good ways to keep the conversation going.

Remember that the applicant should be doing most of the talking. You are the facilitator. It is your job to elicit as complete a response as possible and to gather as much information as you can about the candidate's background and qualifications.

b. Effective Listening Techniques

Ask any businessperson what the number one problem is in management and you will get the same answer — communication. Poor communication is at the root of every business problem, from low productivity to employee theft. And at the root of most communication problems is poor listening.

When you are interviewing for a position, you can't afford to not listen. That means paying more than "ear service" to the applicants you are interviewing. To improve your listening skills, you need to be aware of some of the problems that can prevent good listening.

1. Hearing only what you expect to hear

After you have conducted a number of interviews you may become familiar with the responses you receive to certain questions. So familiar, in fact, that you may tune out after you ask one of these questions — expecting the typical response. You may fall into the habit of automatically nodding with a knowing smile because you know — or think you know — what is going to be said next. Or you may consciously or unconsciously ignore information that you did not expect to hear.

2. Becoming confused by conflicting information

Sometimes what you hear is not consistent with your preconceptions of the speaker. You may have already formed an opinion about the applicant from the resume or from other information that you have. When you hear a message that conflicts with your previous beliefs, your beliefs will usually override the message. Consequently, you come away with a validation of what are often inaccurate perceptions.

3. Letting biases interfere

We all have biases to some degree. If we like somebody (usually if they are very much like us), we are more likely to listen to what they have to say than if we dislike the person. In fact, even negative information is more readily accepted from those we like and respect.

We all have biases. Awareness of your biases can help you be more objective when interviewing candidates who, for whatever reasons, make you uncomfortable.

Biases also affect the way we view the information we are being given. If education is important to you, how will you perceive a job candidate who barely managed to graduate from high school and readily admits that, "School just isn't my thing"?

4. Emotions

Mood is a major determinant of how well we listen. If we are relaxed, we will absorb more. If we have had a rough day or have a million other things on our minds, we won't pay close attention to what is being said to us.

5. Tips for effective listening

The following are some easy-to-use, yet effective, listening tips:

- ➤ Make a positive, sincere effort to listen.
- ➤ Use feedback. Make sure that what you think you heard is actually the message the interviewee intended you to receive.
- ➤ Comment on nonverbal cues you are picking up, especially if you are getting conflicting messages (there is more on nonverbal cues in section **c**).
- ➤ Physically remove yourself from noise that might impede communication. Make sure that you will be free from any disruptions or distractions.
- ➤ Be a committed listener. Don't allow your mind to wander.
- ➤ Be open-minded. Don't let personal biases interfere with the messages you are being sent.
- ➤ Make notes. This is especially important, as one applicant's qualifications fade into another's.
- ➤ Notice your own reactions. Be other-directed. Pay close attention to the people you interview — both verbally and nonverbally.

c. Observing Nonverbal Cues

In the interviews you conduct it will often be not so much what is said as what is left unsaid that determines your reactions and perceptions. The nonverbal cues you receive are an important means of evaluating the verbal information you are hearing.

1. Facial expression

The face is the most expressive part of the body. It has been estimated that we can make and recognize nearly 250,000 distinct facial expressions. The most common of these are interest, enjoyment, surprise, distress, shame, contempt, anger, and fear.

Eye contact is, perhaps, the single most important mode of nonverbal communication. In a conversation, the amount of time you have eye contact may vary from 25 percent to 100 percent. When we are talking, eye contact is reduced, while it is increased substantially when we are listening. Too much eye contact may become dominating, while too little may show a lack of strength or purpose. For instance, we may say that somebody "looked us squarely in the eye," meaning they were assertive, or we could say that they "wouldn't meet my eye," suggesting evasion.

In addition to eye contact, a furrowed brow, quivering chin, or a telltale blush are all easily recognized and interpreted.

2. Body language

Our bodies have the potential to convey various messages. Language experts agree that there are five basic body areas: center, head, posture, hands, and legs.

The total image is important. Before making judgments, you must focus on the sum of the parts. For instance, a smiling face means nothing if it is accompanied by a cold stare and clenched fists. Conversely, we may shake our fists in jest at somebody with a genuine smile on our face.

3. Interpreting nonverbal cues

To become more effective at reading and interpreting the nonverbal cues around you, consider the following suggestions:

> ➤ It is often difficult to read somebody we don't know well. You need to be aware of a person's average expressions and reactions before you can interpret his or her gestures with any accuracy. Keep this in mind as you attempt to interpret the nonverbal reactions of applicants who, in most cases, you do not know well.

> ➤ Keep in mind that you do not know the context of the interview for the applicant. What happened to the applicant immediately prior to the interview? Because some facial expressions are so close — consider the expressions for fear and surprise, for example — you may make incorrect assumptions unless you are aware of the context.

> ➤ Since emotions are fleeting, you must be able to rapidly pick up expressions. Keep in mind that many facial expressions are blends of two or more feelings.

> ➤ When possible, check your interpretations of nonverbal cues. This can avoid misunderstandings resulting from incorrect conclusions.

Actions speak louder than words. In the interview, be aware of the candidate's nonverbal messages and body language.

d. Ten Common Questions

You have carefully reviewed the applicant's resume and application form. You have thoroughly considered the requirements of the job. You have examined your personal biases and have prepared yourself to listen carefully and be alert to verbal and nonverbal cues.

The applicant is at ease. You are ready to begin. To get the responses necessary to make an informed decision, you need to ask the appropriate questions. The best questions will be those that you have carefully prepared based on the needs of the job. However, certain questions are common and fit most interview situations. Following are ten of the most common questions asked in interviews and the type of responses they are intended to elicit.

1. Tell me a little about yourself

This is the first question many interviewers ask. It starts the conversation going and provides information that can lead to further questioning. The answers given will help you determine not only how appropriate this person is for the position but also what he or she considers important. You don't want to hear "I'm 23 and have three sisters and a brother" or "There's really not much to tell." You would like to hear something about the candidate that is appropriate to the position — education, job-related experience, ambition, goals, what kind of person they are.

2. Why are you interested in this job?

Here you are not looking for information about the applicant's financial circumstances or the fact that he or she wants to live in the area. What you are looking for is the applicant's motivation and interest in the position. The applicant's answer should directly relate to the qualifications for the job. If you are interviewing for a sales position in an insurance office you might be looking for a response like, "My educational background prepared me extensively for sales and I have a great deal of professional experience in this area. I am particularly interested in the insurance field because..."

3. What experience do you have that prepares you for this position?

You don't want the applicant to respond with, "I have enclosed my experience and educational achievements in my resume." What you need is a clear idea of why this applicant would be the best candidate for the position. To answer the question appropriately the applicant should reflect back on past experience and interests that directly relate to the job. Even a recent college graduate with no practical experience can emphasize pertinent qualifications by mentioning special projects worked on while in school, groups he or she was involved in, part-time jobs that are relevant, etc.

4. What are your interests outside of work?

Again, you are looking for a response that is job related and, at the same time, one that doesn't potentially interfere with performance on the job. If you are looking for a secretary, you aren't interested in the fact that the applicant is an expert canoeist. You also wouldn't want to hear that the applicant has a side-line word-processing business that he or she is trying to get off the ground and needs this job to raise capital. You would be interested in knowing that the applicant belongs to a professional secretary's association and enjoys taking courses and reading books on office management.

5. What are your greatest weaknesses?

This is a potentially tricky question for applicants to answer. Everyone has weaknesses, so if your applicant sits and ponders for several minutes and finally says, "I really can't think of anything," you have not received an answer and may need to probe further. The benefit of this question is that it may yield some important information as to how this applicant will fit in with the company and the position requirements. A strength in one job may be a weakness in another. For instance, if you are hiring someone for a manufacturing line position involving repetitive work, a weakness like "I get bored easily" may disqualify the person for getting the job. That same weakness, however, would be a strength in a position that involves a great deal of change on a regular basis. In this case, you would not want to hear, "My greatest weakness is that I have a hard time dealing with change." Remember that many savvy job candidates will anticipate this question and attempt to give you an answer they think fits with the job. This is another important reason why you shouldn't describe the position or the type of person you are looking for until after you have asked all of your questions.

> Most candidates are prepared to respond to the question, "What is your greatest weakness?" A good follow up to this question is, "Give me an example of how this weakness affected you on the job and what you did to overcome it."

6. What do you want to be doing five years from now?

This question helps you get a feel for the candidate's level of motivation and lets you determine how interested he or she is in this particular position. If the applicant's future goals fit within the organizational structure, you will probably determine that he or she is a strong candidate for the position. If, however, the applicant's goals can't possibly be achieved at your organization, you may decide not to hire that particular person. A good response might be: "In five years I would like to be working in a position much like this one, in which I have gained additional skills and expertise in the field, and in which I continue to be challenged. I am interested in the possibility of career advancement."

7. I'm impressed by your qualifications, but don't you feel you're overqualified for this position?

Classifying someone as overqualified is a value judgment at best. But if you have found that you have a hard time keeping people in a particular position because they are always moving up, and you would like to have a stable department, you may not want a candidate who is upwardly mobile. The type of response you would then be looking for is one which indicates that the candidate is sincerely interested in this position — not in the advancement potential that it affords.

8. We usually like to hire someone with more on-the-job experience

Although this is not a question, it is a statement that must be responded to. It is especially appropriate if you are interviewing a lot of people who have just completed their educational training. Some recent graduates will be good job candidates — others will not be. The type of response you are looking for here is one in which candidates stress the advantages of their recent education and their openness to new job situations.

9. Why should we hire you for this position?

This is usually one of the last questions asked. At this point you will want the applicant to reiterate the points made throughout the interview and stress the strongest benefits he or she has to offer. You will also want to look for indications that the candidate is very interested in the position and wants to be considered for the job. You do not want a response like "Because I really need this job." What you would like to hear is "Because I'm sure you'll find me to be a dedicated and motivated employee. I guarantee that I'll do the best job I can for you and that you won't be disappointed in my skills."

10. Do you have any questions for me?

Every interviewee should be allowed the chance to ask you questions. By giving the candidate this opportunity you will not only be able to determine his or her level of interest in the position but also how much he or she already knows about the company. A candidate who simply mumbles "no" and slinks out the door will not be high on your list of possibilities. Neither will one who quickly asks about the chances of moving into another department. There are several positive responses you might receive to this inquiry:

➤ What is your management philosophy?

➤ What do you like best/least in the people you supervise?

➤ What is a typical day at the company like?

- ➤ What kinds of training will be provided?

- ➤ Why did the person who previously held this job leave?

- ➤ Are there opportunities for advancement?

- ➤ What are the people I will be working with like?

- ➤ What are the future plans of the company?

The ideal candidate for any position is one who demonstrates potential ability or who has successfully performed the same job before. People who get the jobs take an active part in the interview. They project knowledge and interest in the company; they show how their skills meet the company's needs. They ask questions about the job, its duties and responsibilities, and opportunities. They are enthusiastic and self-confident without being brash. And they establish a pleasant but not overfamiliar rapport with the interviewer.

More often than not, the job goes to the person best able to convince the interviewer that he or she can handle the job better than anybody else. To determine who this candidate will be, you need to draw on your questioning skills. The above ten questions are simply a starting point. From there you will want to go on to develop some specific questions (especially hypothetical questions) that help you narrow your choice. The more pertinent your questions and the more persistent you are in probing for complete responses, the easier your job of making a choice will be and the more likely you will be to make the right choice.

e. A Grab Bag of Questions

Much of the information you are looking for in interviews is the same whether you are hiring a mechanic or a vice-president. Following is a grab bag of questions that you can ask in virtually any interview situation.

Before reviewing these questions, however, keep one caution in mind. Don't make the mistake of using the same set of questions for every interview. You will want to personalize these standard questions to suit your company's hiring needs and your own personal style. They are presented here as a starting point — a baseline to help you get started.

1. Educational background questions

- ➤ What level of education have you achieved?

- ➤ What was your major course of study? Why did you choose that particular major?

- ➤ What were your favorite/least favorite courses? Why?

A candidate who has no questions to ask you about the position may be signifying a lack of interest. Look for candidates who express their interest and enthusiasm in the position by asking questions about the job, the company, and the culture.

- What extracurricular activities were you involved in?

- How did you spend your summers while in college?

- What training beyond your education do you have that you feel makes you especially qualified for this position?

- What are your future educational plans?

2. Personal trait/characteristic questions

- In general, how would you describe yourself?

- If I were to ask your former coworkers/boss/subordinates to describe you, what would they say?

- What do you consider to be your strengths/weaknesses?

- What are you doing to overcome your weaknesses?

- What type(s) of people upset you? How do you deal with them?

- In what ways do you feel your fellow employees would find you easy to work with?

- What are your long-range goals? What do you plan to be doing in three, five, ten years?

- If you could do it all over again, what changes would you make in your life and career?

- How do you like to spend your leisure time?

- How many days of work have you missed in the past year?

- What do you consider to be a legitimate reason for missing work?

- What are your salary expectations? How have you arrived at this figure?

3. Prior job questions

- How did you originally get your job with X Company?

- What were your responsibilities and duties at the time you left the company (or currently, if the candidate is still employed)?

- Tell me about your supervisor. What did you like/dislike about the way you were managed?

- What duties did you particularly enjoy/not enjoy? Why?

- Tell me about some of your major accomplishments.

- ➤ Tell me about some of your major disappointments.

- ➤ How did your job change since you were first hired?

- ➤ How have you benefited from your term of employment with this company?

- ➤ How has this job prepared you for greater responsibilities?

- ➤ Why have you decided to seek employment elsewhere?

- ➤ How long have you been looking for another position? What type of position are you seeking?

4. Motives for applying for this job

- ➤ What first interested you in this job?

- ➤ What qualifications do you have that make you particularly suited to this position?

- ➤ What would be some of the advantages to your joining our company?

- ➤ What are your expectations of this position?

- ➤ What do you feel would be the most challenging aspects of this position for you?

- ➤ If you were offered this position, what would you do first as the job holder?

- ➤ If you were offered this job, in what way do you feel you could best contribute? Why?

- ➤ If you were offered this job, in what areas do you feel you would need further development?

f. Conducting Legal Interviews

The interview is one of the first places to avoid potential problems. As an interviewer, you are attempting to determine:

(a) If applicants are qualified for the job.

(b) How well the applicants will fit in with the company.

(c) To what extent the applicants will be able to grow in the company.

(d) If it would be of benefit to the company to hire the applicant.

During the job interview, questions should be limited to those that pertain directly to the position being filled. You should only ask for information you need in order to make an informed hiring choice.

In most situations, a candidate's age, sex, or race have no bearing on the ability to do a job.

Affirmative Action and Equal Employment Opportunity Commission (EEOC) guidelines in the United States and the Canadian Human Rights Act specifically prohibit certain questions (see chapter 3). Generally, you cannot ask:

➤ Any questions relating to national origin.

➤ Any questions relating to religion (i.e., name of church, minister, or rabbi).

➤ Questions regarding what religious holidays the candidate observes.

➤ Questions about marital or parental status.

➤ Questions about child care arrangements.

➤ For information on where the applicant banks or the status of outstanding loans.

➤ If the applicant rents or owns his or her place of residence.

➤ Whether the applicant has ever served in the armed services for another country.

➤ If the applicant was ever arrested.

While some of this information may be necessary for personnel records, it can be obtained after the person has been hired and should have no bearing on the decision to hire.

There are several areas of pre-employment inquiries that may cause problems from a legal standpoint. Table 3 presents a brief overview of some of the most commonly prohibited areas of questioning:

TABLE 3
Some prohibited areas of questioning

Subject	Legal	Illegal
Race		You may not ask any question referring to race or color.
Religion or creed		You cannot ask any questions about religious denomination or observance of religious holidays.
National origin		You cannot ask any question on lineage or nationality or any question seeking information on the applicant's parents or spouse.
Sex		You cannot ask for any indication of an applicant's sex.

Table 3 — Continued

Subject	Legal	Illegal
Marital status		You cannot ask whether the applicant is married, divorced, or separated or for any information on his or her spouse or children.
Family planning		You cannot ask about any plans for family — present or future.
Age		You cannot ask the applicant for his or her age or birthdate. This is information that you would need after the employee is hired, but it should be obtained at that time — not before.
Arrest	You can ask if an applicant has ever been convicted of a crime.	You cannot ask if an applicant has ever been arrested.
Birthplace		You cannot ask for any information on the applicant's birthplace or the birthplace of the applicant's parents or spouse.
Disability	You can ask about any impairment that would negatively affect an applicant's ability to perform the duties of the position.	You cannot ask, "Have you ever been treated for...?" or "Do you have any disabilities?"
Name	You can ask if an applicant has ever worked under another name.	You cannot ask for the maiden name of a married woman.
Photograph		You may not ask for a photograph before employment.
Citizenship	You may ask, "Are you a citizen of this country?"	You may not ask, "Of what country are you a citizen?" or whether the applicant is a native-born citizen.
Education	You may ask about educational, vocational, or professional schooling.	
Experience	You may ask about work experience.	
Military	You may ask about military service.	You may not ask about military experience in the armed forces of another country.

The number of rules and regulations, do's and don'ts, associated with pre-employment inquiries may seem overwhelming. It is really not that difficult.

Remember BFOQ —
bona fide occupational
qualification. What does
it take to do the job?

What it all boils down to is this: you may ask only those questions that have a direct bearing on an applicant's ability to perform the job. Period. Before going into an interview situation, ask yourself, "What will it take to actually do the job?" That is all that really matters in an interview or a selection decision. Here are some examples:

(a) Disability

Joe is hiring a computer programmer. One of the applicants for the position is in a wheelchair. A person can operate the computer terminal just as readily from a wheelchair as from an office chair. In this case, the wheelchair will not prevent the applicant from performing the duties of the job.

Pam, on the other hand, is looking for a maintenance engineer. The position will involve lifting up to 100 pounds, climbing ladders, etc. In this case, the applicant in the wheelchair would be unable to perform the requirements of the job. The ability to move about freely to meet the requirements of this position is known as a BFOQ (bona fide occupational qualification).

Pam can require that applicants not be confined to a wheelchair.

(b) Sex

Suzanne is the manager of a retail store. She is trying to fill a security position that requires someone to monitor the women's dressing room. A BFOQ for this position is that all candidates be female.

Peter is looking for a tennis coach for a girls' high school tennis team. The coach's office is separate from the dressing facilities so privacy is not an issue. In this case there is not a BFOQ that all candidates be female.

There are several factors that can help determine whether or not a question is permissible. These factors include:

➤ Does the question require an answer that would delve into a protected area (race, sex, religion, nationality, handicap)?

➤ Is the answer to the question necessary to make a hiring decision?

➤ Does the question relate directly to a requirement of the job?

Go through the questions in Exercise 1 and decide which are legal and which illegal. The answers may surprise you.

One special area of caution concerns pre-interview inquiries. Be particularly careful during the first and last few minutes of the interview while making small talk. Illegal questions are just as illegal before the actual interview starts as they are during the interview.

EXERCISE 1
PERMISSIBLE PRE-EMPLOYMENT INQUIRIES

Following is a list of questions. For each of the questions indicate whether you believe it is a permissible pre-employment inquiry.

1. Have you ever worked under a different name?

2. How many children do you have?

3. Will you start a family soon?

4. Would you be able to work on Saturdays to fulfill job requirements?

5. Can we see your birth certificate before we hire you?

6. Do you have any handicaps?

7. Were you born in this country?

8. What training did you receive in the army?

9. If you're hired, will you bring in a photograph for your personnel file?

10. Would you bring in a photograph to attach to your application?

11. Are you a U.S. (Canadian) citizen?

12. I see you attended St. Mark's High School. What kind of school is that?

13. Have your wages ever been garnisheed?

14. Who referred you for a position here?

15. Print a notice on the application that reads, "Any misstatements or omissions may be cause for dismissal."

16. That's an unusual name. What nationality is it?

17. Are you single, married, or divorced?

18. Do you plan to move any time soon?

19. This job requires a lot of heavy lifting. Do you have any physical problems we should know about?

20. You look like you had an American Indian ancestor. Am I right?

21. Do you own or rent your home?

22. What is your church affiliation?

23. Do you speak any languages fluently?

24. What schools have you attended?

25. Have you ever been arrested?

26. Who should we notify in case of an emergency?

27. Have you ever had trouble getting credit?

28. Will you include the name of your minister or pastor with your references?

Exercise 1 — Continued

Answers

1. Yes. Employers need this information for the purpose of checking references.

2. No.

3. No.

4. Yes. If working Saturdays is a requirement of the job, the employer needs to know the answer to this question.

5. No. The employer should ask to be given this information on the first day you report to work.

6. No.

7. No.

8. No. If the employer is looking for specific, job-related training, the question should be phrased to reflect this.

9. Yes. Employers can ask for a photo to be brought in after a job applicant is hired.

10. No.

11. Yes.

12. No. This is a question that might be designed to determine religious background.

13. No.

14. Yes.

15. Yes.

16. No.

17. No.

18. Yes, because this requirement is directly related to the responsibilities of the job.

19. Yes.

20. No.

21. No.

22. No.

23. Yes, if a job-related requirement.

24. Yes.

25. No. Employers may ask only ask about convictions, not arrests.

26. Yes.

27. No.

28. No. This question gets at religious affiliation.

g. Tips for Making Your Interviews Foolproof

Have a plan for the interview before you begin. Determine in advance what type of interview you will be conducting and what questioning approach you will take.

Follow a logical sequence in your questioning. Don't jump back and forth from one major area to another.

➤ Create a comfortable interview environment.

➤ Put the applicant at ease immediately and keep up the rapport throughout the interview.

➤ Keep your reactions to yourself. Learn to guard your own nonverbal responses.

➤ Take notes. You will not be able to effectively remember all the details about each applicant without them.

➤ Don't oversell the position. Present the position and the company accurately.

Learn something from each experience and pinpoint ways you can improve your interviewing style.

Present the position and the company accurately. Don't oversell. You want to find the best match for you — and the applicant.

7

Checking — and Giving — References

A good employee is hard to find. So, in many cases, is a good reference. But if you want to find good employees, you are going to have to do everything you can to assure yourself and others involved in the hiring decision that you are receiving good reference information.

Virtually every employer asks prospective employees to provide references. Few employers actually check those references. They should. If they don't, they may later find that the employee they hired was once somebody else's nightmare — and is now theirs. Or, they may find themselves involved in a lawsuit. Checking references can be a tricky business. When you are hiring, you want to get as much information as you can. But when *you* are being asked for a reference, your attorneys advise you to give only the bare essentials. What is going on here? Why is it so difficult to obtain references? How can you successfully gather the information you need? How can you protect yourself and your company when you are asked to give a reference on a former employee?

> Don't overlook the critical step of checking references — no matter how impressive the candidate may be.

a. Why Reference Checks are Important

Ninety percent of all hiring mistakes can be prevented through proper reference checking procedures. Unfortunately, countless employers neglect to take this important step in the hiring process. They rely, instead, on their own impressions of the candidate based on resume, application, and interview.

This is a major mistake and it can be a costly one. Checking the references of the applicants applying for a position is absolutely essential to obtain accurate information about candidates' qualifications and experience.

One man assumed the identity of a dead man, including his Harvard MBA, to get a job as a middle manager at General Foods and was later dismissed because his performance did not live up to his bogus credentials. A thorough reference check would have certainly determined that the man was not who he professed to be. McDonald's was involved in a negligent hiring suit in which the mother of a three-year-old boy sued the company because her son was molested by a McDonald's employee. This employee had a known past history of this behavior, but McDonald's didn't know about that history because it failed to check the employee's background thoroughly.

b. Why You May Legally be Required to Obtain References

It happens frequently — sometimes in a small way, sometimes in a major way. Employers who fail to check references thoroughly find themselves faced with situations ranging from the unpleasant to the litigious. A startling 75 percent of today's job searchers don't have their references checked by prospective employers according to Challenger, Gray, and Christmas, Inc., an outplacement firm in Chicago. These employers may be opening themselves up to lawsuits due to an emerging theory of employer liability known as negligent hiring.

In negligent hiring cases, an employer may be sued directly for an employee's irresponsible or criminal behavior. You may be liable if it turns out your screening efforts were inadequate and can be logically connected to subsequent wrongful conduct. While courts have rejected the argument that employers should check with law enforcement agencies for possible criminal records, the employer's inquiries must be deemed "adequate." Negligent hiring becomes an issue when an employer knew, or should have known, that an employee presented a foreseeable risk of harm. To avoid negligent hiring liability, an employer must take the necessary steps before hiring to determine if the employee is, indeed, fit for the job.

c. The Catch: Why Many Companies Are Hesitant to Give References

In *Sigal Construction Corp v. Stanbury*, the District Court of Columbia Court of Appeals ruled that the former employer of an employee who was "defamed" through a bad job reference had to pay $250,000 to the former employee because the reference given by a personnel manager with the former company was based on "second-hand knowledge" and was detrimental to the man's chances of getting another job.

In *Holton v. Lockheed Corp.*, a jury awarded close to $1 million to an employee whose former employer provided negative references to a prospective employer. Settlements for wrongful termination suits triggered when prior employers provided negative references for a former employee range from $5000 to $60,000 — awards average $622,000 with some as high as $2 million.

Increasing numbers of such lawsuits have caused former employers and personnel departments to become cautious about giving out information on former employees. Many companies have policies that expressly prohibit the release of employee information other than name, title, and length of employment.

A former employer can be held accountable to prove anything they say about prior employees. A hiring employer has an obligation to make attempts to use every legally available means to determine an employee's fitness for a job. That is the catch. As a supervisor or manager you may find yourself wearing both of these hats. How can you break through the barriers put up by reluctant former employers to get the information you need? How can you cooperate with prospective employers of your past employees to provide them with good information while protecting your legal interests?

d. Avoiding the Catch-22: How to Break the Barriers and Get Good Information

About a third of all job candidates alter their resumes or misrepresent their qualifications when applying for a job. Clearly, beyond the legal requirements, reference checking is an important function of finding the best person for the job you are filling. How much prescreening is enough from a practical perspective? That depends on the position being filled and how critical it is to the smoothly running operation of your company.

How much prescreening is enough from a legal perspective? That depends too — usually on the position being filled and how much risk there is that an employee will be able to harm others in the course of the job.

Many employers call references after interviews have been conducted. This is not necessarily the best procedure. Some employers find that by calling references before scheduling the interview, they are able to screen out undesirable candidates more effectively, thus saving themselves the time they would have spent in an interview.

In addition, checking references before the interview can provide you with additional areas to explore during the interview and let you formulate pertinent questions in advance.

You should always seek permission from the job applicant before checking references. A good method of doing this is to include a statement on the application form requesting the applicant's permission to contact any individuals mentioned on the form. Another way is to ask, "Are there any former employers, coworkers, supervisors, or personal references that you would *not* want me to contact?" By phrasing the question in this way you leave yourself a lot of room to explore potential reference sources.

Many employers are hesitant to give more than the most basic facts about a past employee, but with some creative networking and persistent questioning you can get the information you need.

One of the reasons for leaving yourself latitude in this area is to give yourself the option to network with the references you contact. For instance, suppose you call a former supervisor of a potential employee. During your conversation, the supervisor mentions the name of another supervisor in the organization who has previously managed this employee and who might be able to provide you with additional insight. You are then able to contact this person (providing it is not somebody the candidate asked you not to contact) without going back to the candidate to specifically ask, "Can I contact Jean Smith for a reference?"

Networking is an important aspect of reference checking and one you will want to make full use of. You will want to speak, if possible, to supervisors, coworkers, clients, or customers who are familiar with the person you are considering.

You should ask everybody you talk to if they could give you the name of somebody else in the company who would be familiar with the applicant's qualifications and work performance.

An area of checking references that is frequently touchy is the current employer. Many job candidates do not want their current employer to know they are looking for work elsewhere. While you want to respect the wishes of these applicants, you are also aware that a current employer can provide you with perhaps the best insight into the applicant's qualifications and experience. To get around this problem, let the applicant know that if you make a firm offer of employment it will be contingent on receiving a satisfactory reference from his or her current employer. You reserve your right to withdraw the offer of employment if a satisfactory reference is not obtained.

Following is a recommended approach to use when checking references — an approach designed to give you the best and most complete information possible.

1. Get permission from the applicant to check references

This is frequently done on the application form itself, with a line that reads something like "I hereby authorize (company name) to make a thorough investigation of all statements contained in this application, my past employment, education, and other activities and I release from all liability all persons, companies, and corporations supplying such information. I indemnify (company name) against any liability which might result from making such investigations."

Ask for the name of a superior, a peer, and a subordinate and for permission to talk to them.

2. Conduct a thorough reference check

To conduct a thorough reference check, you need to contact all references for a prospective employee. Never check just one reference. You want a total picture of the applicant — one that will help you spot consistencies and inconsistencies. Ask each person you contact to provide you with additional names of people you should speak with.

3. Do the reference checking yourself

Doing the reference checking yourself can be beneficial. You are hearing the information directly and are in a better position to probe for additional detail if necessary. It is the little bits of information you gather that are often most revealing.

4. Ask the right kind of questions

Reference checks require as much skill in questioning techniques as selection interviews. It is easy to fall into the trap of asking closed-ended questions that don't elicit the full response you need, or backing off when former employers seem reluctant to provide additional information. Use open-ended questions to get at the information you need — yes-and-no responses simply are not revealing enough. Listen intuitively. Sometimes what is not said can be as telling as what is said. For instance, one of the most revealing questions can be: "Would you rehire this person?" An immediate "yes" response can be reassuring. Hesitation, even if the response is ultimately "yes," should set off warning bells.

5. Document the information you receive

Document the source of every piece of information you obtain about an applicant. When and how did you obtain the information? Who gave you the information and what, specifically, did they say?

6. Develop standards and follow them

You should establish standards for checking references and follow them religiously. Being lax in following standards you have set for yourself (using them sometimes, but not others) can create problems.

e. Methods of Checking References

There are three ways to check references — in person, by mail, or by phone.

Don't delegate the task of checking references. Do it yourself. A great deal can be revealed through voice inflection, pauses, and what is not said.

1. Checking references in person

While person-to-person reference checking can be the most effective means of obtaining information about applicants, it is the least practical. If it is possible, however, there are several advantages to be gained from face-to-face meetings with an applicant's former employers and coworkers.

In a face-to-face meeting you will be able to judge nonverbal reactions of the people you are speaking with. You will find that people tend to be much more candid when you are sitting in the same room than if you are speaking on the phone or asking for written information.

Also, in face-to-face meetings you will have the advantage of meeting an applicant's former employer and being able to form your own judgments about the kind of supervisor this person would be. This sort of firsthand information will help you evaluate the candidate's responses to such questions as "What kind of supervisor do you get along best with?" or "What are some of the things you dislike in an employer?"

2. Checking references by mail

Mail is the least productive means of obtaining reference information, for three reasons:

➤ It can be a slow process. You have no way of knowing if your letter was received by the right person and you cannot be assured of a quick response even if your questionnaire did fall into the right hands.

➤ Former employers are twice as unlikely to put their thoughts about former employees on paper as they are to tell you what they think in person or over the phone.

➤ Many people feel that filling out forms, of any kind, is a time-consuming imposition. They simply will not do it — and you won't have a reference.

However, as you might imagine, the same reasons that references may be hesitant to commit their thoughts to paper are the reasons that you may choose this approach — it provides you with clear documentation of the questions you asked and the responses you received.

3. Checking references by telephone

Reference checking by telephone is the most common means of obtaining information about a job applicant. It is also an effective means because it is immediate, providing you reach the person you need right away; it is relatively inexpensive, especially when compared to reference checking in person; and it is possible to pick up on voice cues over the telephone which, though not as helpful as nonverbal body language cues, can still provide you with insights into the speaker's feelings.

(a) How to begin

When you make your initial contact with a reference, begin in a neutral tone. It is often helpful to say something like "I'm considering John Doe for employment and I'm calling to verify some information," rather than "I'm calling for a reference on John Doe."

The initial questions you ask should be nonthreatening and designed to verify factual information that has been provided in the resume or on the application form. You might want to ask about things such as the candidate's job title, the length of time the candidate was with the company, and the responsibilities required by the position the candidate held.

Try to speak to somebody who has direct knowledge of the applicant's performance. Whenever possible, speak with immediate supervisors. This can be difficult because, as we will see, companies often have policies restricting who is able to give out information about former employees.

(b) Overcoming resistance

As we have already seen, many employers will be hesitant to provide anything but the bare facts about former (or current) employees. As a potential new employer, however, you need to be persistent in order to overcome this reluctance. Here are some tips that can help you break through these barriers:

➤ Be confident in your approach.

➤ Begin the call in a neutral way, starting out with questions about factual aspects of the candidate's employment.

➤ Assure the reference that everything covered in the conversation will be strictly confidential.

➤ Stress the fact that you need this information to give the applicant fair consideration and that unless you are able to verify the information you have received, the candidate will not be considered for the position.

If necessary, ask to speak to somebody at a higher level of management.

(c) Using a structured reference guide

It is important to be prepared when you place a call to a reference. One way of ensuring that you will be prepared is to use a telephone reference check form. The telephone reference check form presented in Sample 6 offers a structured

Whenever you speak to a reference, ask for names of additional people you should talk to. Go beyond the names that candidates provide you — it is unlikely a candidate will give you the name of someone who would share potentially negative information.

format that you will find useful. The questions are objective and straightforward, and many simply verify information the candidate has already given you, i.e., salary information, responsibilities, etc.

By using a telephone reference check form, you are able to conduct an efficient and continuous conversation with each reference you contact. You will have the key questions at your fingertips and will be more likely to get accurate, objective information.

One caution however. Do be flexible in your approach. Don't feel that you must be tied to the questions exactly as they appear on the form. Keep in mind that the telephone reference check is really another form of interview and that you need to be open to the idea of pursuing avenues of questioning that you had not originally anticipated.

As well, during all of your telephone or in-person reference checks, remember to listen carefully for not only what is said, but how it is said. Note any signs of hesitation, especially when you ask the crucial question: "Would you rehire this person?"

(d) Other questions for checking references

Many of the techniques and strategies you used in developing and conducting the selection interview (see chapters 5 and 6) can also be used when checking references. You may want to use the following list of questions, in addition to the telephone reference check form, to ask the reference about the potential candidate, or you may want to modify it with some pertinent questions of your own.

➤ What was the quality of the applicant's work?

➤ How much direction did the applicant need?

➤ Did the applicant meet deadlines or delivery dates consistently?

➤ Did the applicant accept supervision well?

➤ How were the applicant's problem-solving skills?

➤ How long did the applicant work for you?

➤ In your opinion: what did the applicant do best? What did he or she do worst? (The law permits employers to offer personal opinions as long as the statements are clearly opinion and are not given with the intent of harming the employee.)

➤ What is your overall evaluation of this applicant?

(e) Other useful information

In addition to checking with past employers, for certain positions it may also be important to conduct credit checks or driving record checks.

SAMPLE 6
TELEPHONE REFERENCE CHECK

1. Was the applicant employed by your company?   ○ Yes   ○ No

2. What were the dates of employment?   From _____ To _____

3. Applicant said he or she was earning $ _____ per _____ when leaving your company.

   Is this correct?   ○ Yes   ○ No

4. What was the position and its responsibilities?

5. Did the applicant fulfill these duties and responsibilities? If not, what areas did the applicant have difficulty with?

6. Did the applicant receive any promotions?   ○ Yes   ○ No   Please describe circumstances.

7. How was the applicant's attendance and punctuality?

8. How was the applicant's overall work performance?

9. How did the applicant get along with coworkers? How did he or she respond to management/supervisors when something was required of him or her? Were there any difficulties, and if so, how did the applicant strive to overcome them?

10. What were the applicant's reasons for leaving your company?

11. Would you rehire?   ○ Yes   ○ No   If not, why?

12. Are there any additional comments you would like to make?

Credit checks are commonly done when hiring for positions that involve financial responsibilities. However, the EEOC has found that credit checks may have an adverse impact on minorities. Use caution, common sense and, as with any employment inquiry, be certain that you have a legitimate purpose for conducting a credit check.

If you are hiring an individual who will be using a company vehicle or will be responsible for operating a vehicle regularly while in your employ, you should check the driving records of that applicant when hiring and periodically after he or she employed.

f. How to Establish a Program For Giving Useful Information

When you are trying to obtain references, you want the prospective employee's previous employer to be as honest and thorough in providing information as possible. However, when the shoe is on the other foot, you may not be as eager to give out information on former employees.

Providing negative references for former employees can be a dangerous (and expensive) proposition. But don't immediately assume that the best posture is a silent posture. Employers have also been taken to court for not providing pertinent information about a former employee. The theory of "negligent referral" centers around the failure to disclose certain types of information. There are three key ways to protect yourself when giving references:

➤ Provide references in good faith without malice and provide only factual, job-related information.

➤ Limit the information you provide and the persons authorized to provide that information.

➤ Provide information only to authorized persons and only in an appropriate manner (not over drinks with a crony at the local watering spot or during a round of golf at the club).

Your personnel procedures should be designed to help you avoid — not win — lawsuits. There are a number of areas that should concern you as you establish procedures to avoid legal liability. To provide a defense, you need to prove one of the following:

(a) The statement was not made. Only give references in writing to avoid any disputes or misunderstandings about what was said or what was asked. Make this a company policy that is followed religiously. No exceptions.

(b) The statement was true. Keep clear, detailed documentation of employee performance and performance problems. When an employee is reprimanded or terminated, have another person present to serve as a witness.

(c) The statement was not defamatory. Make statements based only on actual performance issues that can be clearly documented. Never make comments about an employee's character.

(d) The statement was made with the employee's consent. Ask employees to sign statements giving you permission to release information about their performance. Many companies draft written references for prior employees that the employee sees and agrees to in writing. Conduct exit interviews with each departing employee, whether voluntarily or involuntarily terminated. Have another person present to witness the discussion.

(e) The statement was made by someone acting outside their authority and, therefore, that person must be held personally liable. Have a policy that only a particular department or individual can give references for employees. Adhere to this policy religiously. No exceptions.

Obviously there are a number of gray areas involved in obtaining and giving references. So even though you may be in the right, you may still need to plead your case before a judge or jury at trial. But if you establish clear guidelines for both giving and getting references; stick to verifiable, performance-related issues; and document your activities faithfully, you will be putting yourself in a strong defensive position should the threat or actuality of a lawsuit ever rear its head.

8

Making Your Selection

The last person interviewed for a job is three times more likely to be hired than the first person interviewed. Unfortunately, the last person is not necessarily the best person. You can see from this statistic why it is important to establish an objective system for making a hiring selection.

a. Common Selection Measures

On what evidence will you base your hiring decision? There are three commonly used selection measures for evaluating job applicants. You may decide to use one or a combination of all three. They are: applicant self-report, direct observation, and work samples.

1. Self-report

Self-report is the most commonly used selection measure. An applicant comes to an interview and tells the prospective employer about his or her accomplishments and experience. Obviously this is a biased means of learning about the candidate. As was true with resumes, an applicant is unlikely to provide you with negative information about his or her accomplishments.

Since this is a commonly used evaluation measure, however, it is important for employers to realize the limitations involved and, whenever possible, to combine this measure with one of the other two.

2. Direct observation

If you can directly observe a job applicant performing a representative job task, you will be in a much better position to evaluate job potential.

Unfortunately, direct observation is not always possible. How would you, for instance, observe a managerial candidate making a decision? And you don't want to put an untried job candidate in a position to affect your company's

Are you able to arrange situations where you can actually observe a candidate doing the type of work he or she will be hired for? Asking applicants to perform a simple task or complete a brief assignment can assist you in your selection decision.

99

product, productivity, or credibility. You don't, for instance, ask applicants for a receptionist position to answer the phones for a while so you can observe their competence. There are ways to get around this problem, however.

➤ You can use one of the tests that have been developed to measure analytical and decision-making ability.

➤ Some tasks can be role-played. With a receptionist position, for example, you might develop some scenarios that you could play out with each applicant to evaluate his or her responses.

➤ You can use hypothetical questions or situations to approximate real-life situations. You might present a job candidate with a problem and ask him or her to tell you the steps to be taken to solve the problem.

➤ Some tasks can be directly observed. For instance, you could ask a clerical applicant to file invoices or type a letter, or ask an applicant for an editorial position to edit a page of copy, etc.

If you find that direct observation would be virtually impossible, you may still be able to take a look at work samples.

3. Work samples

Artistic positions especially lend themselves to the use of work samples in applicant evaluation. Graphic designers, for example, might be asked to bring in samples of their design work. A technical writer might be asked to bring in writing samples.

b. Common Selection Criteria

The job specifications you establish before you even start looking for potential applicants should be foremost in your mind as you start to narrow down the choice of people. Applicants should be evaluated both in terms of how well they meet the job specifications and how they compare to other applicants. For this reason it is important to reserve a final decision until all interviews have been completed. Don't make a "yes" or "no" decision after each interview. It is better to wait until all interviews are completed and then rate interviewees on the basis of the criteria you have determined are the best predictors of job performance.

The criteria you use will not necessarily be the same as the criteria another employer might use. There are individual differences based on the qualifications necessary to perform the particular job, the company's historical hiring practices, and the value the company places on certain individual attributes.

Some common selection criteria are intelligence, communication skills, self-confidence, sociability, ambition and motivation, leadership, adaptability, and cooperativeness. These criteria are behavioral traits that you must assess throughout the interview based on your impressions of the candidates.

The applicant selection summary shown in Sample 7 is an example of a form that you might use to compare candidates. The items you enter down the left-hand side of the form will be based on the criteria you established from your job specifications and job description. Fill out a form for each candidate you interview. Later, these forms will prove useful as you rank the candidates in terms of their ability to meet the requirements of the job. Use the notes section to indicate specific observable and quantifiable cues that you used to select your ratings.

c. Steps to Error-Free Selection Decisions

The selection process, by its very nature, is subjective, leaving many areas open to bias and error. Your awareness of the possibility for error is one of the first steps to becoming a fair evaluator of job applicants. The following checklist can help make this demanding task a little easier:

➤ Be prepared.

➤ Identify desired behaviors in observable rather than subjective terms.

➤ Be aware of your own personal biases and work to overcome them.

➤ Try using more than one interviewer and comparing results to determine possible bias.

➤ Don't assume that excellence in one area implies excellence in all areas.

➤ Base judgments on demonstrated performance, not anticipated performance.

➤ Base judgments on observable standards, not on a comparison with other applicants.

d. The Ten Most Common Selection Mistakes

Let's say, hypothetically, that on March 1 you began interviews for an assistant. On March 3 you hired the first person you interviewed. She didn't have exactly the qualifications you were looking for, but she had been sympathetic to your lack of time to prepare for the meeting. You immediately recognized her as an outgoing, hard-working individual — much like yourself. Most of the interview was spent comparing various interests, with you doing most of the talking. Your most probing question was "You don't mind working overtime, do you?" Of course she said "No," and your decision was made. The other candidates paled in comparison and you offered her the position.

A number of mistakes can occur during the selection process. This is arguably one of the most important business decisions you will make. A bad selection choice can be your worst business nightmare.

Position _Marketing Assistant_   **Hiring deadline** _7/1_

For each of the areas listed below, using a rating scale of one to five, one meaning the applicant meets the requirements of the position the least and five meaning he or she meets those requirements the best. For the first half of the form, the information will generally come from the Applicant for Employment form and the Telephone Reference Check. Fill in the second half of the form with the numbers already totalled on the Interview Summary form.

Applicant	#1	#2	#3	#4		
General						
Availability	5	5	4	5		
Education	4	5	3	4		
Experience	4	3	5	4		
References	4	4	4	5		
Salary expectations	3	4	5	5		
Qualities/skills						
Personal	4	5	5	5		
Interpersonal	4	4	5	5		
Communication	4	4	5	4		
Organization	4	5	4	4		
Technical/mechanical	5	4	4	4		
Other						
Total	41	43	44	45		

On April 1, her first day of work, she was late. The second day she called in sick. The third day she just didn't show up. And after putting up with her for the past six working days, you are wishing she would stay home more often.

What went wrong?

Several things. In fact, in the course of your hiring procedure you made every one of the ten most common mistakes in employee selection. They are:

➤ Inadequate screening

➤ Inadequate preparation for the interview

➤ Lack of knowledge of the position to be filled

➤ Unintentional coaching

➤ Ineffective use of questions

➤ Dominating the interview

➤ Stereotyping the candidate

➤ Failing to probe for depth

➤ Evaluating solely in relation to other candidates

➤ Premature evaluation and selection

1. Inadequate screening

You have advertised for an employee and your desk is piled high with applications. What do you do now? The first thing — something you should have done before you ever advertised for help — is to determine the job specifications. What skills and qualifications does the applicant absolutely have to have? Set up your specifications before you ever look at the applications so there is no chance that you will be fooled by impressive though unsuitable resumes.

Now, establish a checklist. Go through each resume, automatically disqualifying those that don't meet your specifications.

Do not be swayed by applicants who write persuasively, who call or visit your office to ask more about the job, who dwell on their on-the-job experience and ignore your educational requirements, or who ignore your request for experience but try to convince you that their extensive education is experience enough.

Some of the questions you should be asking yourself about the position include the following:

➤ What is the primary reason for the job?

➤ What is difficult about the job?

➤ How much supervision is provided?

➤ What types of people must the new employee get along with?

➤ What technical knowledge or experience is required?

➤ Will the position be a challenge to the applicant? Too much of a challenge?

In terms of individual applicants you need to ask:

➤ What is the work history of the applicant?

➤ How often has the applicant changed jobs? Why?

➤ Has the applicant progressed in past positions?

➤ Is the applicant's education appropriate to the job?

The number of qualified applicants per hundred responses is very low. Most hiring consultants suggest trying to weed out the applications and limiting your interview list to a maximum of five candidates.

2. Inadequate preparation

If you set up an interview and immediately proceed to ask the applicant questions that he or she has already answered in the resume, you are not prepared. You are wasting your time, your company's time, and the applicant's time. After the interview is over, you will sit at your desk with no better idea of how qualified the applicant is than when you read the letter of application.

Before you begin the interview you need to determine the job requirements, thoroughly examine the resume or application, plan and organize pertinent interview questions, and arrange to have a private place to conduct the interview.

Three common errors are: failing to read appropriate materials before the interview, failing to develop a questioning strategy, and inadequate knowledge of the position. See chapter 5 for suggestions on how to prepare for an interview.

3. Lack of knowledge of the position to be filled

You need to know exactly what the candidate will need in terms of experience, education, knowledge and skills, characteristics/attitudes, and interpersonal skills. You also need to know what the candidate wants in terms of salary, relocation assistance, availability, and travel.

Lack of relevant job information will increase the chances of your making the wrong choice by using the wrong standards.

The manager of the position is usually the only person who knows the requirements well enough to make an accurate, in-depth assessment of a candidate's qualifications. For this reason, the manager should always be involved in the interview and should play an integral role in making the final hiring selection. Additional people can, and should, be brought in to provide different in perspectives. The hiring manager may wish to include representatives from other parts of the company that the individual will interact with, coworkers from the department, and, in companies that have a formal human resources function, a representative from the HR group.

4. Unintentional coaching

Sometimes, without meaning to, you may find yourself asking leading questions. You may not even realize that you are doing this. Leading interviewees to a response can be a major problem, since you will not know if you are obtaining accurate information or if the responses have been influenced by the tone of your voice or your body language.

One major coaching mistake that is made almost universally, but that can be easily corrected, is telling the applicant about the job and its requirements before you do the interview. You should wait until all of your questions have been answered before tipping off the job candidate in this way.

Another problem is the use of leading questions such as "This position involves a great deal of stress — how well do you handle stress?" Applicants immediately know that to answer this question correctly they should say that they deal with stress positively.

As an interviewer, you need to make a nonbiased choice. To do this effectively, be sure to guard against asking leading questions.

5. Ineffective use of questions

Another common error is overreliance on closed-ended questions. As we have already seen, this type of question yields little in the way of useful information. Asking a majority of open-ended questions can help you gain more extensive information about the job candidate and give you an opportunity to assess the candidate's reasoning and verbal skills.

6. Dominating the interview

Domination can result from failing to be prepared, nervousness, or not knowing when to stop talking! You will learn nothing about the job applicant if you do all of the talking. Your job is to create an atmosphere that will encourage the applicant to talk. You must learn to lead the discussion but not dominate it.

Don't tip off a candidate to the requirements of the position at the beginning of the interview. Wait until the interview is over to provide details on the job and the type of person you are looking for.

7. Stereotyping the candidate

First impressions are hard to forget. As an interviewer, however, you have to watch yourself carefully so that you don't fall into the trap of stereotyping the job applicants. You may have preconceptions of what the ideal candidate will be like. You may even have a picture in your mind of what the successful candidate will look like. But the candidates that fit your picture may not necessarily be the best choices for the job. Be particularly alert for the potential for bias when dealing with these types of applicants:

(a) The likeable candidate

Some people are naturally vivacious and charming. You like them immediately. But you don't have to like the people you hire; you only have to like their work. If you find yourself in an interview with an extremely likeable person, enjoy the interview but remain objective when you begin the selection process for the job.

(b) The mirror image

We naturally tend to like people who are most like us. This holds true in the business world as well as in our personal relationships. Be aware of this tendency when you are conducting interviews. A candidate who attended the same school you did, who shares your political views, and who is near your age is not necessarily the most qualified person for the job.

(c) The poised applicant

Some applicants are poised and self-confident. They present themselves well. Others are nervous and ill at ease. They shift in their chairs, answer your questions in one-syllable monotones, and end up making you feel miserable by the time the interview is over.

Nervous people are not necessarily bad hiring choices. If you are looking for a salesperson, you may have good reason for wanting to hire someone who has sound conversational skills, but for other positions this may not be as critical.

> Each candidate should be evaluated against your selection criteria — not against other candidates.

8. Failing to probe for depth

Many interviewers, particularly those with little experience, will accept inadequate responses to questions. They will accept superficial or ambiguous answers, fail to ask for clarification, and make incorrect assumptions.

Here are some examples of probing statements you should use when you don't feel a question has been answered thoroughly enough:

➤ Could you explain what you meant by...?

➤ Tell me more about that.

➤ How did you feel about that?

It can be difficult to press for answers to questions that you perceive are sensitive. However, the answers to these questions can be vitally important to your hiring decision. Candidates at interviews know they will be asked some tough questions. Don't back down. If you need to know, you need to ask.

9. Evaluating solely in relation to other candidates

Consider the following scenario: the first person you interview doesn't have all of the qualifications and specifications you have established, but somehow you hit it off together. You spend most of the interview talking about mutual interests and you can really "tell" that this person has a "feel" for the job. You have got your mind made up — this is the person you are going to hire.

During the rest of the interviews you are preoccupied, and when you do pay attention to what the other applicants are saying you compare them to the first applicant so that you can legitimize the decision you have already made.

You need to rate all the interviewees on the basis of the criteria you established before you began the interviews. When your first interview goes well — the questions are answered smoothly and the candidate is at ease — there is a tendency for remaining candidates to lose points in comparison.

Objectivity is the most important factor in evaluating all applicants. Go back to the standards you have established and compare each and every applicant to these standards — not to each other. Resist the temptation to add new standards because some glib applicant touted qualifications you did not originally include in your specifications.

10. Premature evaluation and selection

You may be good at not making judgments about the people you have interviewed until all the interviews are over. Or you may be like most other interviewers and make a decision after each person leaves your office.

First impressions can be inaccurate and are assuredly incomplete. When you rely on subjective hunches or let yourself make premature decisions you risk the possibility of creating a self-fulfilling prophecy. The applicants who look good on initial impression will automatically appear to be the best candidates; the "bad" applicants will automatically appear poor candidates.

You should not make any decisions until all interviews have been completed. Many interviewers make the mistake of automatically weeding applicants immediately after the interview is over — sometimes even sooner. Resist the impulse to do this.

Keep an open mind. Make no decision until you have interviewed all applicants.

9
Starting Employees on the Right Track

Making a hiring choice is just the first step in an important process that will determine whether or not your new hire will be effective. The first few days, weeks, and months that an employee spends on the job are critical. Starting off on the right track is extremely important and you want to make sure that you cover all of the bases.

This means preplanning. Your job is not done once the candidate has been selected. In fact, it is just beginning.

a. Making the Offer

If you have religiously followed all of the steps outlined up to this point, you should feel confident in the choice you have made. The next step is to extend an offer.

Try to make the offer as soon as possible after the interview, being sure to provide all of the facts associated with the offer (e.g., salary, terms of relocation, benefits, starting date) and any other information that might influence the prospective employee's decision of whether or not to take the job.

Make the offer personally — by phone or at a follow-up meeting — but follow up your conversation with a letter or written documentation clearly outlining the details of the accepted offer. Sample 8 shows a good format for a letter confirming employment and includes details on the position and its duties as well as working hours and starting wage.

Because you can't always be certain that your first choice for the position will accept the job, you should not turn down your second and third choices until you have received an acceptance from the number one candidate. Keep in mind, as well, that if you only have one good candidate, you shouldn't settle for anyone who is not well qualified for the job. While you may be hesitant to go through the entire search, interview, and selection process again, taking the

SAMPLE 8
LETTER CONFIRMING EMPLOYMENT

Dear Pat Hanson:

I am pleased that you have accepted the position of Marketing Assistant at our company, starting on 7/1/ . You shall perform the following duties and have the following responsibilities:

- general clerical duties including word processing and spreadsheets
- gathering information, tracking and reporting on community relations activities
- coordination of Speaker's Bureau activities
- coordination of print production

Please note that these duties and responsibilities are not exhaustive and that you may be expected to perform other reasonable duties and responsibilities should the need arise.

Subject to statutory holidays, your working hours are from 8:00 a.m. to 5:00 p.m., Monday through Friday, with a 60-minute lunch break and 15-minute coffee break. You are entitled to 5 days of ordinary unpaid vacation per calendar year after your first year of employment, and 6 days of paid sick leave per calendar year.

Your starting salary is $25,000/yr. You will be on probation for 12 weeks during which time we may terminate your employment at any time without notice or payment in lieu of notice. If your employment is continued, we may only terminate your employment without cause on two weeks' notice or payment in lieu of notice; however, we reserve the right to terminate your employment at any time without notice or payment in lieu of notice for good cause.

Your performance and salary will be reviewed after a period of six months and a performance and salary appraisal will then occur annually in July.

The company offers a benefit package which will be outlined to you by our Human Resources Manager on your first day. Other policy and procedure details are contained in the Personnel Manual which will also be given to you at this time.

Your supervisor is Cris Jones. Please see her on your first day and she will help you get settled.

I look forward to working with you. If you have any questions, please do not hesitate to contact me.

Yours truly

Jan Black
HR Director

time now to make the right choice — even if it means a substantial delay in filling the position — will prove to be more than worthwhile later.

b. Orientation and Training

After weeks of wading through piles of resumes and interviewing candidates who were either overqualified or underqualified, you have finally found the person you think can fill the job. Your worries are over...or are they? The problems don't stop once an employee has been hired. Your next step down the road to an effective employee is employee orientation. This important step in the employee development process is often either overlooked completely or hurried through as quickly as possible by an overworked supervisor.

The New Hire Checklist (Checklist 2) provides a summary of the key areas that you should plan to cover during a new employee's orientation:

➤ A letter confirming employment should have been sent and should clearly outline the main elements of the position including start date, duties, conditions of employment, salary, any relocation terms that have been agreed to, a probationary period if relevant, and vacation time and other benefits.

➤ If you have worked through an employment agency to place this employee, the form reminds you to take care of any obligations you may have relative to this relationship.

➤ It can be helpful to new staff members for other employees to have been informed of their background and qualifications before they come on the job. If the new employee will be working with specific customers outside the organization, take the time to notify these people as well. And, depending on the level and visibility of the position, you may also wish to send a news release to area media. Notifying staff, customers, and the media is an important step that is often overlooked.

➤ There are a number of records and agreements related to an employee that you will want to have on file either before, or shortly after, he or she has joined the company. The checklist can help you make sure that you have covered all of the bases.

➤ Job description. The job description should already be up-to-date because you used it in developing criteria and questions for this position. Make sure a copy has been provided to the employee and that a copy is in the employee's personnel file.

➤ There are a number of important items related to work schedule and operations that you will want to go over with each new employee. Sometimes these seemingly basic issues are most important to the new person.

Your new employee is eager to get to work. Don't ask for too much too soon, but do provide an opportunity for the new employee to do something.

CHECKLIST 2
NEW HIRE CHECKLIST

☐ **Letter confirming employment**

Your letter should include some diiscussion of these points.

- ○ Start date
- ○ Salary
- ○ Position
- ○ Relocation terms
- ○ Duties
- ○ Probationary period
- ○ Conditions of employment
- ○ Vacations/days off

☐ **Employment agency obligations**

☐ **Announcements**

- ○ Staff
- ○ Media
- ○ Customers

☐ **Records of agreements**

- ○ Résumé on files
- ○ Union information and contract
- ○ Personnel record
- ○ Credit union information and application
- ○ Employment contract
- ○ Group insurance information and application
- ○ Secrecy and noncompetition covenant
- ○ Life insurance information and application
- ○ Invention covenant
- ○ Medical and dental insurance information and application
- ○ Physical/medical report
- ○ Pension/retirement plan information and application
- ○ Security check

☐ **Payroll**

- ○ Social Security/Insurance No. _____
- ○ Inform payroll of employee's details
- ○ Inform employee of payroll deductions
- ○ Complete tax withholding forms

☐ **Job description**

Discuss with the employee his or her specific, finalized duties and responsibilities

☐ **Work schedule and operations**

Ensure you have explained company policy regarding these matters.

- ○ Lunch break shedules
- ○ Performance evaluation
- ○ Hours of work
- ○ Advancement opportunities
- ○ Summer/flextime hours
- ○ Company training and tuition
- ○ Time cards
- ○ Day care
- ○ Overtime
- ○ Parking
- ○ Statutory holidays amd other days off
- ○ Cafeteria facilities
- ○ Emergency and safety procedures

☐ **Highlights of personnel manual**

- ○ Reporting hierarchy and supervisory structure
- ○ Grievance procedures
- ○ Attendance and absences
- ○ Disciplinary procedures

The Personnel Record is another important form that you will want to immediately fill out for the employee's file. Sample 9 shows a standard personnel record form. This form is intended to be the basis of the employee's file and will be maintained throughout an employee's tenure with your company. It includes information on personal details (employee telephone number, addresses, start date), emergency contact, enrollment details (for various benefits packages), education/training received, employment record, and termination information. There are a number of items that you will want to include in the employee's personnel record or file:

➤ The resume and application form

➤ Reference information

➤ Job description

➤ Records related to the employee's tenure with your company — pay increases, promotions, and job transfers

➤ Disciplinary notices or documents

➤ Performance evaluations

➤ Termination record

In the United States there are other records that you are required to maintain separately from the personnel file. (In Canada you may or may not be required to maintain these types of documents depending on the specific regulations in your province.) These include:

➤ Medical records (physical examinations, drug and alcohol testing, workers' compensation claims). The Americans with Disabilities Act requires that these records be kept separately from the personnel file.

➤ Records related to equal employment opportunity. Documents that identify employees' race and sex may be maintained in separate files for use in the event that there is a need to present records for an investigation of hiring practices.

➤ Safety training records. These records must be made available for Occupational Safety and Health Administration (OSHA) investigations; keeping them separate from personnel files limits the extent of the information that OSHA has access to.

➤ Immigration records should be maintained chronologically by year. It is generally recommended that, as with safety training records, these records be kept separately to limit access of an auditor to unrelated information.

SAMPLE 9
PERSONNEL RECORD

Personal details

Employee _____ Employee No. _____

Social Security/Insurance No. _____ Date of birth _____

Sex ○ Female ○ Male   Marital status ○ Single ○ Married ○ Separated ○ Widowed ○ Divorced

No of dependents _____ Citizenship _____ Military status _____

Years of service with company   1 2 3 4 6 7 8 9 10 11 12 13 14 15 16 17 18 19 20 21 22 23 24 25

Start date _____ Anniversary date _____

Address

Unit No.	Street	City	State/Province	Zip/Postal Code	Telephone	E-mail
Unit No.	Street	City	State/Province	Zip/Postal Code	Telephone	E-mail
Unit No.	Street	City	State/Province	Zip/Postal Code	Telephone	E-mail

Enrollment details

	Date eligible	Date enrolled	Policy No.	Date terminated
Group insurance				
Group medical				
Pension plan				
Union				
Credit Union				

Education/training

Highest grade completed _____

College/university attended _____
   Years completed _____
   Certificate/degree completed _____
College/university attended _____
   Years completed _____
   Certificate/degree completed _____
Company training _____
_____

Employment record

Date	Position	Department	Rate	Grade level	Comments

Termination

Date _____ Reason _____

Comments _____
_____
_____

1. Your expectations for orientation and training

Just as in the interview, you will come to the orientation session with certain expectations. You will expect to provide the employee with pertinent information about the company and its policies, determine the extent of the employee's training and experience as it relates to specific job duties, develop the employee's feelings of belonging and acceptance, and avoid creating unnecessary anxiety.

During the orientation period you also want to provide the employee with copies of the job description, job specifications, and job standards.

2. The employee's expectations for orientation and training

As in virtually every aspect of human relations, you and your new employee will differ somewhat in what you expect the orientation and initial training period to accomplish. This is a natural dichotomy. Each of you will come to this initial meeting with different hopes and fears. The employee, of course, hopes to do a good job. The employee has another, perhaps even more important, expectation — that he or she will get along well with supervisors and coworkers.

As an employer, your major hope is that the employee will succeed and, in essence, make you look good. After all, you were the person responsible for hiring and you are now the person responsible for training. You can see, then, that while training the employee to do a good job is important, your first goal should be to make the new employee feel comfortable by establishing a sense of belonging.

3. Guidelines for an effective orientation

What can you do to make the orientation session successfully meet your training needs while minimizing anxiety for the employee? These guidelines may prove helpful:

(a) Welcome

Initially you should welcome the employee and reestablish the rapport that you had during your initial interview. Begin with some small talk and move slowly into the real business of the meeting. Acknowledge the fact that the employee may be uncomfortable and nervous and demonstrate your acceptance of these feelings. Once you sense that your new employee is more relaxed, move into the information session that begins the orientation session.

(b) Organization chart

It is important that the new employee understands the structure of the company and how his or her position fits into that structure. At the beginning of the

New employees are anxious to know how they will fit in and to meet the people they will be working with. Provide good information about interrelationships and reporting lines.

orientation session you will want to show the new employee a copy of the organizational chart and explain how the departments and divisions are organized and how the new employee's department relates to others in the company. This is also the time to explain the chain of command in operation in your organization.

(c) Company and departmental objectives

What are the goals of the company? The new employee will need to know the answer to this question to understand how he or she can contribute to these objectives.

➤ What is the reason for the company's existence?

➤ What product or service is provided?

➤ What is the history of the organization?

➤ What is the company philosophy?

➤ How does the department in which the new employee will work contribute to the objectives of the company?

The new employee will have to know the answers to all of these questions to be able to understand how he or she fits in.

(d) Working conditions

Much of what you will want to cover in terms of working conditions should be included in the employee handbook. Don't make light of this area, however. Surprisingly enough, the majority of new employees are more anxious, initially, about such things as where to eat lunch and where to park than they are about their job description. By clearing up some of these questions and making sure that the employee is comfortable with the housekeeping aspects of the job, you will be able to move on to areas that deal more directly with job performance. You will want to let your new employee know about such things as —

➤ hours of work and opportunities for flexible scheduling,

➤ lunch hours;

➤ coffee breaks;

➤ location of lunchroom or cafeteria;

➤ location of restrooms;

➤ company policy on personal phone calls and mail;

➤ payday — how often, how much, and how to keep track of this important aspect of employment;

- ➤ special company functions and amenities such as summer picnics, holiday parties, and recognition of employees' birthdays;

- ➤ dress code; and

- ➤ how coworkers and supervisors should be addressed (by Mr. and Ms. or on a first-name basis).

You will be surprised at how much more relaxed your new employee will be once some of these social issues are explained. And be sure to offer plenty of opportunity for questions — there may be something you have neglected to cover that the employee considers important.

(e) Job responsibilities and job standards

At this point in the orientation session you should provide the new employee with a copy of the job description for the position and go over it, point by point, so that every aspect of the job responsibilities and requirements will be fully understood. You also want to let the employee know what the job standards are. What level of performance do you expect? How, and when, will the employee be evaluated? Be clear about your expectations now so you can avoid problems later.

(f) Company standards

You will need to provide the new employee with information on company rules and procedures. What sort of behavior do you expect from employees? How flexible is the company in terms of starting time, lunch breaks, etc.? What are the disciplinary procedures? On what basis would a termination decision be made? These are just a few of the areas you will need to clarify in terms of company standards.

(g) Introductions

It is difficult for anybody to remember the names of a large number of people who they are introduced to in a short time. It is especially difficult for the new employee, who is already feeling apprehensive. Your employee can be effectively introduced to the other employees of the company through a three-step process:

(a) Take the employee around the company to introduce him or her to the members of the employee's department and to other people the employee will work directly with.

(b) Introduce or announce the addition of the new employee through such means as a company-wide meeting or company newsletter.

(c) Encourage other employees to introduce themselves as they have an opportunity.

Some of the little things about a job are most important to a new employee — where to park, how to dress, or when to take breaks.

4. Problems to avoid during orientation

Just as in the hiring process itself, there are several problems you can run into during employee orientation. These six specific areas can cause difficulties:

(a) *Telling too much at one time.* A common problem encountered by many employees during orientation sessions is information overload. They are provided with too much information in too little time. There is no way that they can be expected to retain all of it. In fact, sometimes new employees will come away from the orientation session wondering if they will be able to remember anything they were told. This creates anxiety and can make continued training extremely difficult. What can you do? Provide only the essentials and don't go into too much detail. Provide the same information verbally first and then in written form as well (e.g., in an employee handbook). Watch for nonverbal cues that indicate the new employee is feeling lost, and backtrack if necessary. You certainly can't expect your new employee to recite to you, verbatim, everything you covered during orientation. You can, however, take steps to assure that retention is as high as possible.

(b) *Failure to use demonstration and involvement.* Teachers know that their students will learn and retain more if they are actively involved in the learning experience. Take a minute to think about it. Would it be easier to learn how to bake a cake by simply reading the recipe or by reading the recipe and actually performing the steps? In orientation, you will be much further ahead with the new employee if you involve him or her as much as possible in the areas you cover. For instance, if you are trying to explain how the company's product is manufactured, wouldn't it be more effective to actually take the employee through the plant, pointing out the various steps in the production process as they are being performed? Similarly, it will be much easier for the employee to understand what his or her department does by actually observing coworkers as they carry out their daily tasks.

(c) *Lack of patience.* Most supervisors have more work to do than they can accomplish in an eight-hour day. It is not uncommon for an orientation session to be viewed as an imposition and for a supervisor to try to rush the employee through it as quickly as possible. This is a short-sighted maneuver. Time spent now will pay off, with dividends, in the future. If you fail to cover something adequately during employee orientation, you can be sure that it will come back to haunt you later — and that you will have to spend more time clarifying and re-explaining than you would have spent if you had done it thoroughly in the first place.

(d) *Lack of preparation.* Know what you want to accomplish and how you are going to accomplish it. Have the materials you need gathered together and organized in the sequence in which they will be presented. If you appear disorganized or confused, you will not only lose some of your credibility but you will also lose the attention of your new employee.

(e) *Not allowing for feedback.* Don't just assume that the new employee is understanding and assimilating every fact you present. Ask. Build in opportunities for feedback on everything you intend to cover. Stop occasionally and ask, "Did you understand our procedure on...?" Or, better yet, ask the new employee to explain, in his or her own words, a specific procedure or company policy you just covered. Allow for and encourage questions. You want to do it right the first time so you don't have to redo it later.

(f) *Failure to reduce tension.* If you fail to put your new applicant at ease, all is for naught. After you have hired a good employee, orientation truly is the number one ingredient in assuring positive performance. Make sure you use your new resource as fully as possible. Make every step in the orientation process count!

c. Goals, Roles, and Reporting Lines

Marla felt her first three months working for Acme Construction were a nightmare. The training had been minimal, introductions had been nonexistent; the simple process of finding the breakroom (and the appropriate time to use it) had seemed like an almost insurmountable hurdle. After three months, while she finally felt somewhat acclimated, she resented the wasted time and effort she had spent in a trial-and-error process that she felt was heavy on error.

Mark, on the other hand, found that after only a few weeks on the job for XYZ Insurance he had a good grip on what was expected of him and why. He liked his job and understood how the functions he was responsible for supported the functions of his coworkers' jobs and how, collectively, they fed the success of the organization. If asked, Mark wouldn't think there was anything special about his situation. He had received exactly the kind of direction he expected from a new supervisor.

Marla could tell him how special his situation was, however. Her experience represents the rule rather than the exception in new employee orientation.

When a new employee reports to work, he or she comes with many expectations. The supervisor is the person responsible for meeting those expectations, yet many times the supervisor fails to indoctrinate the employee quickly and effectively into the organization.

If possible, assign a buddy to the new employee to serve as a resource and mentor during the first several weeks on the job.

There are three critical areas that the supervisor must focus on in the early stages — if these areas are handled correctly, the employee's development will be positive and both employee and company will benefit.

(a) *Goals.* What do you expect of me? How do these expectations fit into the company goals?

(b) *Roles.* Who will I be working with? What do they do? How do their job duties relate to mine?

(c) *Reporting lines.* Who do I take direction from? Who do I direct? What is my status in the organization?

Orienting new employees presents a double challenge: the new employee can't ask pertinent questions because he or she is not familiar enough to know what he or she doesn't know, and you can't answer those unasked questions. The key to success in orienting new employees to their jobs is anticipation — and simplification.

There is a tendency to take a lot for granted without even realizing it. It is critical that the new manager attempts to view the situation from the new hire's perspective and realizes that things that may seem common sense or obvious aren't so obvious to the new employee.

1. *Goals.* What do you expect from me?

You hire an employee because you are too busy to take care of everything that needs to get done. Then, when the employee starts work, you are often too busy to take the time to tell the employee what needs to get done and how to do it. You can't just plop someone down at a desk and start giving them assignments. You have to present a framework to them in which those assignments make sense as a whole, not as individual tasks. Goals represent that framework.

First, explain to the employee the purpose of the job. This needs to be a comprehensive explanation. "Your job is data entry" is not a comprehensive description of purpose. "Your job is to enter data on customer rebate amounts and energy savings, accurately and efficiently," is a better description of what needs to be done.

Second, explain why. "The data you enter is used in reports we make to regulatory agencies and also helps us keep track of progress on an individual and departmental basis."

Next, explain how. This is the technical aspect of the job and will involve familiarizing employees with the equipment and processes required to get the job done. Training needs will vary based on the skills the employee brings to the job. For instance, if you are using database software and a system the employee is familiar with, training will focus on the format of the data you are gathering, file names, and system protocol. If, however, the software and system you use are unfamiliar, training will have to start at a more fundamental level.

Finally, explain how success will be measured. "These are the ways in which I will measure your performance — this is how I'll know you're doing a good job; these are the signs that you are not performing up to my expectations."

2. *Roles.* What are my interactions with others in the company?

The social and professional interactions between a new employee and his or her coworkers are critical to that employee's becoming effective in a new position. Who will I be working with? What are their responsibilities? How do my responsibilities mesh with theirs? These are just a few of the questions that new employees have.

Organizational charts are a good way to begin explaining to employees where they fit in the hierarchical structure. Their value is limited, however. The best way for employees to learn their roles and the roles of those around them is to begin working with others. You can't introduce a new employee to everyone in the company and expect that employee to remember who these people are, let alone what they do. Initiate casual introductions with the general work force and then spend more time introducing the new employee to key people he or she will be working with. That extra time might involve staff meetings, project team assignments, or task forces. Other supervisors might set up a certain period of time for the new employee to observe various functions as they are being performed. Perhaps the employee could spend a few hours each day with a different person with whom he or she will work closely.

The organizational chart is a good first step in explaining how your business operates, but spend some time talking about what else goes on as well to round out the picture.

It is important the employee have follow-up time with the supervisor after these activities. This time enables the supervisor to answer questions that may have arisen during these observational sessions. It may also allow the employee to bring up some more subjective issues, for example, "Carmen made a few mentions that I'd be helping her out on the XYZ project. Is that correct?"

Establishing an open, honest relationship with your new employee will allow you to address some of these more subjective, and more touchy, issues.

3. *Reporting lines.* Who do I take direction from?

We are all, like it or not, concerned with status. New employees want to know to whom they can delegate tasks and who will delegate tasks to them.

In addition, employees need to understand the unique climate of your organization. Is the culture structured, with employees expected to maintain strict nine-to-five hours, at their desks, with minimal conversation? Or is the climate more informal, with employees coming and going in a flexible manner and interacting regularly during the day with coworkers?

These seemingly obvious issues need to be addressed with new employees. A new employee who observes others taking long lunches and does the same, may still feel uncomfortable because no policy has been stated.

A request from a manager in another department that conflicts with a more imminent assignment may receive short shrift unless you have previously indicated that this manager's requests need to be given top priority. You are not going to be able to deal with every potential question, problem, or conflict. But what you can do is make clear to your employees that you are open to their questions and make sure that you are accessible. Or if you can't be, designate somebody else who can serve as a mentor in your absence.

New employees are critical resources. They come to you with minimal preconceived notions about what will be expected of them and with a sincere desire to do a good job. The supervisor's role is also critical. It is his or her job to turn that eager new employee into a fully functioning and productive member of staff. You can pave the way by clearly and effectively covering the goals, roles, and reporting lines that shape their new position.

d. Maintaining Ongoing Contact

Training is just the beginning. The key to developing an effective and productive employee is ongoing interaction. The point to remember, though, is that time spent now will more than pay off in the future. Far too many employees who don't last in your company could have been active contributors — if they had received the proper guidance when they first came on board.

In reviewing your orientation and training efforts, make sure that you have —

➤ provided the employee with an up-to-date job description and that you have reviewed it with the employee, point by point,

➤ gathered examples of finished work products that the employee can use as guidelines or samples,

➤ gathered together all pertinent procedural or training materials,

➤ ascertained the level of knowledge the employee brings to the job and taken steps to provide training for any gaps in knowledge that are critical to performing the job,

➤ set tangible and measurable goals for learning and achievement and established a process for regular follow-up to determine progress toward those goals,

Training is not a one-time event. It is a process that will continue throughout an employee's tenure with your organization.

➤ maintained an open dialogue with the employee to determine how the training process is going — backtracking when necessary, and

➤ allowed the employee to learn at his or her own pace.

If you are absolutely too busy to provide training yourself, designate another employee to serve as trainer and supervise these activities. Don't leave it to chance.

1. Establish a schedule of regular one-on-one meetings

It is important to have regular and consistent contact with all employees to discuss work progress, quality, and barriers to performance. By establishing a schedule of regular, one-on-one meetings, you will provide an opportunity for two-way feedback and monitoring of work progress. In addition, you will be able to spot and correct problems as they develop — and before they become major issues.

Once a schedule is established, be sure to keep your appointments. Develop an agenda and a means of following up on a consistent basis. These are developmental meetings and are a critical part of helping your new employee become well acclimated to the needs of the job, the department, and the company.

2. Document performance consistently

The annual (or six-month) performance review meeting is not the time to suddenly let your employee in on some performance problems you have spotted. The time to reveal this information is as soon after the incident has occurred as possible. Most managers conscientiously attempt to provide feedback to their employees. However, sometimes supervisors decide to let the small things slide — they don't want to appear unreasonable or picky. Those small things, though, invariably develop into larger things. When you finally confront the employee with the situation they feel frustrated, angry, and cheated.

Your employees want to do a good job. To do that, though, they need your feedback. If you spot even the smallest problem, you owe it to that employee to point it out and offer some guidance on how to improve.

Keep track of any performance issues as they occur. This documentation not only helps you justify performance ratings, but also allows you to show improvement and milestones the employee has achieved. Be consistent in your documentation. Don't just point out and keep track of the problem situations. Let employees know when they are on the right track, when they have done something exceptionally well. And keep track of those incidents too.

3. Make communication a two-way process

Top-down communication is a thing of the past. Today, employees are much more involved in decision making, job design, and performance evaluation. It is no longer the case where you, as supervisor, says, "Here's what I want you to do and here's how to do it — end of discussion." Today, the two-way communication process is encouraged in most companies — and for good reason.

Good ideas and quality products require the input and creativity of a number of players in the company — not just the supervisors. That old credo that two heads are better than one is adhered to in most progressive, successful companies. It should be in yours as well.

What are some of the statements that hamper this two-way communication? There are many:

➤ "We tried that before and it didn't work."

➤ "Do it this way because we've always done it this way."

➤ "I don't care what you think — this is how I want it done."

➤ "We don't have time to change the process — just do it."

The list can go on and on. You can tell when you are stifling two-way communication by listening carefully to the messages you provide employees. Are you shutting off the opportunity for their input by adhering strictly to the way things have always been done? Do you ram your ideas down the throats of employees, over their objections? Be open-minded when dealing with the thoughts, suggestions, and insights of your employees. Allow employees the opportunity to provide input on how to improve processes and procedures and how to do their jobs effectively. After all, it is the person in the job who knows best how to get it done.

4. Provide ample opportunity for growth

New responsibilities and added challenges can serve as great motivators for employees. Provide many opportunities for employees to contribute to the goals of your organization.

Gone are the days when an employee stayed in the same job for 25 years, happily retiring with the requisite gold watch. Today's employees want — and demand — opportunities for growth and advancement. While a tight job market and flattening of corporate hierarchies mean that fewer promotions may be available for employees, advancement can take place within a position or through lateral moves. Once an employee has gone through the learning curve of a new position and reached a plateau, it is time to explore new opportunities. Those opportunities could take the form of added job responsibilities, additional training, job enhancement opportunities, or promotions.

No two employees will be alike in terms of what they expect from their position or from the company. Some won't want to grow in the job — they are satisfied being at the plateau level, having mastered the position and now feeling confident in their abilities. Others will want the opportunity to learn new skills, while another group will expect rapid advancement and be resentful when it is not available. Again, communication is critical. Don't assume that you know what is in the best interests of your employees. Ask them.

By starting out on the right foot with wise hiring choices, and then providing continuous training and feedback to employees, you can ensure that they will successfully make their way along the development curve and ultimately become successful, productive members of your team.

e. Violence in the Workplace

One last way to start employees off on the right track is to be aware, as a company and as an individual, of the serious nature of violence in the workplace. According to Bureau of Justice Statistics, each year almost one million individuals become victims of violent crime at work. That violence costs businesses more than $55 million each year in lost wages. The cost in terms of physical and emotional injury is difficult to measure, but certainly catastrophic.

It is easy to say, "This couldn't happen to me." The fact is, though, that just one violent incident can be devastating. Violence is the leading cause of fatal occupational injuries for women — and the first, second, or third leading cause of death for all workers depending on the area reporting.

Violence can take a variety of forms: customer to employee, employee to employee, relative to employee, former employee to management, and on and on and on. The first step in averting disaster is acknowledging that violence is an issue. The next step is developing a plan or written policy to address the issue of violence in the workplace. The final step is taking precautions and establishing guidelines for how to react in potentially violent situations.

1. Establishing a policy

Your commitment to employee safety and health can be most readily acknowledged by establishing a policy that clearly makes employee safety a top priority. A commitment from the company's owners to a safe workplace is a critical first step to fighting violence.

Once you have developed a policy, the next step is to communicate that policy to employees and to clearly state your expectations of all employees in terms of how they treat each other and how they treat customers. A policy of zero tolerance for workplace violence and a demonstrated commitment to follow that policy are crucial.

Finally, make sure that employees know how to report complaints of violence or aggression, and make sure that they know how those complaints will be resolved.

2. Employee involvement

Seek employee input when you are developing policies and procedures to address workplace violence. Staff may have ideas on how to keep the workplace safe based on their own experience on the job. They can also help you identify the potential for violent situations.

Addressing the issue of violence is an ongoing concern — not one that is put to rest once a policy has been developed. Keep safety in the forefront through meetings and other communications. You might decide to institute a safety newsletter or hold regular meetings to discuss issues of customer and employee safety. Regular inspections of your facility are another way to ensure that you identify any potential security problems and take steps to remedy those problems.

Depending on your business situation, you may also decide to have training sessions on personal safety, how to respond to assault, or disaster plan response. Local police departments are often available to provide such training.

10

Employee Contracts and Covenants

When Heinz hired Daniel O'Neill, a former Campbell Soup employee, they knew they were obtaining a major talent. O'Neill had been the head of the U.S. soup division for Campbell and had a strong background that Heinz hoped to capitalize on. The company's ability to take advantage of O'Neill's skills, however, was limited by the courts. While O'Neill was permitted to begin working for Heinz in September 1997, he was restricted from working on any soup products until September 1998.

In October 1998 Wal-Mart filed suit against Amazon.com when the bookseller hired 15 of Wal-Mart's former information technology and logistics executives over a two-year period. Wal-Mart accused Amazon.com and a new company, Drugstore.com, of "a wholesale raiding of proprietary and highly confidential information systems." Chief Information Officers (CIOs) of both Amazon.com and Drugstore.com are former executives with Wal-Mart. While all Wal-Mart employees are covered by a "blanket policy against disclosing any confidential information during and after employment," the former executives involved in the suit had not signed noncompetition agreements.

It is a competitive world out there, and one of the issues that large and small businesses alike worry about is the loss of their intellectual capital. The business world has come to recognize that the value of a business extends beyond bricks and mortar, inventory, and cash on hand. The value of a business also includes the value of the information and specialized knowledge possessed by an organization's employees. Obviously every business wishes to protect that knowledge and information and take steps to ensure that trade secrets, confidential information, and specialized knowledge are not shared with competitors.

This is a concern while employees are with your organization. It can become even more of a concern when they leave. From an overall risk-management standpoint there are some important things that any business can do to minimize the damage that can be caused when an employee moves on, including the following:

➤ Making appropriate hiring decisions (see chapter 8)

➤ Providing a positive and motivating employment environment (see chapter 17)

In spite of your best efforts, though, employees do leave — and they may take valuable information with them. Can you protect yourself?

a. Trademarks, Patents, and Copyright

There are certain formal protections available to the inventor or small businessperson wanting to protect a company or product name. Known as intellectual property law, these protections include patents, trademarks, and copyrights. The laws related to intellectual property are complex and require the involvement of an attorney knowledgeable in these areas. Here, though, is a brief review of the protections afforded by patents, trademarks, and copyrights.

1. Patents

A patent provides you with the exclusive right to make or use an invention for a specified period of time — usually 20 years. Patents can only be obtained for inventions that are unique and did not previously exist. Both the U.S. and Canada have a first-to-invent system, which means that the first inventor, with a provable date of invention, is entitled to obtain patent protection. Certain things are not patentable — laws of nature and things that occur naturally in nature, for example. The process of obtaining a patent can be extensive and costly, involving an attorney well-versed in patent law. It is important to note that a separate patent must be obtained in each applicable country. So, for instance, to protect an invention in both the U.S. and Canada, two separate patent applications must be filed — one in the U.S. and one in Canada.

2. Trademarks

The process of applying for a trademark is quite similar to that of applying for a patent. A trademark affords the small business person the right to use a specific name, word, phrase, symbol, logo, design, sound, color — or combination of these elements. As with patents, to qualify for a trademark, the design must be new and unique. Generic terms — i.e., ice cream shop or beauty salon — cannot be trademarked. The application process for a trademark involves both the determination of whether the mark is proper and subject to trademark protection and also if the mark is already in use. Again, the process can be complex and costly and requires you hire an attorney specializing in trademark registration.

Once you receive a trademark it is important that you be alert to unauthorized use to keep your mark from becoming a generic term. Consider how the words Kleenex and Xerox have become commonly used beyond their specific application to the unique product brands they originally referred to. Once your trademark becomes a generic term, your right to enforcement can diminish — or be eliminated.

3. Copyrights

A copyright is the right to reproduce a work in a certain fixed form. This book, for example, is subject to copyright. Unlike patents and trademarks, copyrights are obtained quite simply. A copyright exists automatically when the work is created — for instance, when a poem is written or when a painting is painted. The mere act of creating the work affords the creator certain legal rights. Those rights extend for the life of the creator plus 50 years. While copyright is created automatically, you can protect your rights to your creation most effectively by registering your work with the U.S. or Canadian Copyright Office. A much simpler process than filing for a patent or trademark, copyright application involves completing a form and paying a fee.

If an employee develops a new product while working for you, does your business own that product? To avoid disputes and misunderstandings you may want to consider developing formal agreements to address these issues.

b. Who Owns It?

If an employee invents a product for your company, who owns the right to that product — you or the employee?

If an employee creates a brochure to promote a product for your company, does he or she have the right to use that brochure design for other purposes?

Ownership is a question that plagues many businesses — particularly small businesses — when dealing with the issue of employee inventions or creations. A legal doctrine known as "work for hire" covers the ownership of copyrightable material created during the course of employment. The Copyright Act states that if an employee creates a copyrightable work during the course of employment (a newsletter, for instance), the work is considered to be a "work made for hire" and the copyright is actually owned by the employer. However, if the individual who created the work is not an employee but a contractor or consultant, or if the work was created outside the employee's scope of employment, the copyright does not belong to the employer.

An area where this issue has become increasingly prevalent is in the development of software. Software that has been developed by an employee who is hired as a computer programmer and who creates software under the direction of the company for a specific use is, based on the definition provided above, owned by the company. But what about software that is developed by an employee who is not a programmer? What if that software was developed by an accounting clerk who simply wanted to simplify some job process?

Obviously these issues can become complex. Even though it is generally true that the work products of employees directly related to the position they hold are the property of the company they work for, you can provide yourself with added security by asking employees to sign an invention covenant, similar to the one in Sample 10.

c. Employment-at-Will

Employment-at-will means that a company may terminate an employee, with or without cause, at any time, with or without notice. Conversely, employees may leave with or without notice at any time. One of the major differences between American and Canadian employment law is that Canadian law does not recognize the concept of "employment-at-will." In the United States, virtually every state operates under the presumption that unless a company has an employment contract with its employees, it is operating under the employment-at-will guidelines.

While the employment-at-will doctrine has long served to provide protection to employers, companies in the United States have faced legal problems when they have inadvertently included language in their personnel handbooks that has been construed as establishing a contractual relationship that supersedes employment-at-will. Employees in the United States have argued that language in the employee manual guaranteed job security, guaranteed them that certain progressive disciplinary steps would be followed, or guaranteed them the right to permanent employment with a company.

Section **b.** of chapter 11 covers this issue in more detail. Suffice it to say here, however, that your company handbooks may inadvertently create contractual arrangements that you had not intended.

d. Employment Contracts

Employment-at-will does not exist in Canada. In Canada, employers may terminate employees upon providing reasonable notice or for just cause. Because of this and because employees in Canada can waive or limit rights under common law by contract, Canadian employers are much more likely than employers in the United States to use written employment contracts for employees at all levels of the organization.

Employment contracts are written agreements that outline the services and pay arrangements for employees. In addition, employment contracts frequently include sections related to the protection of trade secrets and confidential information, and sections that limit competition from the employee should his or her employment be terminated.

In both Canada and the United States, make sure that —

SAMPLE 10
INVENTION COVENANT

The undersigned Employee (the "Employee") of _____XYZ Company_____ (the "Employer") hereby
promises the Employer: *(Name of Employer)*

1. to promptly disclose to the Employer in writing all inventions, discoveries, developments, innovations, and computer programs ("inventions") made, in whole or in part, by the Employee during the course of or in relation to the Employee's employment with the Employer, whether conceived or developed during working hours or not, including but not limited to inventions:

    (a) resulting from work performed by the Employee or any other employee of the Employer for the Employer,

    (b) relating in any manner whatsoever to the present or contemplated business of the Employer, or

    (c) resulting from the use of the Employer's time, equipment, materials, or work facilities;

2. to assign and hereby does assign to the Employer all the Employee's interest in and title to inventions required to be disclosed by the Employee to the Employer;

3. to execute at the Employer's request, whether made during or after the Employee's employment with the Employer, any instruments prepared by or on behalf of the Employer or the Employer's successors in title acknowledging or assuring the Employer's interest in and title to inventions required to be disclosed by the Employee to the Employer or assisting the Employer or the Employer's successors in title to obtain any registered copyright, design, patent, or any other industrial property rights whatsoever.

Given under seal on _____7/1_____ .
                              (Date)

Signed, sealed, and delivered in the presence of:

_____   _____
(Signature of Witness)   *(Signature of Employee)*

for the Employee

- your job offers are made in writing. See chapter 8 for a sample,

- any employment contract is executed before employment begins, and

- employment contracts are reviewed and updated regularly to reflect changes in an employee's position.

Provisions that should be included in the employment contract are:

- Length of employment/provision for termination. This section may specifically outline a term of employment (i.e., one year), indicate that the contract will be automatically renewed at certain time periods unless either party provides written notice to end the contract within a certain time frame prior to the automatic renewal, or reinforce the employment-at-will doctrine, indicating that the employee may be terminated at any time or that either party may terminate the agreement.

- Duties of the employee. These can be detailed within the body of the contract or you may wish to attach the job description as an addendum.

- Confidentiality. This section prohibits the employee's disclosing any information that is considered confidential or proprietary. Nondisclosure agreements will be discussed in more detail later on in this chapter.

- Compensation and benefits.

- Noncompetition covenant. Many employers wish to restrict former employees' activities with regard to who they work for after the employment relationship has been terminated. This is a particularly difficult issue, with courts generally favoring the rights of employees. Noncompetition agreements will be discussed in more detail further on in this chapter.

When dealing with any type of employment contract, it is critical that the document be signed before the employee begins work with the company. Contracts can be instituted for existing employees under certain circumstances: if an employee is offered a raise or promotion conditional on the signing of a contract, or if the company is implementing a new policy requiring the entire work force to sign employment contracts. However, for the contract to be a contract, each employee must be offered some form of "consideration" — something of value — for signing the agreement. When an employee signs a contract at the time of hiring, the "consideration" is the job. If a company wants to implement a policy where all members of an existing work force sign a contract, the "consideration" might be an across-the-board pay increase.

Generally, the best way to use contracts is to require them for certain critical positions and to have them completed prior to embarking upon the employment relationship.

e. Nondisclosure Agreements

Your marketing information, your financial information, information on how your products and services are manufactured and distributed — all of this knowledge is proprietary and valuable. In the wrong hands it could potentially have a detrimental impact on your sales, profitability, and long-term success.

While employees are on your payroll, the more information they have, the more effectively they can do their jobs and the more positive impact they can have on the bottom line. On the other hand, if those employees leave your company, the more information they have, the more potential there is that this information could find its way to the competition. What can you do?

While common law and the Uniform Trade Secrets Act (in the U.S.) clearly limit employees' ability to misappropriate employer trade secrets, many businesses also have employees sign confidentiality or nondisclosure agreements. Some important points to include in a confidentiality or nondisclosure agreement include:

(a) *A definition of confidential information.* It is not enough simply to say, "Employees will not share confidential information." You need to specifically indicate what type of information you view as confidential (for example, sales figures, new products planned for introduction, marketing plans, etc.; basically any information that is not generally known). And even doing this doesn't guarantee that the courts will agree with you. Information that is generally not viewed as confidential is information that was already known by the employee, information revealed to the employee by a third party, information that has become publicly known, information that has been requested by and provided to a government agency, or information that has been obtained independently.

(b) *No disclosure.* The recipient of the information agrees that this information will not be shared with third parties.

(c) *No use.* A statement that clearly indicates that the recipient of the information will not use that information for any purpose other than what has been set forth in the agreement.

(d) *Term.* While the term during which the confidentiality agreement is applicable should be long enough to protect the interests of the company, it cannot be so long as to place an unreasonable burden on the employee.

In a competitive business environment, your proprietary information represents exceptional value. Nondisclosure and noncompetition agreements can help you minimize the risk of losing valuable information to competitors.

f. Noncompetition Agreements

When you've spent time and resources training an employee to carry out a function in your company, the last thing you want is to have that employee take those skills and that knowledge to your competition. Employers have their employees sign noncompetition agreements so they will not take their abilities to a competitor and so they will not set up a competing business and solicit the employer's customers. The courts have generally recognized two legitimate reasons for an employer to enter into a noncompetition agreement with employees:

➤ To protect customer contacts and relationships

➤ To protect confidential information

However, courts have been notoriously reluctant to uphold these agreements due to concern over limiting competition and concern over interfering with an individual's ability to secure employment. California's Business and Professions Code Chapter 16600, for instance, says that "every contract by which anyone is restrained from engaging in a lawful profession, trade, or business of any kind is to that extent void."

Courts have also tended to take an all-or-nothing view of these agreements — either upholding them or throwing them out in their entirety. Illinois is a state that has traditionally taken a hard-line approach against applying restrictive covenants such as noncompetition agreements. For example, in *Prudential Insurance Co. of America v. Semptrean*, the defendant, an insurance salesman, signed a termination agreement that prohibited him from soliciting customers that he had served while employed by Prudential. While this may seem reasonable, the court in this case determined that the agreement was too vague because it lacked time and geographic limitations.

Since these agreements have been historically difficult to uphold, you should make sure that any agreement you use meets the following requirements:

(a) *Is designed to protect a legitimate business interest.* For example, an agreement could not prohibit a lawyer from practicing law. It could, however, forbid that lawyer from sharing proprietary information in the course of his or her legal practice. You should clearly and specifically define the type of business activity from which the employee would be prohibited from engaging.

(b) *Is limited in time.* In general, two years is considered the maximum time limit that is considered reasonable.

(c) *Is limited in geographic scope.* Trying to keep an employee from getting a job in a related field anywhere in the country would generally be viewed as unreasonable. However, language that restricts an employee from working in a particular city, county, state, or province would be viewed more favorably.

(d) *Is consistently applied.* Employees in similar jobs should each be required to sign a noncompetition agreement if one is used by your company. You could not, for instance, ask one of five software engineers to sign an agreement without requiring the other four to do the same.

Noncompetition agreements should be used sparingly and only with employees who hold certain key positions — i.e., salespeople, software designers. Sample 11 shows an example of a basic nondisclosure and noncompetition covenant. Since the interpretation of these documents varies widely, and because employers have traditionally found these agreements difficult to uphold, you should always check your state statutes or municipal guidelines and have an attorney review any document you use to help ensure that it will stand up to scrutiny should an employee leave your company.

SAMPLE 11
NONDISCLOSURE AND NONCOMPETITION COVENANT

The undersigned Employee (the "Employee") of ___XYZ Company___ (the "Employer") hereby promises the Employer:

1. to keep the Employer's business secrets, including but not limited to customer, supplier, logistical, financial, research, and development information, confidential and not to disclose the Employer's business secrets to any third party during and after the term of the Employee's employment;

General noncompetition clause

2. that, on the termination of the Employee's employment with the Employer for any reason, the Employee will not operate a ___Widget Marketing___ (type of business) business or in any way aid and assist any other person to operate such a business in ___a 45-mile radius___ (geographical area) for a period of ___24 months___ (time period) from the date of termination of the Employee's employment;

Specific account noncompetition clause

3. that, on the termination of the Employee's employment with the Employer for any reason, the Employee will not solicit any customer of the Employer that was a customer of the Employer during the course of the Employee's employment with the Employer, whether or not still a customer of the Employer and whether or not knowledge of the customer is considered confidential information, or in any way aid and assist any other person to solicit any such customer for a period of ___24 months___ (time period) from the date of termination of the Employee's employment.

If any part of these promises is void for any reason, the undersigned accepts that it may be severed without affecting the validity or enforceability of the balance of the promises.

Given under seal on ___7/1___ (date).

Signed, sealed, and delivered in the presence of:

_____   _____
            (Signature of Witness)   *(Signature of Employee)*

for the Employee.

11

Company Policies

The best advice I can give about developing a personnel handbook is: DON'T. The logic is that for everything you spell out there are five things you'll miss which can be construed (by contingency fee lawyers) in a manner unhealthy for your business. Little traps like listing a few grounds for dismissal, then having all the grounds not listed being considered invalid. Like having an AIDS policy, but not a hepatitis policy. In short, leave handbooks to the pros or leave them alone.

This statement was made by a business owner and expresses a common feeling. Many small- and large-business owners feel much the same way. And there are grounds for their trepidation. Employee handbooks can open your company to potential legal problems. But so can the lack of an employee handbook.

Just as a society needs rules to function effectively, so does a company. Those rules frequently start out informally — we will come to work at 8 a.m. and leave at 5 p.m. — and this system works quite well for a period of time. As time elapses, however, and as the company grows or changes, the rules need to be formalized. They need to be written down.

It is that process of writing down the rules that constitutes the development of a personnel manual in its simplest form.

The role of the personnel manual is to establish rules and guidelines by which everyone in the company can operate. The handbook provides a structure for presenting these rules as well as a source of information for employees and managers alike. It provides consistency so that employees can be assured they will be treated fairly, and it offers an authoritative source for managers who need to know how to handle specific situations.

> Every society has rules. Your business can be considered a small society and your personnel manual serves as a compilation of the rules and procedures that govern your work force.

Within the handbook are rules, but also information on insurance benefits, vacation and holiday issues, disciplinary procedures, and anything else that is relevant to company personnel.

Because of the breadth of information included in the personnel manual, as well as its importance, it will also have legal implications. For this reason, whether your handbook is a simple two-page document or a more comprehensive 300-page tome, it is advisable to have a legal review of the completed piece — or legal involvement in its development.

a. Why Does My Company Need a Personnel Manual?

A personnel manual serves a number of purposes within an organization. It establishes the rules and guidelines by which employees will function on the job. It outlines benefits. It serves as an arbitration device in the event of disputes. It can be useful as an orientation and training tool. It can outline hiring and promotion policies as well as employee development opportunities.

By far the most important use of the manual, however, is to lay down the guidelines by which all members of the organization — your society — will operate.

By requiring the company to define and set down its policies, the personnel manual also helps a company work toward —

> ➤ recognizing each person as an important individual;

> ➤ establishing appropriate objectives or standards for each position within the organization;

> ➤ reviewing regularly the performance of all staff members to inform them of their status and to provide them with guidance to help them progress in their positions and in the company;

> ➤ promoting from within the company those individuals qualified to fill job vacancies or new positions;

> ➤ maintaining salary scales that compare favorably with those maintained by other companies and the local business community for similar work, and administering salaries in a manner that recognizes the relative importance of each position and rewards competent and meritorious performance;

> ➤ providing an efficient environment by maintaining good physical working conditions and by fostering harmonious relationships among employees;

> ➤ providing planned training, education, and staff development activities and regarding them as an investment for the mutual benefit of employees and the company; and

➤ establishing and maintaining a truly open-door environment with all members of the staff to encourage open communications at all levels of employment.

For company owners, the personnel handbook should be viewed as a legal document establishing a form of contract with employees. It is your documentation that employees have been informed of certain rules and policies, that they do know which actions are grounds for dismissal, and that they understand and agree to the terms of employment. Recognize, though, that you will want to downplay the contractual nature of the handbook for legal liability reasons (see section **b.**).

For managers as well as company owners, the personnel handbook is a repository of information that might otherwise be forgotten, misinterpreted, or miscommunicated.

For employees, the manual is a reference that provides information to answer their questions. Here, in one convenient, easily accessible place, employees can find answers to such questions as:

➤ What are the standard work hours?

➤ What are the paid holidays?

➤ What are the health benefits?

➤ What rules of conduct must I abide by?

➤ What is the dress code for my position?

In short, the personnel manual is an indispensable tool to keep your company, large or small, running smoothly. By creating and using such a reference, you ensure that everyone in the company understands the parameters of his or her job, the overall organization of the company, and what conduct is expected in this particular society. With clear guidelines, both employees and managers can do their jobs better.

Checklist 3 is a Company Policy Outline that you can use as a guide to identify items that you may want to include in your own company policy document. This form can also be useful as a guideline for discussing company policy with new employees.

b. Watch Your Language

As mentioned in chapter 10, the employment-at-will doctrine is a legal concept that has been followed on a widespread basis in the United States. Employment-at-will means that either a company or an employer can terminate an employment relationship at any time for any reason that is not illegal. The most obvious exceptions are the following:

Give examples in your handbook, but be sure to include language that clearly indicates these are examples only and that you will reserve the right to use discretion in dealing with unanticipated issues or situations that may arise.

CHECKLIST 3
COMPANY POLICY OUTLINE

The Company

- ○ Mission statement
- ○ Corporate philosophy
- ○ Organizational chart
- ○ Job descriptions

Issues of pay and performance

- ○ Performance review
- ○ Attendance polocies
- ○ Changes in employee status
- ○ Reduction in staff
- ○ Reimbursement for expenses
- ○ References
- ○ Hours of operation
- ○ Employee classifications
- ○ Hiring relatives
- ○ Outside employment
- ○ Exit reviews
- ○ Work hours
- ○ Salary reviews
- ○ Hiring policies
- ○ Issues of pay
- ○ Termination
- ○ Use of personal automobiles

Benefits

- ○ Vacation
- ○ Dental insurance
- ○ Jury duty
- ○ Personal leave
- ○ Unemployment compensation
- ○ Funeral leave
- ○ Training
- ○ Life insurance
- ○ Holidays
- ○ Sick leave
- ○ Workers' compensation
- ○ Military leave
- ○ Employment assistance program
- ○ Health insurance
- ○ Doctor and dental appointments
- ○ Disability income
- ○ Sharing of company profits
- ○ Family and medical leave
- ○ Employment education
- ○ General leaves of absence
- ○ Extended benefits after leaving the company (e.g., pensions)

Standards of conduct

- ○ Problem resolution
- ○ Voluntary termination
- ○ Grievance procedures
- ○ Disciplinary appeals process
- ○ Disciplinary procedures
- ○ Involuntary termination

General information

- ○ Telephone procedures
- ○ Automobile liability coverage
- ○ Company property
- ○ Other contributions
- ○ Sexual harrassment
- ○ Company vehicles
- ○ Personal property
- ○ Contributions for gifts
- ○ Personnel records
- ○ Smoking/chewing tobacco
- ○ Business gifts
- ○ Traffic amd parking violations
- ○ Confidential nature of business
- ○ Personal mail
- ○ Emergency and safety procedures
- ○ Alcohol on company premises or on business travel

> An employer cannot terminate an employee if that termination would violate anti-discrimination laws.

> An employer cannot terminate an employee for any situation that would contravene public policy (for instance, an employee could not be fired for refusing a superior's order to break the law).

Employment-at-will has traditionally meant that employers have the right to terminate employees whose performance is not up to standards. Employment relationships were interpreted to be "nonpermanent."

A poorly drafted handbook can change this relationship. For instance, if your handbook lists specific work rules, a court could determine that an employee could not be disciplined for something that is not included. Or if your handbook contains a progressive disciplinary procedure, your company could be in legal jeopardy if you fail to adhere strictly to these procedures.

The key to avoiding these problems is to understand where the potential for trouble lies. The problem with many personnel handbooks is that by including certain statements they challenge the employment-at-will concept and make it difficult to legally discipline or terminate employees.

The proper language can help you avoid these problems. The sample contracts and forms in this book contain noncompromising wording for you to use in your personnel manual. For example, "This list is intended as an example only and is not intended to indicate all of those acts that could lead to employee discipline" or "This progressive disciplinary policy is intended as a guideline only. An action could start at any point in the process, including immediate termination."

To avoid legal problems with your handbook, consider the following tips.

1. Promises, promises...

Don't make promises in the handbook that you don't intend to keep. For instance, don't state in your handbook that all employees will be reviewed twice a year, in March and September, unless you fully intend to adhere to this statement. Watch out for implied promises both in your handbook and in statements made by you or your employees. The type of statements you should be wary of? Any that imply guarantees of job security or advancement opportunities could cause problems. So could statements about probationary versus permanent employment status. Such statements might be interpreted to mean that once an employee has worked for a specified period of time, he or she is guaranteed a job for life. Stay away from wishy-washy language like "We will be fair to our employees." The term "fair" is open to wide interpretation and can get you into trouble.

2. Revise regularly

Revise your employee handbook regularly. Be aware of the rules and regulations governing your jurisdiction. Laws vary by state or province — sometimes even by county. Laws can change so dramatically within a short period of time that you may be liable to a lawsuit if the appropriate sections in your handbook are not modified. Know the rules that affect you and stay current on the changes in those rules. Keep your job descriptions up-to-date and tied to the actual requirements of the job. Outdated job descriptions can lead to problems if discharged employees claim they were terminated for failure to do work for which they were not originally hired.

3. Don't limit yourself

When discussing reasons for termination decisions in your handbook, avoid references to dismissal only for "just cause" or vague terms like "fair" that could cause you problems later. The following qualifying statement would be appropriate to include in your handbook:

> *We recognize our employees' rights to resign at any time for any reason; similarly we may terminate any employee at any time, with or without cause. No one other than the company owner has the authority to modify this relationship or to make any agreements to the contrary. Any such modification or agreement must be in writing.*

Do include a list of potential causes for discharge though. Such a list can help alleviate employee fears about arbitrary dismissal. But make sure that you also include a statement to the effect that this list is intended to be a guideline only and that management retains the right to discharge an employee for any reason. This language might read as follows:

> *While it is impossible to list all the rules associates are expected to follow, some of the more serious infractions that will subject you to discipline (up to and including termination) are outlined herein. This list is not meant to be all-inclusive. Management reserves the right to terminate associates for any reason, at any time.*

This language may seem harsh and may certainly be cause for concern among your employees. It is necessary to include it, though, to protect yourself and your company — to help allay some fears, explain to your employees why you must include such language.

Be cautious when outlining layoff procedures. Today's business climate has made downsizing and reductions in the work force a fact of life and one that your company may, unfortunately, have to deal with. Statements in your handbook related to this issue should avoid indications that layoff decisions will be based on length of service. You will want to retain the right to terminate employees based on performance — not seniority.

4. Subject to change

You will want to indicate in your handbook that the information it contains can be changed or modified at any time.

> *Management reserves the right to change the provisions of this handbook at any time, with or without notice. In almost all cases, changes to the handbook will be announced in a timely fashion.*

c. The Handbook As a Contractual Document

> *The contents of this handbook are presented as a matter of information of employment only. This handbook does not constitute an express or implied contract for employment. It provides guidelines only and may be changed or disregarded when, in the opinion of management, circumstances so require."*

An employee handbook is viewed as a contractual document in most locales. Because of this, it is especially critical that you carefully consider each statement you include in the handbook so you don't obligate yourself to meet conditions that you are not prepared to meet.

To help avoid some of the inherent contractual problems with employee handbooks, many companies include disclaimer statements at critical points in the handbook itself. Some of these points might include the following:

Your personnel manual can be construed as a contract. Exercise caution in the information you include and use disclaimers freely and prominently.

- ➤ The introduction
- ➤ The discussion of orientation or training periods
- ➤ The section on complaint or dispute resolution
- ➤ The listing of standards of conduct and work rules
- ➤ As part of the statement acknowledging receipt of the handbook by the employee

Such disclaimers should appear prominently when they are included and should not be buried in the text or printed in such small type that attention is diverted from them.

Following is an example of a statement of purpose that might be included in the introduction to a personnel handbook. Notice that language is included in this statement relating to the rights of employees conferred by the handbook and touching on certain legal issues. This same type of language could be included in other parts of your handbook and might serve to protect you from various legal problems that sometimes develop based on implications of a "right to employment" or contractual agreement.

This handbook has been produced by the company for the guidance and orientation of our employees. None of the benefits or policies in this handbook are intended by reason of publication to confer any rights or privileges, or to entitle you to be or to remain to be employed by the company. The contents of this handbook are presented as a matter of information of employment only.

This handbook does not constitute an express or implied contract for employment. It provides guidelines only and may be changed or disregarded when, in the opinion of management, circumstances so require. Management reserves the right to change the provisions of this handbook at any time, with or without notice. In almost all cases, changes to the handbook will be announced in a timely fashion. We will use one, some, or all of the following to announce changes when needed: staff meeting, department or division meetings, memos, and the bulletin board. However, we retain the right to implement some changes immediately without advance notice.

Each manager is responsible for maintaining a completely updated copy of this handbook available to all employees at all times. Copies of all changes will also be distributed to all associates and it will be up to you to make sure your handbook is current. In the event of a dispute, the most recently updated and announced version will be used. All changes will be issued through the Human Resources Department; however, no one other than the president has the authority to effect changes pertaining to the plans, policies, or procedures described herein. Any changes must be in writing.

We recognize our employees' rights to resign at any time for any reason; similarly we may terminate any employee at any time, with or without cause. No one other than the president has the authority to modify this relationship or to make any agreements to the contrary. Any such modification or agreement must be in writing.

It is important to include a statement to the effect that "this handbook does not constitute an express or implied contract for employment" because it can dissuade employees from suing and will be sufficient evidence of intent in most locales. However, in a lawsuit, the matter of whether or not the handbook was a contract can be open to interpretation by the court, even if such language is included.

In addition to the language concerning the lack of any implied employment contract, this statement also illustrates two other points about the handbook: how management will communicate changes and modifications, and the manager's responsibility to maintain an updated version of the handbook.

In your handbook, you will also want to make explicit the rights and responsibilities your company has in relation to its employees. The following statement provides an example of the type of language you might use:

> *Certain rights and responsibilities are imposed on the company by state, provincial, and federal legislation and court decisions. Many of these have implications for policies and procedures governing employment. For this reason, please be advised that we hereby reserve any and all management rights regarding employees' employment status. These rights and responsibilities include, but are not limited to, the following:*
>
> *To manage and direct company employees, including hiring, promotion, scheduling, transfers, assignment or retention of employees in positions within the company, and to establish work rules; to lay off employees; to discharge or take other appropriate disciplinary action when necessary; to schedule overtime work as required consistent with the requirements of the company; to develop job descriptions, bearing in mind that such descriptions are usually guidelines and not rigid limitations, and that associates shall perform any reasonable assigned duties; to introduce new or improved methods or facilities, or to change existing methods or facilities; to fulfill its obligations in contracting out for matters relating to the operation of the company; to discontinue certain operations; and to direct all questions of the company.*

Before distributing your employee handbook, be sure to have it reviewed by legal counsel. It is a small investment to help ensure you have adequately protected your interests.

d. The Legal Review

Employee handbooks are complex documents and subject to interpretation by employees and the courts. To avoid legal liability, always have these documents reviewed by a lawyer. If you have legal counsel on staff, that may suffice. However, you will be best served by a lawyer who specializes in employment law. You can locate such a lawyer through your local bar association, legal referral service, or legal directory at your local library.

Fees lawyers charge for reviewing your manual will vary depending on your locale; however, expect to pay between $50 and $100 per hour. View this fee as insurance against potential lawsuits that could carry with them exorbitant legal fees as well as costly judgments if your handbook is not legally sound.

e. Living by the Book

Whether you decide to produce a handbook that is 200 pages long and bound, 10 pages long and stapled in the upper left-hand corner, or computerized and accessed through your company's Intranet, your job is far from done once the handbook is printed or introduced. Handbook development is not a finite process with a recognizable end in sight. Handing out those first drafts is just the beginning.

One of the common problems with personnel handbooks is that they are not used. Seldom read, they sit on a shelf and gather dust. Revisions are stuffed into the binder but not looked at. The result is that employees are unaware of the benefits available to them, the sanctions that apply to various aspects of their performance, and the opportunities that exist within their company. A frequent comment is, "I didn't know that!"

Your best weapon for combating the "I didn't know" syndrome is to ensure that employees *do* know — through effective communication. In any company, communication plays a major role both in terms of imparting important information to the work force and in terms of maintaining morale and engendering an atmosphere of teamwork.

What are some common forms of communication that companies have at their disposal? Staff meetings, newsletters, annual reports, bulletin boards — these are just a few examples.Whatever your unique communication tools, awareness — and organization — are the keys to effectiveness.

"Communicating" your personnel manual involves more than simply handing it out and asking employees to sign a form stating that they have received it. The handbook and its contents should be introduced to employees.

1. Meetings

Perhaps the best way to introduce your handbook is in a meeting, either with the entire company or by department. At the meeting, each section of the book should be reviewed and employees allowed the opportunity to ask questions or receive clarification on the information. Make overheads of the critical and complex portions of the handbook so they can be reviewed in the meeting.

At this meeting you can also provide employees with specific information on how the handbook is to be used and where to go if they need additional information.

When the general meeting is complete, ask your managers and supervisors to continue the discussion in their own staff meetings. Require that supervisors and managers be intimately familiar with the handbook and its contents so they can serve as resources to employees. Both you and your managers should make the handbook a part of ongoing employee communications. Refer to it in such situations as staff meetings and one-on-one discussions.

Don't be afraid to talk about the handbook and its contents too much. Repetition is the key to retention. To avoid the "shelf syndrome" with your handbook, make it an integral part of the day-to-day activities of your company and all those in it.

As changes come up or revisions are necessary, call employees back together to discuss those changes. Make sure that they add or delete the appropriate pages and that they understand the implications of any changes made.

2. Bulletin board

When new handbooks are introduced or as changes are made, make use of your company bulletin boards to post specific items. Consider developing posters that highlight the availability of the handbook or point to critical new bits of information.

3. Suggestion box

To ensure that employees feel that the company handbook is their handbook, invite input. Have a suggestion box or a similar system in place so employees can contribute their ideas or point out areas that need clarification or modification. Be responsive to the suggestions submitted. One of the failings of many suggestion systems is that managers and company owners don't respond promptly to the suggestions submitted. Get back to employees immediately — whether their ideas will be implemented or not. If you are not going to implement a suggestion, explain why and encourage the employee to continue to submit ideas in the future.

4. Testing

Consider implementing some form of testing on the contents of the handbook and make it an ongoing process — not a one-time activity. Offer an incentive to employees for reading and retaining the information in their handbooks. One company has a quiz it gives to employees after they have received the handbook to show whether they have understood the basics. You might tie performance on such a quiz to some token incentive — movie tickets or gift certificates.

5. Making your manual user friendly

Here are some additional tips that can help you create a personnel handbook that will be used — and useful:

➤ Gather handbooks from other companies to generate ideas. How are the books laid out? How is information organized and arranged to aid readability? What makes these various handbooks good or bad? What do you like about these handbooks? What do you dislike?

➤ Talk to other business owners or personnel managers about the process they went through in putting together their employee handbooks. What did they learn in the process? What tips can they offer you on pitfalls to avoid or suggestions to make your handbook more effective?

➤ Aim, above all, to increase employee understanding of the operation of your business. Write with the employees' interests in mind. Use a level of writing neither above or below your average reader.

➤ Establish an ongoing handbook committee with a responsibility to ensure that the handbook is kept up-to-date. The committee might meet on a regular basis to update and modify the handbook, determine when a revision should be issued, and develop ways to best communicate changes to the work force. The committee should be made up of a broad cross-section of employees, including both management and nonmanagement representatives.

➤ Hold orientation sessions for new employees to go over the handbook and to familiarize them in other ways with the company, its organization, and operations

f. Some Do's and Don'ts of Preparing Your Employee Handbook

1. Do be sure to comply with all applicable laws

It is a big, complex minefield out there with federal, state, and local regulations changing all the time. You have to be proactive and make sure you are staying on top of any court decisions that can have a great influence on your handbook.

In some areas, this task has been simplified through software programs. In the state of New York, for instance, a system is in place whereby credit unions can receive software updates on applicable changes in the law and recent court decisions. Similar programs may be available in your area or within your industry.

There are countless laws — state, provincial, federal, and local — that impact what you should or should not include in your employee handbook. Keeping up with these laws is a momentous task, but one that must be taken on nevertheless. An out-of-date handbook is useless and, in fact, may create unnecessary risks for your business.

2. Don't be a copycat

Even though it can be helpful to look at other handbooks to generate ideas, make sure you include well-thought-out policies that conform to the realities of your workplace. Don't just take someone else's handbook, change the name, and make it yours. A handbook that is appropriate for one employer may be totally inappropriate for another. Tailor policies to your work force and only include policies that you intend to implement and have them follow.

3. Do include adequate disclaimers

Employers are often hesitant to use adequate disclaimers in their handbooks — they view disclaimers as somehow harsh or negative. Disclaimers should, however, be included throughout the handbook; they are critically important. Make them large, clear, and bold.

4. Don't be overly restrictive

Draft your handbook to give maximum flexibility to your company and its managers. You want managers to handle violations of company policy at their discretion and as they feel appropriate. Each circumstance does not have to be handled identically. But if you have mandatory policies, no deviation is allowed.

5. Do require signed employee acknowledgments

When you distribute your handbook or any handbook updates to employees, you should make sure to have employees complete an acknowledgement form. This form should indicate that employees have read the handbook, that they had an opportunity to ask questions, that they understand the handbook, and that they agree to abide by the handbook and its policies. This form should be signed and maintained in the employee's personnel file. These acknowledgements should be completed each time a change is made to the handbook. You want to create a paper trail to show that employees have indeed updated their manuals and signed off.

6. Don't forget the importance of communication

The key to an effective employee handbook is communication. You have to do a good job of educating employees and supervisors to make sure there is internal consistency in the policies and procedures they are using.

Employee handbooks are a wonderful resource for employees and employers. Ultimately, they can save a lot of time and money for the company and reduce miscommunication between employer and employee.

12

Issues Related to Pay and Work Hours

State, provincial, and federal regulations exist that govern issues of salary and hours. Being familiar with the regulations that affect your business can save you a lot of trouble — and money. Small businesses are required to abide by the requirements of fair labor and pay laws just as large corporations are. No matter what the size of your business, you don't need a lawsuit from an employee who feels he or she was badly, or unfairly, treated.

To avoid this, make clear, legal, fair policies and put them in your personnel manual so all employees understand them. There are a number of policies and procedures related to pay and work hours that you may wish to include in your handbook depending on the size of your company, the type of business you are in, and the unique characteristics of your management staff and work force.

a. Issues of Money and Hours of Work

There are a number of basic issues regarding pay and work hours that your employees will want to know about. For instance:

- ➤ How often am I paid?
- ➤ When am I paid?
- ➤ What about overtime?
- ➤ Do I get paid more for working on holidays?
- ➤ Do I need approval for overtime?
- ➤ How do I keep track of the time I work?
- ➤ When I leave employment with unused vacation or leave, do I receive pay in lieu of time off?

These issues should be clearly outlined in the personnel handbook. In addition, supervisors and managers should be familiar with the company's policies and should ensure that those policies are applied consistently for all employees. Some common handbook sections are outlined here.

1. Salary reviews

Your handbook should cover the issue of salary reviews and explain how pay decisions are made. Typically, these decisions are tied to the evaluation process. Explain how that system will work in a general sense. Avoid stating the process in such specific terms that you create rigid expectations that you must comply with. A statement such as the following would be appropriate: "An employee will receive a salary review after the first six months of performance and again after one year of performance. Thereafter, salary reviews will occur on an annual basis. Salary reviews are based on an evaluation of performance by the employee's manager and will be reviewed by the company president."

2. Work hours

Again, provide general information about work hours, but don't be so specific that you create rigid expectations that you will be held to. Offer information on the number of hours considered to be a typical week in your company related to your hours of operation. Include a statement that allows you the option of rescheduling individual hours in any given week at your discretion based on workload or staffing requirements.

3. Breaks

Another area of concern to employees is when they will have lunch and work breaks. These guidelines should be indicated in your handbook and can be based on the number of hours worked. For example:

TABLE 4
Breaks for hours worked

Working Hours	Breaks
0–2 hours	None
2–4½ hours	One 15-minute break
4½–6 hours	½ hour lunch and one 15-minute break
6+ hours	½ hour lunch and two 15-minute break

4. Tracking time worked

An employee time card is a standard way of tracking the hours that an employee works. Whether you use a paper format, an electronic timecard system, or a computerized timekeeping system, it is important to clearly communicate with employees your expectations for tracking and reporting the time they have worked and the days they have not worked — i.e., vacation time, sick time.

When employees are absent from work, you may want them to complete an absentee report. This form should include a checklist of possible reasons for an employee's absence, along with space for remarks. Keep completed forms in the employee's personnel file.

A vacation request form should be divided into three sections to be completed by the employee, the employer/manager who authorizes the vacation, and the personnel department. It is designed to keep track of the number of vacation days the employee has used and still has available, and it ensures that all departments have the information they need related to employee vacation time off.

Employees should be informed of policies related to how they request time off, the amount of notice required, and issues related to a supervisor's authority to deny a vacation request based on workload and staffing issues.

For supervisors with larger departments, a vacation schedule form can be a convenient way to manage and plan all employees' vacation schedules to ensure an effective and productive department. Such a form can be divided into monthly segments or smaller increments — i.e., weekly, bi-weekly.

An attendance record (see Sample 12) can help you keep track of an individual employee's attendance. It spans one year, divided into months and days. This form allows you to track leave for a variety of reasons so that you can quickly identify any patterns (i.e., frequent accidents, excessive sick leave, etc.)

5. Accident/injury report

Employee safety is important for all employers whether they operate in higher risk manufacturing environments or seemingly risk-free office situations. Quickly responding to and investigating any accident incident is important, both to provide documentation of the action taken and also to provide a record of the incident so trends can be identified and appropriate safety measures instituted.

The accident/injury report in Sample 13 is a comprehensive document that captures a great deal of information. On this form you will enter employee information and provide a description of the accident and a list of witnesses. You

SAMPLE 12
ATTENDANCE RECORD

Employee __Pat Hanson__
Department __Marketing__

Employee No. __12345__
Position __Marketing Asst.__

Year __2000__

Vacation due __5 days__
Sick leave due __6 days__

Vacation taken __5 days__
Sick leave taken __4 days__

Notes _____

	1	2	3	4	5	6	7	8	9	10	11	12	13	14	15	16	17	18	19	20	21	22	23	24	25	26	27	28	29	30	31	PI	FI	HI	LA	V	PB	OA	A	JD	D	LO	X	O	Monthly total
Jan	H																																												1
Feb				✓																																1									1
Mar																																													1
Apr								✓																												1									1
May											✓	✓	✓																							3									3
Jun				H																																									1
Jul					PI																											1													1
Aug																																1													1
Sep														PI																		1													1
Oct					FI	FI																											2												3
Nov																									H																				1
Dec																								H																					13

Yearly total: 13

Codes

PI	Personal illness	PB	Personal business
FI	Family illness	OA	Off-duty accident
LA	Leave of absence	A	Off-duty accident
V	Vacation	JD	Jury duty
H	Holiday		

D	Discipline	
LO	Laid off	
X	Unexcused	
O	Others	_____

SAMPLE 13
ACCIDENT/INJURY REPORT

This form should be completed as soon as possible after an accident or injury. Try to provide as much information as you can, as these details are necessary for insurance and workers' compensation claims.

Employee Information

Employee name   Pat Hanson   Employee No.   12345

Department   Marketing   Position   Marketing Assistant

Date employed   7/1   No. of months in this position   6

Accident information

Location   outside front door

Date   1/3   Date reported   1/3

Time   7:45 a.m.   Time reported   8:00 a.m.

When did the accident occur?   ○ On-duty   ☑ Off-duty

Where did the accident occur?   ○ Inside   ☑ Outside   ○ Driving

Describe the accident in detail   Pat slipped outside on the way in to work — scheduled work start time is 8:00 a.m.

Witnesses

Were there any witnesses to the accident?   ○ Yes   ☑ No

1 Name _____   **2** Name _____
Address _____   Address _____
Telephone No. _____   Telephone No. _____

Written report prepared?   ☑ Yes   ○ No   Written report prepared?   ○ Yes   ○ No
Written report attached?   ☑ Yes   ○ No   Written report attached?   ○ Yes   ○ No

3 Name _____
Address _____
Telephone No. _____

Written report prepared?   ○ Yes   ○ No
Written report attached?   ○ Yes   ○ No

Sample 13 — Continued

Nature of injuries and medical attention received

The following injuries were sustained (describe parts of body affected and severity of injury): _____

_____sprained wrist_____

_____

_____

First aid _____NA_____   **Doctor's examination**

Given by _____   Doctor ____Smith_____

Address _____   Address ____333 Wellness Dr._____

Contact No. _____   Contact No. __555-777-1234_____

Comments _____   Date of examination __1/3_____

_____   Time of examination ___8:45_____

_____   Comments ___sprained wrist_____

_____   _____

Hospital treatment

Hospital _____   Address _____

Contact No. _____   Doctor _____

Date of treatment _____   Time of treatment _____

Comments _____

_____

Prepared by __Jan Black_____   Date __1/4/99_____

Action

Reviewed by __Cris Jones_____   Date __1/5/99_____

Comments _____allowed Pat to take one day sick time on 1/3_____

_____

Action to be taken

_____

_____

_____

_____

_____

will also describe the diagnosis and treatment, doctor's information and examination, and hospital information and treatment. Space is also included for employer comments and recommendations for further action.

b. Rates of Pay

When you make a new hire, you agree to a certain rate of pay and process for payment. For instance, you may make an offer to hire an employee on a salary basis at $X/month, to be paid bi-weekly. At the time of hire, and in the letter confirming the offer, you may also indicate the process for reviewing this rate of pay. Issues of pay are critical for both employer and employee. You want to ensure that you are paying employees equitably both in terms of the marketplace and in relation to other employees who are on staff.

In addition, you should be concerned with legal issues that impact your payroll decisions and actions.

1. Comparable worth and pay equity

One issue you need to be aware of in terms of salary administration is that of comparable worth or pay equity. These terms refer to equal pay for equal performance and are closely tied to the issue of job discrimination.

Is a janitor's job worth as much as a secretary's? Is an administrator's job as important to the company as an engineer's? These are tough issues that are not easily addressed.

To help fairly evaluate the worth of jobs, some companies develop systems whereby jobs can be rated based on various criteria determined to be important to the company, for instance, educational requirements, decision-making ability, or control.

Obviously salary administration is a complex issue and beyond the scope of this book. Suffice it to say that it is an area that needs careful consideration, and you need to take steps to ensure that your pay practices are fair, consistent, and legal.

2. Exempt versus nonexempt

Another important pay issue concerns exempt versus nonexempt employees. Nonexempt employees are entitled to overtime pay at one-and-one-half times their regular rate of pay for all hours worked over 40 in one week. Exempt employees, on the other hand, can work any number of hours without being paid overtime.

As an employer your first thought might be, "Great, I'll make all of my employees exempt and save money on overtime pay." It is not as simple as

What you pay employees will be determined by your budget, of course, but you should also do some research to determine what the market rates are for various positions in your area to help you remain competitive.

that. There are strict guidelines that govern whether an employee can be classified as exempt. Employees who are improperly classified as exempt when they should be nonexempt can create problems for employers when they ask for payment of overtime that has been inappropriately withheld.

Exempt employees are those who are exempt from the pay rules that have been established by the Industrial Welfare Commission (IWC). The status of being exempt has nothing to do with whether the employee has a title or receives a salary versus an hourly wage. Instead, the exempt classification relates to certain categories of employees, which include the following:

➤ Licensed professionals such as doctors, architects, and CPAs

➤ Managers with responsibility for hiring, firing, and training and who spend less than 50 percent of their time engaged in the same type of work as their employees

➤ Top administrators who have responsibility for creating business policies

➤ Outside salespeople

In Canada the criteria related to whether employees are paid overtime are similar to those in the United States. While there is some variance between provinces, in general hourly wages are paid to employees who are in support staff positions, work in a trade, or are covered by union agreements. Salaried employees are those who work in jobs that can be considered professional or managerial.

3. Independent contractor versus employee

Classifying a member of your staff as an independent contractor or employee has ramifications related to payroll withholding issues. When working with independent contractors, employers are not required to withhold taxes, unemployment insurance, or social security benefits. Nor do these individuals receive other benefits of employment such as vacation time. However, misclassifying someone as an independent contractor and not withholding these items or providing these benefits may lead to liability at some later date if it is determined that the individual was, indeed, an employee and not an independent contractor.

How can you distinguish between the two? It is safest to err on the side of classifying workers as employees and to handle withholding in the same manner as with anyone else on the company payroll. If you wish to avoid the withholding requirements, however, IRS Revenue Ruling 87-41 outlines 20 factors used to determine whether a person can be classified as an independent contractor.

Many businesses have been surprised to find that someone they thought was an independent contractor should have been considered an employee. Make sure you clearly understand the distinction — when in doubt err on the side of classifying workers as employees.

(a) The contractor must assume the risk of profit or loss from the association.

(b) A relationship with a contractor represents a limited time frame marked by the completion of a project, while employees are hired for an ongoing period of time.

(c) A contractor controls where and how the work is performed.

(d) Contractors are not trained by the company that purchases their services.

(e) Contractors may delegate aspects of the work they are doing to others, while employees are required to do the work themselves.

(f) Contracted services are not an integral part of the company's operation.

(g) Contractors control the hiring, firing, and supervision of any assistants they might work with.

(h) The contractor's work hours are not dictated by the organization.

(i) There are no full-time work requirements.

(j) The contractor is not required to work at the employer's business location.

(k) The sequence in which the work is performed is not dictated by the organization.

(l) Contractors are less likely than employees to be required to complete and submit regular reports to management.

(m) Contractors are paid based on a project or commission basis, not on an hourly, weekly, or monthly basis.

(n) The contractor is responsible for the payment of work-related business or travel expenses.

(o) Independent contractors provide their own work tools and supplies.

(p) The contractor has a significant investment in the facilities they use for work.

(q) Contractors are able to work for more than one company at any given time.

(r) The contractor regularly makes his or her services available to the public.

(s) Independent contractors cannot be fired. The relationship can, however, be terminated if the contract agreement is violated or the work is not performed as outlined in the contract specifications.

(t) Employees are free to sever their relationship with a company at any time; independent contractors may be liable for breach of contract if they do not complete the work they have been contracted to do.

4. Payroll/expense forms

Pay advice forms provide a convenient way to keep track of regular, overtime, and vacation hours and rates of pay and a place to record all payments and deductions.

The payroll change notice provides a checklist of reasons for a change in employee pay — i.e., a new hire, promotion, increase in pay, layoff — with space to record additional information.

The employee earnings card is a convenient way to track an individual employee's progress with the company (see Sample 14). Here you can record the employee's status, performance reviews, rates of pay, and comments. Over time, this form will provide both you and the employee with a historical perspective on the employee's tenure with your company.

If employees are likely to be travelling or otherwise incurring expenses for the company, you will need to create forms for expense reports and vehicle operation reports. An expense report allows employees to record trip or travel expenses, including details and descriptions, while the vehicle operation report covers a one-month period and provides spaces for each day where employees can record distance traveled, expenses (i.e., fuel, oil, repairs, parking), and additional notes.

SAMPLE 14
EMPLOYEE EARNINGS CARD

Use this form in conjunction with the Appraisal Package to keep track of the earnings and promotion of employees.
The comments column can be used to schedule new review dates or record additional information.

Employee Information

Employee name   Fran Green   Employee No.   32123

Date hired   4/1   Starting wage $5.75/hr.

FT/PT/Temp	Date	Position	Wage	% Increase	Comments
FT	4/1	Clerk I	$5.75/hr.		
FT	7/1	Clerk I	$5.92/hr.		
FT	10/1	Clerk II	$6.22/hr.	3%	probationary increase
FT	10/1	Clerk II	6.53/hr.	5%	promotion
FT	5/1	Admin. Aide	$7.53/hr.	5%	performance review

Prepared by _____   Approved by _____   Date _____

13

Benefit Administration

Why offer benefits to employees? To keep up with the Joneses. And the IBMs. And the corner grocery store. Due to the competitive nature of hiring qualified employees, more and more companies are finding that they must offer attractive benefit packages to retain the best workers.

In the early twentieth century, few companies offered any benefits to employees. In the 1940s and 1950s this began to change, and in the last 20 years we have seen an explosion of new benefits, new benefit plans, and a growing number of companies offering benefits to their employees. Some benefits, such as holidays, minimum vacation time, and worker's compensation coverage, are legislated in some areas of North America. Be sure to check the laws in your area to determine what benefits you must offer your employees.

Benefits can fall into a number of areas including social programs (social security, worker's compensation), insurance and retirement benefits (health, life insurance), payment for time not worked (vacation, sick time), extra cash payment to employees (educational allowances, suggestion awards), and services (recreational programs, free parking, day-care centers).

Benefits represent a high cost to employers and that cost is continuing to grow. In March 1998, employer costs for employee compensation in the United States averaged $19.76 per hour worked according to the U.S. Department of Labor's Bureau of Labor Statistics. Wages and salaries, which averaged $14.30, accounted for approximately 72 percent of these costs, while benefits, which averaged $5.47, accounted for the remaining 28 percent. These compensation costs increased with establishment size, ranging from an average of $15.92 per hour in companies with less than 100 workers to $25.56 per hour in companies with 500 or more workers. The proportion of compensation costs represented by benefits also increased with establishment size, from 24.6 percent in establishments with less than 100 workers to 30.4 percent in establishments with 500 or more workers.

> Benefits represent a major cost to any organization but also serve as a way to attract employees.

Part-time employees are less likely to be covered by most benefit programs, although it is relatively common for employers to prorate benefits to time worked — for example, paid leave. A Bureau of Labor Statistics survey indicates that 30 percent of part-time employees received a paid vacation; 24 percent received paid holidays. Part-time employees had a far smaller chance of participating in benefits that had substantial per capita costs, however — for example, only 6 percent of part-time employees participated in employer-sponsored medical plans.

a. Commonly Provided Benefits

The most commonly provided benefits include paid time off for holidays, vacations, and personal leave; sick leave; health and life insurance; and retirement plans. Table 5, from the Bureau of Labor Statistics, indicates the percentage of full-time employees at small private companies who participate in various employee benefit programs in the United States.

TABLE 5
Percentage of full-time employees at small private companies who participate in employee benefit program

Employee benefit program[1]	All full-time employees	Professional, technical, and related employees[2]	Clerical and sales employees[3]	Blue-collar and service employees[4]
Paid time off				
Holidays	80	86	91	71
Vacations	86	90	95	79
Personal leave	14	21	18	8
Funeral leave	51	60	60	42
Jury duty leave	59	74	68	47
Military leave	18	25	23	12
Sick leave[5]	50	66	64	35
Family leave	2	3	3	1
Insurance				
Short-term disability coverage[5]	29	32	33	25
Long-term disability insurance	22	39	30	10
Medical care	64	76	69	56
Dental care	31	40	35	24
Life	62	72	68	54

Table 5 — Continued

Employee benefit program[1]	All full-time employees	Professional, technical, and related employees[2]	Clerical and sales employees[3]	Blue-collar and service employees[4]
Retirement				
All retirement[6]	46	56	53	37
Defined benefit plans	15	12	16	15
Defined contribution plans[7]	38	51	46	28
Savings and thrift	23	2	29	16
Deferred profit sharing	12	13	17	9
Employee stock ownership	1	2	2	1
Money purchase pension	4	6	3	3
Tax-deferred earnings arrangements				
With employer contributions	24	30	31	17
Without employer contributions	4	8	4	3

1. Except for certain tax-deferred earnings arrangements, employers pay some or all of the costs for each benefit.

2. Includes professional, technical, executive, and administrative occupations.

3. Includes clerical, administrative support, and sales occupations.

4. Includes production, craft, repair, laborer, and service occupations.

5. The definitions of paid sick leave and short-term disability (previously, sickness and accident insurance) were changed after 1994. Paid sick leave now includes only plans with an unlimited or specified number of days per year. Short-term disability now includes all insured, self-insured, and state-mandated plans that provide benefits for each disability, including unfunded plans reported as sick leave in 1994.

6. Includes defined benefit and defined contribution plans. Some employees participate in both types, but are counted just once in all retirement.

7. Total participation is less than the sum of individual plan types because some employees participate in two or more types of plans.

Note: For paid time off, participants include all employees in occupations offered the benefit.

(Source: US Bureau of Labor Statistics, 1996)

1. Time off

Paid time off for recreation and other purposes was the most frequently available employee benefit for full-time employees in small private industry establishments in 1996, according to the Bureau of Labor Statistics, U.S. Department of Labor. Four-fifths of full-time employees received paid vacations and holidays. Half received paid sick leave, and more than a quarter received another form of short-term disability protection (for example, sickness and accident insurance) in addition to, or in lieu of, paid sick leave. Three-fifths received paid leave for jury duty, half received paid funeral leave, and one-fifth were eligible for military leave.

The length of paid vacations, the time available for sick leave, and the number of paid holidays in 1996 were all similar to results obtained in 1994. On average, vacations varied substantially by length of service. For example, in 1996, employees received about 8 days after completing one year of service, but almost 16 days after 25 years. To a lesser degree, paid sick leave also reflected length of service. In 1996, the average days of sick leave were 8 days after one year of service and about 11 days after 25 years. On average, small private employers granted 7.6 paid holidays in 1996. Table 6 shows the average paid holiday and days of vacation and sick leave provided to full-time employees in small private establishments in 1996.

TABLE 6
Average paid holiday and days of vacation and sick leave provided to full-time employees in small private establishments in 1996

Leave category	All full-time employees	Professional, technical, and related employees	Clerical and sales employees	Blue-collar and service employees
Paid holiday	7.6	8.5	7.7	7.0
Paid vacation days after specified years of service:				
1 year.	8.1	10.0	8.6	6.8
3 years	10.2	11.7	10.5	9.2
5 years	11.9	13.8	12.3	10.7
10 years	13.9	16.0	14.3	2.5
15 years	14.8	17.0	15.4	13.4
20 years	15.4	17.6	16.1	3.8
25 years	15.7	17.8	16.4	14.1
Paid sick leave days after specified years of service:				
1 year.	8.0	8.5	7.0	8.8

2. Health benefits

About two out of three full-time employees (64 percent) participated in employer-sponsored medical benefit plans in 1996 according to the U.S. Department of Labor. More often than not, employees had to contribute to the cost of their medical benefits, and those benefits were contained in a managed care health plan. Employee contribution requirements for medical plan coverage changed little from 1994 to 1996. In both years, 52 percent of participants were required to contribute toward the cost of single coverage, on average $41 per month in 1994 compared with $43 per month in 1996; 75 percent of participants had to contribute for family coverage in both years. However, the average monthly cost rose from $160 to $182 over the period.

Nontraditional or managed care plans continue to make enrollment gains among participants in employer-sponsored medical plans. In 1996, 27 percent of all full-time employees participated in health maintenance organization plans (HMOs), where care is managed and benefits are prepaid.

In March 1996, employer costs for the health plans of all employees in small private establishments averaged 74 cents per hour worked. Health plans include dental and vision care plans in addition to medical plans.

According to the Bureau of Labor Statistics, private industry health benefit costs averaged $1 per hour or 5.4 percent of total compensation in March 1998; these health benefit costs varied by industry, occupation, bargaining status, region, and establishment size.

3. Retirement benefits

Bureau of Labor Statistics data indicate that in 1996, 46 percent of full-time employees participated in one or more employer-sponsored retirement plans, compared with 42 percent in 1994. Retirement plans are typically classified in two broad categories — defined benefit or defined contribution plans. In the first, the earned benefit at retirement is specified, and the employer bears the investment risk over the years to fund the benefit. In defined contribution plans, the employer's current cost (contribution) is specified, and the benefit at retirement is unknown in advance. Fifteen percent of all full-time workers were enrolled in defined benefit plans in 1996, the same as in 1994. On the other hand, 38 percent of all full-time workers were enrolled in defined contribution plans. Some participants were enrolled in both forms of retirement plans.

Some types of defined contribution plans were more prevalent than others. Participation in savings and thrift plans was highest at 23 percent of full-time employees, followed by deferred profit-sharing plans at 12 percent and money purchase pension plans at 4 percent. Participation in savings and thrift plans

Health insurance is a highly valued benefit for many employees, but can represent a high cost, especially for small businesses. Most companies pay a portion of the health care expense and ask interested employees to pay a percentage of the total cost.

was higher in 1996 than in 1994, while participation in other types of defined contribution plans was not noticeably different from two years earlier.

In savings and thrift plans, participants are required to contribute, and their contributions are matched by employers, at least in part. There is a maximum amount participants can contribute, with 15 percent of earnings being the most common limit. There is also a limit on the amount of employee contribution that will be matched by the employer. In plans with specified employer matching rates, for example, 49 percent of participants had an employer match on their contributions of up to 5 percent of earnings. Another 38 percent of participants were in plans with matches on more than 5 percent and up to 6 percent of earnings, and the small remainder were in plans with matches more than 6 percent of earnings. The most common rate of employer match (applicable to 36 percent of participants) was 50 cents for each dollar contributed by the employee. Thirty-one percent of participants were in plans with lower match rates, and 33 percent were in plans with higher (such as a 100-percent match).

In March 1998, the average cost for retirement and savings benefits was 55 cents per hour in private industry (3 percent of total compensation). Included in this amount were employer costs for defined benefit plans, which averaged 24 cents (1.3 percent), and for defined contribution plans, which averaged 30 cents (1.6 percent).

4. Employee stock ownership plans (ESOPs)

An employee stock ownership plan (ESOP) is a benefit plan that provides employees with stock in the company where they work. The benefits of ESOPs are many and include increased employee motivation, and tax and financial advantages for your company.

The rules for establishing an ESOP differ between Canada and the United States and between provinces or states, but the basic concept is that a company develops a trust and makes annual contributions to that trust. Contributions are allocated to individual employee accounts; these allocations can be made based on a variety of different formulas. The most common provides allocations to employees based on their rate of pay.

Generally employees must be employed for a specific period of time before they are able to participate in the plan and, after participating, they must be vested before they are able to receive any of the funds in their account. Employees receive the vested portion of their accounts upon termination, disability, death, or retirement. These distributions may be received in a lump sum or in installments over a period of years. Vested portions of ESOP accounts may be received immediately by employees or their beneficiaries if the employee becomes disabled or dies.

If you are interested in establishing an ESOP, there are a number of steps you should follow:

(a) Talk with other business owners who have established ESOPs. They can give you information on pitfalls and benefits and provide you with practical insights on how to proceed.

(b) Select a company to help you establish the plan. There are many qualified consultants available who can help you establish a plan that is best for your company and your needs. The businesses you spoke with in step (a) may be able to provide you with some names to get you started.

(c) Determine whether an ESOP is a feasible alternative for your company. If your company is privately held, the value of your company's stock will need to be valued by an independent appraiser. The effect on existing stockholders will need to be determined.

(d) Determine the type of plan that is most appropriate for your company.

(e) There are a number of questions you will need to answer before establishing a plan: Who will participate in the plan? How will stock be allocated to participants? What vesting schedule will be adopted and how will distributions of ESOP accounts be handled? How will voting rights be handled?

(f) Once your ESOP design has been determined, you will need to work with an attorney to prepare the formal plan document. An appraiser will prepare a final formal evaluation report addressing the plan's purpose and operation, eligibility and participation requirements, company contributions, investment of plan assets, account allocation formulas, vesting and forfeitures, voting rights and fiduciary responsibilities, distribution rules and put options, employee disclosures, and provisions for plan amendments.

Setting up an ESOP can be complicated, but working with qualified advisers will help you move through the process efficiently.

b. Flexible Benefit Programs

The work force is growing increasingly diverse. Employers are coming to realize that satisfying employees through a single benefit program is a difficult task indeed. People work for a variety of reasons and what motivates one employee will not necessarily motivate another. While Employee A may appreciate a generous vacation plan, Employee B may value health insurance more, and Employee C may be concerned about retirement. One way to accommodate

> An employee stock ownership plan (ESOP) can be a good way to generate commitment, enthusiasm, and involvement among employees — and to interest them in the financial well-being of the organization.

all the diverse needs of a work group is through a flexible (or cafeteria) benefit plan. Employers benefit as well through tax savings.

The first flexible benefit programs were implemented in 1974 by the Educational Testing Service and a division of TRW, an automotive products remanufacturing company in Cleveland, Ohio. American Can, a packaging company, then developed a program that was tested in 1978 and started in 1979. Since then, a number of companies have established flexible benefit plans. These plans accommodate the needs of today's work force by allowing individual choice from among several benefit options. Employees receive credits or "flexible compensation dollars" to spend on the benefits they want. They are not forced to accept fixed benefits as part of a standard employment package. A flexible plan allows employees to sacrifice some of one benefit in order to gain more of another.

The benefits usually included in these plans are: medical expense reimbursement; accident, health, and hospitalization insurance; disability insurance; group term life insurance; group legal services; dependent care assistance. Each benefit area has a core plan that provides a basic level of coverage that the company feels each employee should have. The flexible plan allows employees to supplement the core coverage in the areas that are most important to their individual needs.

If you feel that such a plan might be well received in your organization, you will want to —

> develop employee understanding so the plan is used appropriately — with advantage to both employee and company,

> provide a core of benefits that provides minimum coverage for employees,

> determine whether the savings will outweigh the costs (both actual and administrative); and

> monitor changes in tax laws.

Determining which benefits to include may at first seem like a monumental task. For many companies, however, it has involved no more than a brief survey to determine which benefits employees are most likely to take advantage of. The results of such a survey allow you to determine the best way to set up the program.

Another important factor in program success is employee understanding. The options available and the tax implications can be confusing. If employees do not understand the plan, they will not make use of it.

Many small businesses are successful at motivating employees through a variety of creative means — and sometimes the "little things" can have a big impact. Take time to celebrate successes and to show employees in many ways how much you appreciate all they do.

c. Low Cost/No Cost Benefits

There are countless benefits that small businesses can provide to employees that don't cost a great deal, yet still serve to improve morale and generate loyalty and enthusiasm among employees.

Simple efforts like taking employees to lunch on occasion, providing birthday cakes or some other form of recognition for special events, rewarding employees for a job well done with tokens of appreciation that could include T-shirts, buttons, movie tickets, or gift certificates, are all ways of expressing gratitude. Appreciation efforts could also be more elaborate and involve banquets and other types of celebratory events.

Educational benefits are provided by many organizations, benefiting both the employee and the organization. Employees appreciate the opportunity to improve their skills and, perhaps, place themselves in a better position to move forward within the company. Employers benefit through the goodwill of employees taking advantage of this benefit, as well as the improved skills and knowledge that employees obtain.

Wellness programs and activities are another win/win benefit for employee and employer. Employees appreciate the opportunity to exercise at work, learn about health care issues, and relieve stress. Employers benefit from improved health of employees (less absenteeism), improved staff morale, and the potential for lower health care costs. Because of these direct benefits, companies may opt to subsidize employee wellness efforts in a variety of ways including providing employee fitness centers, contributing to the cost of participation in health clubs, providing low-interest loans for the purchase of exercise equipment, or providing financial incentives for employees who reach certain fitness goals.

d. Communicating Benefits

Your personnel handbook should outline all the benefits available to employees and refer employees to other sources (such as an insurance program booklet) for more information if needed.

In addition, you should take steps to ensure that employees realize the value of the benefits with which they are provided. The cost of providing benefits to employees is, as we have seen, substantial. Providing good benefits is a competitive advantage — but only if employees realize what they are getting.

Use whatever communication tools your company has — staff meetings, newsletters, annual reports, bulletin boards — to ensure that employees are well aware of the many benefits offered to them through their employment with your organization.

14

Dealing with Employee Absenteeism

Any company's successful operation depends in large part on the regular attendance of each of its employees. Each job fits into a pattern of production. Unnecessary or unexcused absences or tardiness affect company operations and place an unfair burden on other employees. A uniform attendance policy helps inform all employees of the importance of adhering to certain guidelines and establishes the basis for disciplinary action should it be necessary.

Certainly there will be times when even the best of your employees will be absent or tardy. In these cases, employees need to know the procedures for notifying the company. A statement such as the following works well: "If you are going to be absent or more than 30 minutes late to work, telephone your manager as far in advance as possible or at least within a half hour after you are expected to be at work. Asking another associate, friend, or relative to give this notification is not considered proper notification except under emergency conditions or as previously approved by your manager."

If your company is located in an area that receives heavy snow during the winter or sudden floods during the spring or summer, you know that unforeseen circumstances can create difficulties for employees trying to get to work. While you don't want employees risking their lives, you do need to establish guidelines so that inclement weather doesn't become an excuse to take a day off.

When an employee fails to come to work on time — or at all — it affects not only productivity, but the morale of other employees. There comes a time when a manager or business owner has to say, "I empathize with you and understand your problem. I believe you want to be here when you're scheduled to be here, but you're not, and I have to consider the needs of the company."

There are two different types of absenteeism: culpable absenteeism and innocent absenteeism.

> When an employee doesn't show up for work, or doesn't show up at the appointed time, it can have a dramatic impact on your operations. Some absences are unavoidable — others are worth taking steps to control.

173

For example, an employee of a small construction company is on disability leave. While out picking up materials, another employee spots his supposedly injured coworker working at a job for another contractor — a side job.

Or a secretary suffers from chronic migraine headaches. Her excessive absences create hardships for the small office that employs her.

The first example is a case of culpable absenteeism; the second a case of innocent absenteeism. Both can create serious problems in the workplace — and result in substantial costs to the business.

a. Trends in Absenteeism

Absenteeism costs companies more each year. Consider just the cost of providing employees with paid sick time. A company with 100 employees that offers six days of sick leave each year, at an average hourly rate of $7, could experience a cost of $33,600 for the time alone. This does not take into account the cost of benefits, the cost of replacement help, overtime pay, lost productivity, impact on morale, impact on customer service, and so on.

According to the 1998 CCH Unscheduled Absence Survey (a survey conducted annually since 1991 by CCH Incorporated, a provider of human resources and employment law information), the unscheduled absenteeism of American workers reached the highest level in seven years and, as a result, businesses lost millions of dollars. The 1998 survey found the overall rate of unscheduled absenteeism had increased by 25 percent and the dollars lost to absenteeism jumped 32 percent since 1997. Both the absenteeism rate and costs incurred were at the highest level since 1992, the second year of the CCH survey.

The overall mean average unscheduled absenteeism rate in 1998 was 2.90 percent, compared to a rate of 2.32 percent in 1997, indicating a 25-percent increase in unplanned absences. The 1998 rate is the second highest on record since CCH began the survey in 1991, when the rate was 3.08 percent.

Absenteeism rate by organization size varied, as shown in Table 7. Increases were highest among small and mid-size companies, while large companies were the only categories to report declines in their unscheduled absenteeism rates.

The study also showed an increase in the cost of unscheduled absenteeism of 32 percent, from $572 per employee in 1997, to as high as $757 in 1998. (Table 8 shows the percentage increase in cost for companies of different sizes.)

TABLE 7
Increase in absenteeism rate from 1991 to 1998 by organization size

Company size	Percent change
Up to 100 employees	14% increase
100–249 employees	28% increase
250–499 employees	29% increase
500–999 employees	32% increase
1000–2499 employees	0% increase

TABLE 8
Increase in the cost of unscheduled absenteeism from 1991 to 1998 by organization size

Company size	Percent change
Up to 100 employees	3% increase
100–249 employees	21% increase
250–499 employees	42% increase
500–999 employees	52% increase
1000–2499 employees	52% increase

Small businesses, with fewer than 100 employees, reported the smallest increase, but still had the highest absenteeism cost per employee at up to $1,044, according to CCH.

As for why employees are not showing up for work, family issues now is the most-cited reason for last-minute absences. Personal illness as a reason continued to decline, while taking sick days due to stress or to an entitlement mentality reached all-time highs.

Businesses are seeing the cost of absenteeism increase and attribute these increases to a variety of factors including the following:

➤ A work force that is less loyal and committed to the organization than in the past

➤ A more mobile work force

➤ Two-career families

➤ The pressures of caring for dependents (children and dependent adults)

Surveys have shown that the higher the rate of pay and the longer the length of service for employees, the lower the rates of absenteeism. Small businesses with fewer employees, lower wages, and higher turnover generally see higher levels of absenteeism. Female and single employees tend to be absent more frequently than male or married employees. This can be attributed to issues related to child care; women are still disproportionately responsible for child care. Studies have also shown that younger employees are absent more frequently than older employees — but older employees are absent for longer periods of time.

Why are people absent from work? There are a variety of reasons and, perhaps not surprisingly, many of those reasons have nothing to do with the employee actually being medically indisposed. In fact, it is not unlikely that you have missed a day of work sometime during your business career, not because you were physically sick, but because for whatever reasons you simply did not feel like going to work.

> The work environment may contribute to absenteeism if employees feel overburdened, have difficulties dealing with coworkers or supervisors, or don't feel valued for their contributions.

The reasons for "not feeling like it" can range from interpersonal problems with coworkers, supervisors — or even customers — to poor working conditions, a poorly designed job, or an employee who is a mismatch with the system. Absenteeism can occur for a variety of reasons, including actual illness, accidents, personal problems, poor working conditions, low morale, lack of job satisfaction, poor management, stress, and boredom.

b. Examining Absenteeism

What is the rate of absenteeism in your organization? While percentages will vary by geography and industry, absenteeism rates between 2 and 3 percent are generally considered average. If your levels of absenteeism are higher — or high for your industry — the first step you need to take is to examine the pattern of absenteeism within your work place.

To calculate a rate of absenteeism, you will need to consider the number of work days during a particular time period, the number of days lost, and your total number of employees. Then —

(a) multiply the number of work days in the time period by your total number of employees,

(b) divide the answer obtained in (a) by the number of days lost, and

(c) multiply by 100 to obtain a percentage.

For example: during a one-month period there are 20 work days; you have 100 employees and have lost 75 days through absenteeism.

(a) 20 x 100 = 2000 total days worked

(b) 75/2000=.0375

(c) .0375 x 100 = 3.75

Compared to an average expected rate of 2 to 3 percent, your absenteeism rate is slightly high based on this calculation.

In addition to calculating the level of absenteeism, your analysis should include a look at where and when absenteeism is occurring. For example, is there a certain department or work area that has a higher rate of absenteeism than other areas? Is there a certain day of the week (Monday or Friday, for instance) when absenteeism is higher?

If absenteeism is a problem for your business, it pays to take some time to determine the cause of the problem. For example, if 25 percent of employee absences are caused by sick children, perhaps your company could subsidize the cost of sick child care. If 75 percent of the employees who participate in the Wednesday night volleyball league fail to show up for work on Thursdays, or show up late, you may need to reconsider the wisdom of a Wednesday night volleyball league!

c. Your Absenteeism Policy

Your policy on absenteeism will not solve a problem with unscheduled absences from work, but it is an important way to ensure that employees know you are concerned about absences and will serve to provide a clear indication of your expectations and the sanctions that will be applied if time off is abused. Clearly outlining those expectations, and ensuring that employees are familiar with the policy, is a good starting point. Clearly indicating that you take the policy seriously is another important step in controlling abuse.

Be careful, though, about including language or sanctions in your policy that you do not intend to follow with all employees. A good way to decide if the language you have used is appropriate is to consider your best employee. Then ask yourself: "If he or she violated this policy, would I be willing to act in accordance with the sanctions I've established." Be honest. If you would not be willing to apply the sanctions to your best employee, change the policy.

Your policy should include specific disciplinary action for failure to properly notify the company of an absence. A poorly designed attendance policy can result in costly legal action by employees who claim they have been wrongfully disciplined or terminated. These employees may claim protection under a variety of laws such as the Family Medical Leave Act (FMLA), the

Americans with Disabilities Act (ADA), and other federal or state/provincial anti-discrimination laws — the policies and approaches to employee absenteeism in Canada and the U.S. are similar. The ADA covers employers with 15 or more employees and protects those employees whose illness or disability is severe enough to limit a major activity. The FMLA covers employers who have 50 or more employees within a 75-mile radius of their business and allows employees the ability to take time off from work to care for immediate family members.

These laws are designed to protect employees against unfair treatment in the workplace. However, as an employer, you do have the right to —

➤ require that an employee be examined by a doctor to determine whether he or she is able to work;

➤ expect that employees who accept a job are available to work as the job requires, unless that employee qualifies for a job accommodation (under ADA) or a medical leave of absence (under FMLA); and

➤ expect the employee to take responsibility for making you aware of a health condition that interferes with his or her ability to work.

Following are some guidelines for designing, implementing, and communicating your absenteeism policy:

(a) *Be consistent.* You can't allow one employee to miss work on a routine basis, but lower the boom on another employee who does the same thing. Your policies should be applied consistently with all employees.

(b) *Consider establishing a "paid leave bank."* A number of companies have found that the paid leave bank can be an effective way to control absenteeism. A paid leave bank rewards employees who have regular attendance by giving them extra vacation time. It allows people to schedule time away from work without having to find an excuse to call in sick. Consequently, it minimizes unscheduled absences. You might also want to consider rewarding employees who come to work regularly. Some companies do this by issuing a certificate of attendance, others with monetary rewards that may represent a portion of the value of unused sick time.

(c) *Address problem situations immediately.* Don't let troublesome situations drag on. If an employee is abusing the system, confront that employee immediately. The purpose of the meeting should be to make the employee aware of concerns regarding his or her attendance and the effects on the company and the rest of the work group (see section **e.**).

d. Combating Absenteeism

Absenteeism and tardiness can be controlled, but employees need to develop the motivation to control their behavior. As one astute manager asked a frequently tardy employee: "How many times have you been late for a place when you're going on vacation?"

There are three primary ways that employers can help to combat unscheduled absenteeism:

(a) Address the physical and emotional needs of employees. It may seem simplistic, but one good way to ensure that employees will come to work is to make work a place that they want to be. A high level of absenteeism can be a clue to underlying issues related to working conditions and management practices.

(b) Communicate to employees why their presence at work is so important — both in terms of the high cost of absenteeism and in terms of the value they provide to the organization. When employees understand the impact their absence has on their coworkers and the company, and when they feel their contribution is valued, they will be less likely to abuse the organization by inappropriately using time-off privileges.

(c) Deal with abuses of the absenteeism policy promptly and consistently. Your enforcement of your absenteeism policy will clearly indicate to employees that you take the policy seriously and that you will apply it fairly and consistently throughout the organization.

When employees feel that their jobs are meaningful, they are more likely to be motivated to come to work on a regular basis. Coworkers also play an important role in encouraging attendance — or absence — of others. As the saying goes, "One bad apple can spoil the whole bunch." Motivated, enthusiastic employees can have a positive impact on those around them. Disgruntled employees will have the opposite effect. This is just one more good reason to ensure that you respond promptly to absenteeism issues within the work group.

Recognition of good attendance can be another good way to encourage employees to come to work regularly. Some companies offer year-end bonuses for high attendance records. Others provide extra time off to employees who don't use their allocated time off. Still others will pay employees for a portion of their unused sick time. All of these methods can be useful in encouraging attendance.

To better understand how companies can reduce their unscheduled absences, the 1998 CCH Unscheduled Absence Survey also asked employers about their experiences with work-life programs. These are programs that take into consideration the demands employees face outside the workplace; they attempt to provide resources or programs to assist them in meeting their needs. Day care is one example. Flexible work schedules another. Survey results indicate these programs can help reduce unplanned absences among workers. However, the organizations didn't necessarily offer these programs to their workers.

On a scale of one to five (with five being most effective), the work-life programs ranked highest for reducing unscheduled absences were Flexible Scheduling (3.78), On-Site Child Care (3.62), and Emergency Child Care (3.55). As for what programs they actually have in effect, more than half (51 percent) indicated their companies offer Flex Scheduling. This was up significantly from the 1997 CCH survey, when less than a quarter offered Flex Scheduling.

Employers acknowledged that work-life programs and paid-time-off (PTO) programs — which provide employees with a bank of hours to be used for various purposes instead of the traditional separate accounts for sick, vacation, and personal time with a specific allotted number of days — both had a positive effect on reducing last-minute no-shows by employees. However, these programs are not widely instituted and are just now being embraced by companies, according to CCH.

While PTO was seen as the most effective absence-control program, only 25 percent of organizations reported they had implemented such a program, and most of these reported having done so within the last two years.

By company size, PTO programs were most popular, preferred by companies with up to 499 employees as well as companies with 5,000 to 9,999 employees. Those companies with 1,000 to 2,499 employees saw no-fault programs as more effective, while organizations with 2,500 to 4,999 employees and those with more than 10,000 employees, saw a bonus program as more effective.

e. Dealing with Individual Employees

While it can be helpful to view absenteeism from a broad standpoint, ultimately it comes down to the actions of individual employees who choose to come to work — or stay home. As an employer or manager, you should view attendance records regularly to spot any indication that an employee's absence from work is excessive. Consider both whether the employee's absence is higher than it has been historically and whether this employee is absent from work more often than other employees.

It is critical that employee absenteeism issues are confronted immediately and directly. When employees who abuse the system are not dealt with, it sends a signal to other employees that management really doesn't care. In

> Paid time-off (PTO) programs offer employees flexibility in determining how they will use their time-off benefits. PTO programs have also been shown to have a positive impact on unplanned absences.

addition, inconsistently treating absenteeism issues can result in legal charges of discrimination.

Upon noticing a problem, the first step is to talk to the employee individually. Share the information you have gathered and explain why you are concerned. Keep the conversation focused on work-related issues and based on factual information. For instance: "I've noticed that you have been absent from work each Monday for the past six weeks. This is a new pattern that I have not noticed in your prior work records, and it is a pattern that is creating concern here at work. When you are absent, your coworkers must step in to cover for you. This is disruptive."

Once you have presented this information and stated your concern, offer the employee the opportunity to present his or her response. Listen carefully. Again, focus on facts and the impact of the employee's absence on the workplace.

Work with the employee to implement solutions where appropriate — solutions that are consistent with your company's policy and actual practice. These might involve flexible scheduling, arranging for car pooling, or adjusting hours. Whatever options are offered, however, must also be available to other employees.

A number of "reasonable accommodations" are required by the ADA if the nature of the employee's absences stem from a disability covered by the act. Bear in mind that you only have to make accommodations that are reasonable.

At the end of the meeting, you should clearly indicate to the employee what your expectations are for future attendance. Review your attendance policy and clearly indicate to the employee what the consequences of noncompliance will be. State your expectations in terms of specific time frames: "As it says in our policy, unexcused absences in excess of twelve days per calendar year will result in termination. You have missed ten days through August. If you miss more than two days the remainder of this year..." Document the meeting, your discussion, and your agreement in the employee's personnel file.

The attendance policy may be established through written notification in a personnel or policy manual, or through practice. So while you may want to allow some flexibility for the organization in dealing with employee absence, you should be certain that whatever standards are applied are applied consistently for all employees.

Your decision of how to respond to employee absence will also be affected by whether the absences were innocent or culpable. Obviously, an employee who misses 3 more than the allowed 12 days in a year due to serious illness will be dealt with differently than an employee who misses 12 days with no documented medical reason.

However, even innocent absenteeism can place an undue burden on a company — particularly a small company. While you will want to work with the employee to the extent you are able, there may come a point where the employee's medical problems create too great a strain on the business and the employee must either be reassigned or terminated. Only after every effort has been made to accommodate the employee should termination be considered.

Generally, you will find that after such a discussion, attendance will improve — often permanently. In some cases, while attendance improves for a period of time, the employee may fall back into previous habits. If this occurs, you should meet with the employee again and implement whatever sanctions had been detailed at the previous meeting. Following are some additional tips on dealing with absenteeism issues:

> Give employees the benefit of the doubt — even those who have a history of abusing sick time. Don't jump to conclusions, but gather as much information as possible to help you determine if this is a legitimate absence.

> Review your absenteeism policy regularly and make sure that it adequately represents your actual practice in terms of granting time off.

> Base any decisions related to disciplinary action with respect to absenteeism on business-related issues. If an employee is legitimately absent frequently and is operating within the guidelines of your policy, even if the absences are disruptive, you may not be in a position to take disciplinary action.

> Make sure that employees understand the importance of having all staff present by communicating to employees the importance of their positions and the value they bring to the workplace.

> Employees should be encouraged to take care of their health proactively. It is far better for an employee to miss one day of work to get needed rest and return to work well, than it is to push too hard and create a more serious or long-term illness. While absent employees can stretch the resources of your company, it is ultimately in your best interests — and the interests of other employees and customers — to encourage employees who are ill to stay home.

> Cross-train other employees to cover for their coworkers to ensure unexpected absences are covered. There should be no such thing as an indispensable employee in your organization.

> Develop a good relationship with a temporary employment agency and become familiar with its staffing services.

15

Performance Evaluation

What are the most common laments heard from today's employees?

➤ "I just don't know what my boss expects from me."

➤ "I thought I was doing a good job — then all of a sudden...wham!"

Clearly identifying what is expected of employees and providing the proper incentives for meeting those goals is an important part of human resources management.

Performance evaluation is not a once-a-year event. It is a process that begins the moment an employee is hired and continues throughout the employee's tenure with your organization. It involves clear communication of expectations and standards; development of specific, measurable goals; and ongoing feedback.

An employee's job description is a good starting point for indicating what is expected of that person. But it is just a starting point. In addition to the job description, job standards can help indicate to employees the specific expectations for their positions. Employees also need to know the goals of their positions and how those goals tie into department and company performance. Finally, employees need to be provided with both formal and informal feedback about their performance and accomplishment of the goals that have been established.

a. Job Standards

A job description merely describes what tasks are intrinsic to a specific job. This is a crucial step in establishing goals, but you need to go one step further by indicating how each task must be performed to meet the requirements of the position. You need to develop standards of performance — or job standards. Without standards, performance issues can become extremely fuzzy.

The first step in developing job standards is to identify the critical aspects of the job. What elements of the position are necessary to keep the department and the company operating efficiently?

Most jobs have between three and six major areas of responsibilities. When you are trying to pinpoint these responsibilities, don't think of the routine or regular tasks that are performed, but the end result or purpose of those tasks. For instance, in a clerical position, filing would not be a major responsibility. The major responsibility would be "maintaining accurate files that are readily accessible to those who must rely on this information."

Once the areas of responsibility have been identified, three or four standards (or key results) that represent satisfactory performance levels need to be established. It is critical that these standards be measurable. If they are not, they become merely subjective indications of how a job should be performed and help neither the employee nor the manager. Effective standards use numbers, time limits, or error/rejection tolerances to establish objective measures of performance. More specifically, managers can use measures of quality, quantity, timeliness, or cost efficiency in establishing standards.

1. Quality

Quality standards are usually written as tolerance for variances from the ideal. In other words, how many errors, omissions, or complaints would you tolerate over a given period of time? Depending on the task being performed, the period of time specified could be anywhere from one hour to one year. One company requires that "errors or omissions in payroll changes shall not require special adjustment in more than one percent of all payroll checks issued each month." Another specifies that "phones will be answered prior to the fourth ring. Callers on hold shall be recontacted or connected within one minute. Message forms will include a legible name, number, and time of call."

2. Quantity

Suppose you manage a manufacturing department. A common standard might be: "produce X amount of widgets in X amount of time." This is a measurable standard based on quantity of work produced.

3. Timeliness

Time standards can be written in terms of daily, weekly, monthly, or quarterly deadlines for task completion or amount of turnaround time permitted. For example, a company might require project reports to be submitted on the last working day of the month. The reports could include project status, budget to date, problems, causes of problems, and an action plan for the next month.

Another standard related to timeliness might specify that all internal correspondence will be ready for distribution not more than 16 working hours after it is received by staff.

4. Cost efficiency

Some positions have responsibility for meeting budgets or affecting costs. In these cases your standards might reflect a maximum dollar budget or a plus or minus variance from the stated budget.

Standards should answer such questions as: What final results are expected? How well must the work be performed? How much work must be performed? When must the work be performed? and so on.

Standards should be established based on clearly and objectively defined performance levels — not gut instinct. Before determining a specific performance level, it can be helpful to establish a baseline of performance for the type of work being examined. This can be accomplished by asking employees to keep records, by reviewing past performance records, or by checking industry standards.

Once baselines have been developed, you can establish minimum expected levels of performance. This minimum level becomes the standard and defines performance at an acceptable level. This accepted level will tie to your performance evaluation. For example, if you use an evaluation scale of one to five, meeting the standard would provide the employee with a rating of three, where three represents the expected level of performance.

Based on the minimum accepted level, you can define increments of excellence and increments of unacceptable performance. For each standard you would determine what level of performance exceeds your expectations and what level of performance falls below your expectations.

Not all job tasks readily lend themselves to establishing clearly defined standards, and it can be challenging to come up with quantifiable measurements for certain tasks. Remember, though, that your objective is to define the most critical elements of the job and, at a minimum, to establish standards for those elements. It is not necessary (although it can prove useful) to develop standards for every task. Table 9 gives some examples of common jobs and job tasks and appropriate standards for measuring performance.

TABLE 9
**Common jobs and job tasks and appropriate standards
for measuring performance**

JOB	TASK	STANDARD
Salesperson	General leads	X leads/day, week, month, etc.
	Selling product	$X week, month, quarter, year, etc.
Accountant	Reports	Identify specific reports which are to be made avaialble by a certain date each month,quarter, year, etc. A standard might also be developed relating to accuracy of the reports.
Computer programmer	Program development	Specify timeframe from consutation to implementation based on various common programming tasks required by the organization.

b. Establishing Goals

The unifying force that exists in any organization is that, theoretically at least, everyone in the organization is working toward the same end — success of the business. From the smallest company to the largest multinational conglomerate, a clear understanding of the goals that drive the organization and how each individual employee contributes to those goals can lead to improved morale and increased productivity.

It sounds simple — unfortunately it is not as easy as it seems. But it is worth the effort. There are several benefits from establishing clear, quantifiable goals. Specific, measurable goals provide a sense of order and purpose for the entire company. Clear goals allow both employee and manager to develop a broader outlook on company objectives. Once goals are developed, management is better able to make decisions based on company and employee direction. Once goals begin to be achieved, the confidence of both employee and manager increases.

Goal setting itself is a process that allows managers and employees to continually work for improvement. When goals are set, they should have the following characteristics:

➤ *Specific.* A goal should state "increase sales by 20 percent," rather than simply "increase sales." It is important for goals to be measurable and specific. When organizational or departmental goals are unclear, motivation is decreased.

➤ *Mutually agreed upon.* You should encourage managers and supervisors to set goals in cooperation with their employees. Once two people are working toward a common goal, the chances of meeting that goal increase substantially.

➤ *Difficult, but achievable.* Goals should be realistic. They should not be too easy or too difficult; they should be challenging yet attainable.

➤ *Comprehensive.* As goals are set, they should cover every area of the company's objectives. Goals can be developed for both line and staff activities.

The process for setting goals, regardless of company size, is straightforward:

(a) The company establishes its overall goals and strategic objectives.

(b) Each department or business unit receives a copy of those goals and objectives and establishes department or unit goals to support them.

(c) Working together, each employee and his or her manager establish individual goals that support departmental goals.

To ensure that the process continues to move forward, you must establish methods to communicate progress continually. How is the company doing? How is each department doing? How are individual employees doing?

1. Involving employees in goal setting

Goals should not be developed in isolation and then handed down to employees as edicts. Employees need to be involved in the goal setting process. They will be more willing to work toward goals if they have been allowed to give input based on their personal experiences and aspirations. It is a standard management principle: commitment is engendered from involvement.

Goal development in isolation or failure to pay heed to the input of your employees are both good ways to sabotage your efforts in this area.

An employee's life is not segmented into two distinct parts: one part that runs from 5 p.m. to 8 a.m. and the other that runs from 8:01 a.m. to 4:59 p.m. An employee's life extends beyond the office — personal and professional goals are integrally intertwined. Your efforts at setting goals need to focus on personal goal achievement as well as professional achievement.

For example, suppose you are establishing goals with a clerical employee. The employee is a high-school graduate and has worked with your company for ten years. This employee could have a personal goal to receive a bachelor's degree. Or to learn how to facilitate meetings. Or to learn new software programs. Or to become involved in community events. Each of these personal interests may, in some way, also benefit your company. A bachelor's degree will provide the employee with additional knowledge and insights that can be applied in the workplace. The ability to facilitate meetings can be applied in your company. Perhaps once these skills have been learned the employee could lead a task force, or facilitate a planning process. Learning new software can help the employee be more efficient at job tasks. And involvement in community activities can reflect positively upon your company.

The employee will be more committed to goals that draw upon personal interests as well as company needs. That commitment will be exhibited through more effective — and faster — goal attainment.

However, while personal goals are important, they should not be the driving force behind establishing goals. The goals of the company should drive the establishment of departmental and individual goals. When employee efforts are not directed at tasks and goals that are aligned with a company's goals, nothing has been accomplished. The employee is not being productive.

> When goals are committed to writing they are much more likely to be achieved. Write down the goals you establish and refer to them regularly, using them as a way to measure employee progress.

2. Additional considerations

Relationships are strengthened when people know what to expect from each other. Consider these points when establishing your goals.

(a) *Don't assume that goals are known.* The most important element of establishing goals in the first place is to help employees understand what is expected of them so that they can monitor their own performance. Make sure that you communicate goals to your employees, make sure that they understand those goals, and make sure that they know what you have determined as an unacceptable level of performance. Don't assume that employees know what is expected of them.

(b) *Make sure goals are written.* Committing goals to written form makes it much more likely that they will be met. Having forms in writing is a good way to ensure that both you and the employee know about the goal. It also provides a reference point as you proceed through the review period — a written document that can be referred to, revised, and updated as necessary.

(c) *Allow employees to participate in measuring their jobs.* Don't cloud the goal-setting process in an aura of secrecy. Give employees responsibility to measure and report on their success in attaining their goals. Allow them to take ownership of the goal.

(d) *Review progress frequently.* Don't establish goals and review them only once a year during a formal review process. Set frequent reporting periods when you and the employee can review progress and modify the goals as necessary.

(e) *View goal setting as a dynamic process.* Just because a goal has been established doesn't mean it can't be modified. The key is ensuring that individual goals work to support organizational goals. If it becomes apparent that a goal is not supporting organizational goals, or if you learn that the goal is not realistic, eliminate or change it. Goal setting should not be viewed as a punitive process. It is a process that ensures consistency of purpose throughout the organization and, whenever possible, a process that encourages individual employee development.

(f) *Spell out clearly the consequences of not meeting goals.* What are the consequences of not meeting a goal? A lower rating on the employee evaluation form? A written warning? Suspension? Termination? There must be a consequence associated with failure to meet goals. If there is no consequence, your employees will soon feel that it really makes no difference whether they do what you ask them to do. Make sure that as part of the goal development process, you clearly communicate the impact of not meeting goals. Further, once you have established a consequence, follow through.

No company can function without goals. There is nothing more frustrating to employees than not knowing how their jobs contribute to the overall working of the company. By establishing specific, quantifiable, and obtainable goals, you are taking the first step toward recognizing employee accomplishments.

c. Feedback

"How am I doing?"

While some employees ask this question directly, many simply sit back hoping that someone — specifically, their supervisors or managers — will tell them.

Many companies have formal systems in place to provide evaluations of employee performance. But while these evaluation meetings serve an important purpose, they don't fulfill an employee's ongoing need for consistent and constructive feedback. What can happen when employees are not provided with appropriate feedback? Let's look at an example.

Nancy started her job as a secretary for a small company five years ago. She was well liked, even though her performance wasn't all that it might be. Because of her pleasant personality and the family-like structure of the company, she was kept on and shifted from one job to another, wherever her skills could be best used. For a time she was a receptionist because she was good on the phones. Then she worked as an assistant for a few people because she followed instructions well and was pleasant to work with.

During this time, Nancy was never told that her typing skills were below par. She was never told that her letter and report compositions were inadequate. She was never given the opportunity to improve. Eventually the company grew beyond her limited means, and when it was no longer possible to find positions that were suitable for her, she was terminated. Neither Nancy nor her coworkers saw it coming and they didn't understand when it happened. The termination was a troublesome one — for Nancy, for her manager, and for her fellow employees. Long after she was gone, other employees suffered from feelings of insecurity. "If it could happen to her, it could happen to me." "How can I tell if I'm really doing a good job?" These comments were heard throughout the firm time and time again.

Had Nancy been told of her inadequacies at an early date, she could have been trained in the areas where she was lacking. She could have grown with the company and been a valued and loyal employee. Because this didn't happen, the company was forced to let her go.

You owe it to employees to provide them with feedback, not only so you can get the most productive use of them, but also so they can develop their skills and grow with you.

Good employees can also be lost due to inattention.

Chris was hired as a secretary at a small firm and grew with the company to eventually hold a management position. She took courses at a local college to enhance her skills, joined numerous professional groups to establish her credibility, and worked hard. Her managers valued her contributions and felt she was a model employee — but they never felt the need to tell her because she always seemed to be "self-motivated." Because Chris never heard the positive comments she craved, she felt unappreciated. She felt that because she had been promoted from within and not hired as an expert, she would eventually be replaced. She began to look for employment elsewhere and eventually left the company. The day she resigned was the first time she could remember anyone telling her just how important she was to the company. Unfortunately, by then it was too late.

1. Giving positive feedback — how to recognize employees

Suppose you have an employee who meets all of your expectations and does the job exactly right, but is not a stellar performer. You feel insincere about going out of your way to tell this employee what a great job he or she is doing.

Well, positive recognition can be more subtle than blatantly praising an employee for doing a good job — sometimes it requires little more than recognizing the employee's efforts. Let's look at some examples.

Sometimes the best employees are the ones who are most likely to be overlooked. Employees crave feedback — it is the least expensive and most effective of employee motivators.

Sam has worked at ABC Corporation for 25 years. During that time he has had a series of managers. None of them ever noticed (or recognized) him for performing any better than the other ten members of his work group.

A new manager was recently hired. After reviewing production reports and individual evaluations of worker performance, the new manager is surprised to see that Sam was a high performer during his first 13 years of employment. His performance declined, though, after his 13th year. He now works at a pace that could most accurately be termed satisfactory.

The new manager calls Sam into her office to talk, not about his performance, but about his interests (at home and at work). She wants to know what he likes about his job and what he dislikes. After the meeting she remarks, "Sam, your records indicate that you have consistently been one of ABC's best employees. I hope you will keep up the good work."

She continues these individual meetings and always makes a special effort to comment on any increase in Sam's output. In a relatively short period of time, Sam's level of performance is exceeding the point it had been at 12 years earlier! He had been recognized.

Suzanne was excellent in her position as sales clerk in a large department store. In fact, she was so good that she was quickly promoted to the position of women's wear sales manager. In this position she was responsible for a large staff of other sales clerks.

As sales manager, however, Suzanne quickly lost the drive she had had as a clerk. She no longer felt the personal reward that accompanied a large sale. She was also growing envious of others in her department who seemed to get all the credit while she merely monitored results.

One day Suzanne had the opportunity to speak to the store manager about this problem. The store manager listened closely and assured Suzanne that her problem was not unique. Several other department sales managers felt much the same way.

A few weeks later the store manager called all the managers together. He told them about a new program the store was implementing: sales teams. Each department manger would be responsible for a team of salespeople. Managers were responsible for encouraging and motivating members of their teams to increase sales. After a three-month trial period, a reward system would be established. Each month a specific department would be recognized for outstanding sales achievement.

The new system was, in effect, no different from the old system. The store manager had been smart enough to realize that it was not enough for department sales managers to watch their staff succeed. Managers needed to feel that they played an important part in this achievement.

Six months later the store's sales had increased dramatically. The monthly reward dinners were also well accepted. Department sales managers felt better about the work they were doing and the role they played in improving sales. Department members felt part of a team with a clear goal in mind. They had been recognized.

If you want to get the same kind of action and see the same results from the people you manage, you should recognize them — frequently, sincerely, and consistently.

2. Giving credit and praise for accomplishment

What happens when employees in your company meet or exceed the goals you have set?

Your answer should be: "I acknowledge their accomplishments."

If your answer is "nothing" or "the achievement of the goal should be reward enough," don't be surprised if morale and productivity are low.

There is no such thing as a self-motivator. Each of us is motivated by something. For many of us that something is praise.

Fail to praise your employees and they will fail to perform. They will fail to perform time after time after time until you replace them or they seek employment elsewhere. The end result, of course, is that you have lost a valuable resource.

When do you offer praise? The answer to this question is directly related to the establishment and monitoring of employee goals. You should praise employees when they meet or exceed one of the goals you have mutually established. Praise should be:

(a) *Immediate.* Employees should be recognized as soon as possible after accomplishing a goal. Keeping a list of accomplishments to bring up at the annual review is a good way to remind yourself of events over the past year — but it is not a good way to provide feedback. When you consistently note and comment on achievements and accomplishments *when they happen*, morale and productivity are enhanced.

(b) *Specific.* If your administrative assistant stays late to finish an important report and you say, "Good job," should your assistant assume that the report was well formatted, that it was prepared in a timely manner, or that it was error-free? In fact, your assistant will have no idea what you mean unless you say what you mean. "Thank you for staying late to finish this report. I appreciate your dedication and dependability" is much more specific — and meaningful — than "Good job."

(c) *Sincere.* Sincerity is crucial when offering praise to employees. The people that work for you will be able to tell immediately if your comments are sincere or meaningless. Giving praise simply because you know you should is not enough. You need to give praise because you honestly believe that a good job was done.

3. Giving constructive feedback

Most employees want to do a good job. If you are remiss in letting them know when they are *not* doing a good job, they cannot possibly improve their performance. Constructive feedback should not be considered negative. Constructive feedback focuses on identifying behavior or action that is not contributing to meeting employee (and therefore company) goals.

As important as it is to offer constructive feedback to employees, many managers hesitate to do so. Why? Because it can be unpleasant. Because it can make a manager feel like a bad guy. There is the possibility that the employee will react defensively. There is the possibility that the employee will feel resentful. On the other hand, an unresolved triviality may later on evolve into a major disciplinary problem. Unresolved issues can have a negative impact on the organization in many ways.

Without constructive feedback, your employees will not have the information they need to improve behavior or performance. In chapter 16, we will take a more detailed look at constructive feedback and disciplinary intervention.

4. Motivation through recognition and involvement

Recognition is an effective and accessible way to motivate employees. The following guidelines can help you recognize employees and ensure that they are receiving the feedback that is so important to them.

➤ Be available to talk to employees. Simply being there is very important. If you say you have an open-door policy, demonstrate it by being available. Your undivided and sincere attention to employees can be motivating.

➤ Encourage people to work with you, not for you. Teamwork is more than a buzzword — it is an important way to encourage employees to meet department and company objectives. To reword a familiar saying: when your employees feel that they are part of the solution, they won't be part of the problem.

➤ Tell employees in advance about changes that will affect them. Involve them in those decisions whenever possible.

Just as employees have a need to hear when they are doing well, they need to know when their performance is not meeting your standards. Prompt and direct corrective feedback is critical to the successful development of employees.

➤ Give credit freely. Be quick to compliment and to recognize good performance.

➤ Make sure each employee understands what is expected and how he or she is doing. Employees need to know what behaviors will be rewarded and what behaviors will be criticized. Make your expectations clear. Be sure employees understand the expectations you have of them and how those expectations fit into the overall goals of the department and the company.

d. Formal Evaluation

Employees want to know how they are doing. They need feedback to help them improve — to help them develop. Why then are annual reviews often such stressful interactions?

➤ The annual review is often the only time that employees receive feedback. In some companies, if it weren't for the required annual review, employees would have no idea how they were doing. Then, once a year, they sit down with their manager and wait for the bomb to drop. Sometimes it does. Sometimes it doesn't. Either way, this annual meeting is stressful, for both employee and manager.

➤ The annual review is often tied directly to pay. It can be difficult for employees to focus on the developmental aspects of their annual review when they are most concerned about how much their pay increase will be.

➤ Employees have learned that a review can be a disheartening and ego-damaging experience.

How do you turn this situation around and move to a more positive and productive interaction?

(a) Make sure employees understand the review process. Explain how the review process works when the employee is hired. Show the employee a copy of the evaluation form and explain how it is used.

(b) Directly tie the evaluation to the job standards and goals you have already established with the employee.

(c) Clearly communicate your expectations and explain how performance will be measured and tied to the evaluation.

(d) Provide feedback regularly throughout the year — not just at the annual review. Have a policy of no surprises for the evaluation meeting. Anything that is brought up at this meeting should have been discussed with the employee at some point throughout the year. Never save an issue for the review session.

1. New employee evaluation

Most companies with formal review programs review employees on an annual basis and provide more frequent reviews for new employees — often at three- or six-month intervals. The end-of-probation appraisal (similar to the performance evaluation in Sample 15) includes sections on technical skills, interpersonal qualities, and personal qualities as well as a section for new goals and objectives. This section presents you with a formal opportunity to commit individual goals to writing. These goals will then serve as the basis for your next review.

The end-of-probation appraisal provides definitions for each factor being reviewed. For instance, job knowledge is defined as having the skills and knowledge needed to meet required standards. Suppose you are meeting with an employee after three months on the job. A key part of the employee's job is working with database programs. Is the employee's knowledge in this area what you would expect? That would earn the employee a "satisfactory" rating. If the employee's knowledge is somewhat higher than you might expect, a "good" rating would be appropriate. If the employee's knowledge far exceeds your expectations, you may choose to give an "excellent" rating. Conversely, if the employee does not meet your expectations in this area, you may select a "poor" or a "fair" rating.

Whenever your rating of an employee's performance falls below satisfactory, it should be a signal to you that there is a need for some developmental work. This might involve more training, more coaching, an extension of the probation period, or even transfer to another position where the employee's skills could be most appropriately used.

Every attempt should be made to quantify ratings whenever possible. Obviously there is a certain amount of subjectivity associated with any evaluation process. To the extent you can, however, include examples to support your ratings, and tie ratings to observable, measurable performance.

2. Ongoing evaluation

All employees should have the opportunity for a regular, formal review. While feedback should be given frequently and directly throughout the year, a formal session once a year — or more often — provides a formal opportunity to discuss development issues and to focus specifically on performance improvement.

The evaluation form you use should be based on the unique characteristics of your company and the position being reviewed. It should incorporate elements of the job standards and goals you have developed with your employees. The examples included here can provide you with some formats to use as a starting point.

Be cautious in the way you define your probationary period for employees. You do not want to suggest that, after this time period, employees will be permanent.

The performance evaluation form in Sample 15, designed for sales personnel, includes an area to record some quantitative measurements of job success — net sales, sales quota, sales calls per week, etc. Note also that there is space to review goals established at the previous review session, as well as space to record new goals for the next review period.

The performance appraisal form in Sample 16 takes a slightly different approach, eliminating the poor/excellent rating categories of the performance evaluation form, allowing, instead, for more open-ended discussion of performance. Your comments should still be tied to specific requirements of the position and should include examples to support your impressions. Note that you can easily add or substitute items that are unique to the position you are evaluating.

3. The 360-degree evaluation

No longer is employee evaluation the sole responsibility of that employee's direct manager. Today many companies look to a variety of sources for feedback, including supervisors, peers, subordinates — even the employees themselves. Comments come from literally all around the employee in what is called the 360-degree evaluation. Feedback from vendors and customers may also be used in the review process. Samples 17 and 18 show an employee self-evaluation form and a peer evaluation form, both useful evaluation instruments.

Gathering feedback from a variety of sources can help you get a broader perspective of an employee and how he or she interacts in a variety of settings.

Many large companies have embraced the concept of 360-degree evaluation; some purchase customized programs that can cost several thousands of dollars. But even the smallest of companies can take advantage of this feedback process at little or no cost.

While the concept itself may seem simple, though, success depends on attention to some important details.

(a) *Tie the program to business goals.* Before implementing a 360-degree feedback program you need to have a good idea of why you want to take this direction. What is it that you are trying to achieve? Once you have made the decision, it is equally important to communicate your reasons to your employees.

(b) *Sell the program to employees.* Employees may understandably feel threatened by the introduction of a 360-degree feedback program. Comments like "Only my supervisor should be able to judge my work" are not uncommon. To ensure that the program will work effectively and to minimize unnecessary anxiety for employees, make sure to invest time in selling the program and its benefits to the company — and to individuals.

SAMPLE 15
PERFORMANCE EVALUATION

Employee name   John Doe

Department   Information Systems

Start date   3/1

Supervisor   Stacy King

Current salary $30,000/hr.

Reasons for appraisal   [x] Scheduled   [   ] Salary increase   [   ] Promotion

Last evaluation   3/10/

Employee No.   23456

Position   Help Desk Support

Appraisal period   3/1/

Last date of increase   3/1/

Present date   3/3/

Technical skills	Poor	Fair	Good	Excellent	Comments
Job knowledge Has skills and knowledge to meet standards required				X	John clearly has the skills necessary to respond to internal customer requests. He is proficient in all company systems.
Quality of work Accuracy, thoroughness, consistency, and completeness of work assigned or performed			X		John provides consistently high quality service, is thorough and accurate.
Productivity Output of work, promptness				X	John excels in this area; he handles more calls, per reporting period, than any other helpdesk rep and had fewer callbacks.
Comprehension Ability to learn, grasp concepts essential to the work, and follow instructions/procedures			X		
Organization Ability to handle many projects simultaneously, prioritize tasks, and complete projects on schedule				X	John's organizational skills allow him to be consistently on time, to handle a large amount of work and to provide exceptional customer service.

Interpersonal skills	Poor	Fair	Good	Excellent	Comments
Independence and initiative Ability to work without supervision				X	John works very well independently and requires minimal supervision
Teamwork Ability to work well with coworkers, management, and subordinates		X			As discussed in earlier meetings, there are outstanding issues with regard to interaction with help desk peers. John has high standards of performance for himself and frequently conveys those high standards, sometimes inappropriate to others.
Customer relations Understanding of customer's importance to us, demonstration of concern for him or her				X	Feedback from users of the help desk is consistently high.
Attitude Enthusiasm, willingness, and motivation					

Sample 15 — Continued

Personal qualities	Poor	Fair	Good	Excellent	Comments
Attendance				X	
Punctuality				X	
Customer relations				X	

Sales personnel

Territory covered _____

Sales performance

    Net sales _____

    Sales Quota _____

    Above/below quota by _____ %

Period from _____ to _____

Sales activity

    Sales calls per week _____

Sales reports

    Quality of reports _____

    Timeliness of reports _____

General comments

John is an excellent performer but needs to focus on interpersonal relationships, particularly with help desk peers. We will work together on this over the coming months and monitor performance through peer feedback.

List goals from last review period and rate the progress of achievement

Establish tracking system for call-ins on new XYZ software (completed)

Respond to all inquiries within 24 hours (John's actual response time averages 12 hours)

Recommendations

Position in company   [x] Remain in present position   [ ] Promote to _____   [ ] Transfer to another position _____

Salary $32,000 _____

Training   Interpersonal skills training _____

Others _____

This appraisal was discussed with employee on   3/3/ _____

Reviewer's signature _____   Date _____

I have read this appraisal and made my comments on the back of this form.
My signature does not necessarily indicate that I agree with this appraisal.

Employee's signature _____   Date_____

SAMPLE 16
PERFORMANCE APPRAISAL

Employee name Cary Dobbs

Department Accounting

Start date 4/15/

Supervisor Joan Brown

Current salary $7.75/hr.

Reasons for appraisal [x] Scheduled [ ] Salary increase [ ] Promotion

Last evaluation 4/15/

Employee No. 45678

Position Account Clerk

Appraisal period 4/15/ -4/15/

Last date of increase 4/15/

Present date 4/13/

Technical skills
Job knowledge
Consider whether the employee has the skills and knowledge required to perform his or her job to the standards required.

Cary is adept at using the software required to perform job duties. However, her understanding of accounting principles is an area that needs continued focus. She performs well tactically, but could contribute more if she were more comfortable offering strategic recommendations.

Job skills
Consider the employee's ability to gather information, grasp concepts essential to the work, generate creative solutions to problems, make and implement efffective decisions, and organize and prioritize tasks.

Cary performs any task given to her quickly. Increased comfort level with her role and the requirements of the position may help her to be more proactive in making recommendations and problem-solving.

Interpersonal qualities
Communication
Consider clarity, accuracy, and timelessness in oral and written communication.

Cary is pleasant and has strong written and verbal communication skills. She is well liked and works effectively as part of the accounting team.

Independence and initiative
Consider the employee's ability to work without supervision and to initiate appropriate action.

Cary needs frequent supervision and direction. This will be an area of focus over the next year.

Teamwork
Consider the employee's ability to establish and maintain effective working relationships with coworkers, management, and subordinates.

Excellent! As mentioned previously Cary is highly regarded in her work group; she is also seen as an eager and efficient contact point for internal customers. Peer review are consistently high.

Attitude
Consider the employee's levels of enrthusiasm, cooperation, and motivation.

Cary is very motivated and enthusiastic about her work. She is eager to learn and to be able to grow in this position.

Leadership
Consider the employee's desire to assume leadership role and his or her ability in motivating, directing, delegating, and coaching.

At this point, this is not applicable.

Personal qualities
Attendance, punctuality, and appearance.

No problem.

General
What are the employee's strengths that enhance the performance of his or her job? (Consider technical skills, interpersonal qualities, and personal qualities.)

Cary's strengths are her enthusiasm, her strong communciation skills and her excellent interpersonal skills.

What job accomplishments has the employee achieved over the last review period?

Familiarity with the organization and departmental procedures and policies.

In what areas can the employee improve his or her performance? (Consider technical skills, interpersonal qualities, and personal qualities).

More confidence in ability to do the work, less reliance on supervisor. Reduction in errors.

How can improvement be achieved? (Consider job-related training, leadership training, and personal development.)

Cary will attend a series of training programs designed to improve her skill levels. She will also work with her supervisor, one on one to address the above-mentioned concerns.

Sample 16 — Continued

List of goals from last review period and evaluate them.

1.　Learn accounting software (accomplished).

2.　Become familiar with company and departmental procedures (done).

3.　

4.　

5.　

Set goals for the next review period.

1.　Become proficient with departmental software and procedures.

2.　Reduce errors (no more than 3 substantive errors in the coming year).

3.　Work to be more proactive, provide evidence of proactive consultation with three internal customers.

4.　

5.　

List any concerns or comments raised by employee during the review, and any solutions or suggestions made to resolve them.

Cary recognizes areas in which she needs to improve and is anxious to work together to improve her performance.

Recommendations

Position in company　[x] Remain in present position　[ ] Promote to _____　[ ] Transfer to another position _____

Salary　$7.75/hour (reevaluate in three months)

Training　skills training

Others _____

This appraisal was discussed with employee on　4/13/

Reviewer's signature _____　Date _____

I have read this appraisal and made my comments on the back of this form. My signature does not necessarily indicate that I agree with this appraisal.

Employee's signature _____　Date _____

SAMPLE 17
EMPLOYEE SELF-EVALUATION

Employee _____ Employee no. _____

Department _____ Position _____

Start date _____ Appraisal period _____

In preparation for your upcoming performance review on _____, consider the following questions. Bring this sheet to your appraisal meeting for discussion.

Objectives	Achieved?	Comments
1.		
2.		
3.		
4.		
5.		

1. Are your performance goals reasonable and appropriate for your position?

_____

_____

_____

2. Consider the strengths that enhance your job performance.

_____

_____

_____

3. In what areas can you improve your job performance?

_____

_____

_____

Sample 17 — Continued

4. Do you feel that you need additional training? What training would you find helpful?

_____

_____

_____

5. What are your short-term career objectives? How can you achieve them?

_____

_____

_____

6. What are your long-term career objectives? How can you achieve them?

_____

_____

_____

7. If you could change your job or company policies, what changes would you suggest? How can we work together to improve the company?

_____

_____

_____

8. Are there any other aspects of your job or the company that you would like to discuss?

_____

_____

_____

SAMPLE 18
PEER EVALUATION

Employee _____ Employee no. _____
Department _____ Position _____

All responses will be compiled in a single report.

	Poor				Excellent
Responds promptly to my requests	1	2	3	4	5
Provides consistently high-quality service	1	2	3	4	5
Is considerate of my needs and project deadlines	1	2	3	4	5
Keeps me informed of issues that affect me in my job	1	2	3	4	5
Communicates with me effectively	1	2	3	4	5
Provides me with adequate and appropriate feedback	1	2	3	4	5
Consistently provides creative solution and ideas	1	2	3	4	5
Is flexible and willing to adapt to change	1	2	3	4	5

*If you respond with a 1 or 2, please indicate on the back of this form:

1. If you have spoken with your coworker about this issue.

2. If not, why not?

3. What your coworker could do to improve in this area.

_____ 's most valuable contributions to our department are:

_____ and I could work together more effectively if:

Thank you for your feedback.

(c) *Emphasize development — not dollars.* Evaluation is a stressful activity for employees in any circumstance. Add to that stress the idea that the evaluation is tied to pay and the situation can become volatile. For 360-degree feedback systems to work effectively, it is important that the process is tied to development and not dollars.

Communication is the key to success. Before implementation, spend time with employees, both in groups and one-on-one, discussing the benefits of the feedback and how it can be used to improve performance and guide future development. Help employees view the system as a positive means of identifying areas for potential improvement or increased focus rather than as a threatening source of subjective feedback.

(d) *Focus on performance-related measures.* The best way to avoid non-constructive feedback is to ask for ratings of job-related items only. For instance, a request for evaluation on comments such as "Responds promptly to requests" or "Is prepared for meetings" will generate feedback directly related to job performance. Comments like "Is well respected by peers" or "Is a value to the organization" call for more subjective responses that can become personal.

(e) *Use constructive candor.* Candor is critical for the success of a 360-degree feedback program, but that candor should be constructive. Evaluation forms that allow written comments, in addition to numerical scores, can be enlightening, but only if the comments are constructive.

Written comments can also be used to help clarify any negative ratings. For instance, on a one to five scaling system, where one is considered poor, you might suggest that any employee giving another employee a score of three or lower also include a written comment clarifying that score.

(f) *Emphasize employee involvement.* Each employee should be involved in identifying the people who should evaluate him or her. Working together, the employee and supervisor can select a workable balance of representative peers and customers. Again, it is critical that the employee view the process as a helpful source of feedback — not a witch hunt.

(g) *Protect anonymity.* In a perfect world, employees would feel comfortable providing constructive feedback openly to their peers. Unfortunately, we don't live in a perfect world. To ensure the integrity of a 360-degree feedback system, anonymity should be ensured. At the same time, though, employees can be encouraged to identify their comments if they feel comfortable doing so and should at all times be coached to provide constructive feedback.

(h) *Share results.* One of the administrative burdens of this type of program is that somebody needs to be responsible for compiling results. It is important that employees be given the opportunity to review their ratings and comments; however, most companies compile the results as opposed to showing employees individual rating sheets. This is an additional means of protecting rater anonymity.

4. Relieving employee evaluation stress

The evaluation process is not stressful only for the employee. Supervisors and managers often dread these meetings as well. The following guidelines can help relieve that stress and make the evaluation meeting a more productive and rewarding experience for the employee.

(a) No surprises

It bears repeating — have a "no surprises" policy for the evaluation meeting. Nothing should be covered here that hasn't already been covered throughout the year. It is unfair to hold issues for the annual review and spring them on the employee. No surprises also refers to the review process itself. Make sure that employees know what to expect from the review process. What information will you be gathering? From whom? What forms will be filled out? Will the employee be asked to bring any information to the meeting? Do you want the employee to be prepared to discuss progress toward goals and to discuss ideas for new objectives for the coming year (you should!)? Will pay be discussed at this meeting? How are decisions regarding pay made? How much time have you set aside for the meeting? Will anyone else be present?

(b) Ask the employee to speak first

Even if you feel you have been direct with the employee throughout the year, a good way to gain information on the employee's perspectives and viewpoints on performance and areas for improvement is to ask him or her to speak first.

You could say something like, "Before I share my thoughts with you, I'd like to hear your perspectives. Why don't you tell me what you consider your strong points and areas where you would like to improve." Then listen carefully and take notes. If you've been providing good feedback throughout the year, you will likely hear the employee tell YOU about the very issues that you were planning to bring up during the review.

By giving the employee the opportunity to speak first, you change the environment from one of passing judgment to one of collaboration. You are

Nothing you say in a formal employee evaluation setting should come as a surprise to the employee. Always address performance issues as soon after they occur as possible and take steps to ensure an open, two-way channel of communication with employees.

working together to identify areas where improvement can be made to benefit the employee, the department, and the organization.

Once the employee has shared his or her perspectives, tie your comments to the issues the employee has raised. If your organization uses an evaluation form, share that form with the employee and point to areas that support what you just heard, commenting, "Well, as you've already pointed out, I've noted your strengths of..." or "I've also noted that a potential area for improvement is..."

What if the employee hasn't noted something that you did? To the extent you can, try to bring the employee to discuss these issues before you go over the formal document. Your objective is to have employees identify areas of strength and weakness within themselves. If this doesn't occur, though, you will need to bring those issues up. "I'm surprised that you didn't mention your excellent group facilitation skills — that's something that I've included in my comments. I may not have given you enough positive feedback about this over the year."

(c) Discuss peer/self evaluation

If you do peer and self-evaluation you will also want to review and discuss that feedback. The forms or process you use to gather this information should be designed to elicit objective, work-related information. You do not want to receive nonconstructive feedback on personal issues or personality factors unless those issues can be directly tied to performance. That is why an open-ended statement like, "Employee X and I could work together more effectively if..." will provide constructive feedback that is directly related to job performance.

(d) Focus on development

The majority of time during the evaluation meeting should be spent on plans for development and on setting objectives and goals for the following year. Again, focus on information you have gained from the employee in terms of his or her career objectives and professional goals. How can you and the company support the employee in meeting those goals? Are there educational or training opportunities that would be appropriate? Are there task forces or special projects in which the employee would be willing and able to participate?

(e) Solicit feedback on your performance

Finally, be sure to get feedback from the employee about his or her interaction with you. Are you providing adequate feedback throughout the year? Does he or she have the tools and information necessary to perform effectively and efficiently? Are your assignments clear? Do you provide enough direction? Enough autonomy?

Don't stop with giving feedback to employees — ask for their feedback on the company. Do they have the tools they need to perform their jobs effectively? Is their supervisor supportive? What suggestions do they have for improving the organization?

Close by asking the employee for feedback about the evaluation process. Was it useful? Does he or she have enough information or the right information to meet his or her goals and objectives for the coming year?

The employee evaluation process is not a once-a-year event. It is a process that begins the moment an employee is hired and proceeds through the establishment of job standards and goals, ongoing review of performance, and formal evaluations based on your company guidelines. It is a process that does not flow from the top down, but is rather a collaborative effort that involves feedback from many different sources, as well as input from the employee.

Optimally, if you have been successful to this point — if you have hired correctly, oriented and trained properly, and provided adequate and appropriate feedback — you may never have to move on to the next step in human resources management: dealing with problem employees.

16

When Employees Become Problems

Ginny has been a manager for five years, and even during that relatively short period of time she has already encountered a number of employee problems — in fact, her boss recently spoke to her about the fact that the involuntary turnover rate in her area was significantly higher than anywhere else in the company.

"I can't help it," Ginny responded. "I've gotten stuck with some real duds. And besides, I think some of the other managers are just too hesitant to lay it on the line with their employees or more people would be out the door."

Does Ginny have a valid point? Probably not. As difficult as it may be to accept, when you have to fire someone you hired in the first place, it is probably your own fault.

For Ginny and other managers, blaming it on the employee is a mistake that could lead to more firings in the future. While no manager wants to reach the point where an employee must be let go, many inadvertently make critical errors that can have a major negative impact on an employee's tenure with the company.

a. How to Create a Problem Employee

1. Hiring in haste

When faced with a vacant position, you may be anxious to get another body on board so productivity can be maintained and things can get back to normal. That urge to fill a position, though, can lead to hasty decisions. It is important to realize that the time you spend now will pay for itself later.

Make the time to carefully consider where to advertise the job opening, to develop a list of requirements for the position, to compare applicants to those requirements, and, if necessary, to go back to the drawing board. It is possible that you will run an advertisement for an available position and receive a stack of resumes from candidates who are okay, but nothing special. Resist the impulse to hire the best of the worst. Realize that you do not have to interview any of the applicants if they are not what you are looking for. Send them all polite letters and start over again. But this time, take a critical look at the ad you are running to be sure that you are being specific enough about the qualifications you are looking for in an applicant.

2. Misrepresenting the job

There are aspects about any job that are undesirable. Hiding these things from prospective employees won't help you out in the long run. Let's look at a typical example. Larry is hiring an administrative assistant. His department is a fairly new one and it has been difficult to get approval for new staffing. While his hope is that eventually the administrative assistant position will operate on a more administrative level, currently the position is a glorified clerical job. Because of his future hopes for the department, he wants to hire the most qualified person he can find. Yet he is afraid that if he tells it like it is, the better candidates won't be interested. So he decides to be as general as possible when discussing the job. Larry has just made a major mistake — one that plagues many people making hiring decisions to some degree. If you want to hire the best employee for the job and avoid problems later, be sure you are honest about what the job entails — good and bad. And make sure you are clear about your expectations. If you expect a high level of devotion to the job and this translates into late hours and some weekend work, make that clear.

3. Letting personal bias/ego interfere

You are interviewing for a new position and one of the top candidates appears overqualified. You are worried that this candidate may eventually be after your job, and you're afraid that he or she just might get it! While you certainly would not admit this to anyone else — and may not even admit it to yourself — your fear is a common one. Yet it is usually unfounded. Remember — when your employees look good, you look good. The best person for the job is the most qualified person for the job. Most job candidates agree that one of the most frustrating things they hear when they are told why they didn't land a certain position is "You're overqualified." "Let me decide whether I want the job or not," one still-unemployed recent college graduate laments. That is a common complaint and one that supervisors should work to overcome. If you are fairly representing the job, and the overqualified candidate is still interested, why not hire the best?

Another problem that keeps some supervisors from making sound hiring choices is that they let personal biases interfere with decisions. A female manager may be hesitant to hire an older male employee. A college graduate may

Many hiring managers worry that a very qualified candidate represents a threat. That is a narrow-minded viewpoint. The better your employees, the better your company.

be hesitant to hire a candidate with substantial on-the-job experience but minimal educational requirements. An outgoing supervisor may be leery of a quiet interviewee, even though that applicant seems to have the best skills for the position. Affirmative action issues aside, making hiring choices based on personal bias will almost always fail to place the most qualified person in that open position. The advice is simple — hire the best person for the job, period.

4. Not providing adequate training

Another critical error that many employers make is not providing adequate training once a person is hired. You can't just show someone his or her desk and say, "Go to it." Unfortunately, hard as it may be to believe, many managers do little more. If you want an employee to succeed, you must provide that employee with the tools to succeed. That means training. The time that you spend now will more than pay off later once the new employee has developed into a valuable contributor.

What is adequate training? It is whatever that particular employee needs to do the job as you want it done. It may, and probably will, vary from one employee to another. While one person may need only a few hours of instruction and will pick up the rest on his or her own, another may need a few weeks before he or she feels comfortable in the job.

To train effectively, you need to determine what you really need from this position. From there you can develop a list of job responsibilities. These responsibilities are the areas that will require training. How you train is not as important as the fact that you do train. Whether you provide written documentation of what needs to be done, designate another employee to serve as the trainer, or do the training yourself, the key is that the individual being trained is provided with clear-cut guidelines on how to do the job.

Part of the training process is providing the employee with easy access to information and resources for answers to questions and further direction. Having an open-door policy means nothing if you are seldom available or if you act put upon when an employee comes to you with a question. Remember, also, that training is an ongoing process. Today's business environment is evolving, with changes occurring on a regular basis. Even the employee who has been on the job for several years needs to be involved in ongoing training.

5. Not being clear about expectations and goals

How many supervisors have you heard lament, "He just doesn't do the job"? Maybe you have said it yourself. But have you been clear about what, specifically, the job is? If you feel that quality is a key issue and that the job must be done right, even if deadlines are missed, you need to communicate that to the employee who always meets deadlines but sometimes cuts corners. If you expect employees to contribute in meetings and are frustrated with somebody who doesn't, you need to make your expectations clear. Never assume that your expectations are clear or that they are understood. Check out employees' perceptions of your expectations by asking them what they think you expect from them. When something is done wrong, ask the employee if he or she knows what is wrong. If the person doesn't know what the problem is, you haven't been clear enough. Don't be nebulous about your expectations. Have regular meetings with employees to establish standards and goals, and monitor those goals on an ongoing basis.

6. Not providing adequate, timely, and appropriate feedback

Feedback, both positive and negative, must be provided on a regular basis. You need to tell employees what you liked about what was done — specifically. Employees, without exception, want to do a good job. But they need you to help them do a good job. That is your role — and your responsibility.

7. Examining past employee failures to prevent future problems

What has your history been with employee problems? While every supervisor will experience employee trouble from time to time, if you are having more than your share, it is time to look at your habits and actions.

The first step is to review all of the problems you have encountered over the past few years. What similarities can you find? Look at common traits shared by employees (e.g., lack of motivation, incompetence). For example, if you take a critical look at your record with employees and discover that every problem employee you have dealt with has been a recent college graduate, that should tell you something. Perhaps the experience level of the people you have been hiring is not extensive enough.

It is far easier to avoid a performance problem than to tackle it head on, but it is far costlier in the long run.

Be brutally honest with yourself and, if possible, ask for some input from those you work with. Good employees are always a valuable resource. They are developed over a period of time through ongoing communication, clear direction, and appropriate feedback. If you are faced with the prospect of firing an employee, take the time to review the role you have played in the development of this problem. Then, if the situation isn't already beyond repair, take steps to mend it. If it is too late to fix it, make the decision that must be made, but learn from the process — learn what you have been doing wrong.

b. Addressing Poor Performance

Unresolved disciplinary issues can have a negative impact in a number of ways.

There may be direct monetary cost to the organization. Incompetence may cause inefficiencies, result in damage to company equipment, contribute to the loss of customers or clients, or result in costly errors.

There may be productivity costs. Work bottlenecks may be created since most jobs interrelate with others. You may find yourself having to spend more time on training, counseling, and disciplining an employee while the rest of your job is put on hold.

There will almost certainly be morale problems, especially if you fail to take action. Other employees will quickly become irritated if someone in their work group is not pulling his or her weight and is getting away with it.

One of the most common mistakes is to avoid dealing with poor performance. Few people welcome conflict, and it is far easier to avoid than to confront — at least it appears to be. In fact, avoiding a problem may actually result in greater frustration, effort, and cost to the organization at some later date.

Issues that require disciplinary action do not develop overnight. In most cases, early warning signs were present. Addressing a problem at an early stage provides an opportunity for intervention, coaching, and counseling. Signs of developing problems may include the following:

- ➤ Declining performance

- ➤ Increased complaining

- ➤ Interpersonal conflicts

- ➤ Difficulty accepting constructive feedback

- ➤ Behavior that has a negative impact on the work group

After these early warning signs, the problem typically becomes more serious. By ignoring these signs, you may find yourself faced with an issue that is much more damaging — to the employee, to you, and to the organization.

1. Before taking disciplinary action

Once you have identified a problem, it is time for you to take action. But before you do, there are several questions that you should ask yourself:

- ➤ Did the employee know and understand the rule that was broken or the procedure that was not followed, and was the employee warned of possible disciplinary consequences? Was this rule clearly outlined in the employee manual or policy guidelines, along with details about company response if the rule is not followed? Is there a system in place to ensure that employees are made aware of these rules? Can you document that the employee was aware of this rule?

➤ Is the rule or procedure that was violated necessary for the orderly, efficient, and safe operation of the business? In the event that an employee brings litigation against your company, it may be necessary to defend the rule itself. If the rule is judged to be capricious and not directly related to the work environment, you may be at risk for legal action.

➤ Was a fair and objective investigation conducted to determine whether the employee actually violated the rule? You should not act upon second-hand information or "rumor" in reprimanding an employee. For any infraction it is important to conduct an investigation before taking any disciplinary action.

➤ Has the company applied rules, procedures, and penalties fairly and consistently to all employees? If you have explicitly stated the rules of the organization and the penalties that will be applied if the rules are not followed, but then apply those rules inconsistently, you open yourself to the potential for legal liability. Rules — and penalties — should be consistently applied.

You should determine all the facts before having a discussion with the employee. If you don't, you may find that your decision to discipline was inappropriate.

Let's assume that you are working with an employee who, it has been reported, is consistently coming in late and has been intimidating other employees into covering up for this tardiness. Before you confront the employee, you should gather all of the facts and be as specific as possible in terms of —

➤ what happened,

➤ when it happened,

➤ how often it happened, and

➤ who knew it happened.

You will want to review the employee's past history to determine length of service, specifics of past performance, and the possibility of other disciplinary action.

You will want to compare this situation with other similar situations that have occurred at the company. How have other employees who have exhibited the same or similar problems been disciplined?

2. Characteristics of effective discipline

Effective discipline is immediate, predictable, impersonal, and consistent.

Before confronting an employee with a performance issue, be sure you have gathered all of the pertinent facts — who, what, when, and where. Then you can get together with the employee to determine how to resolve the issue.

(a) Immediate

When discipline is necessary, you should approach the employee as soon as possible after the violation has been noticed or reported. At this point the incident will be fresh in both your mind and the employee's mind. If you wait too long, the impact of your confrontation will be lessened.

You should, however, time your confrontation so that you approach the employee at an appropriate moment. For instance, you don't want to corner the employee the minute he or she comes to work on Monday morning or just as he or she is leaving on a Friday afternoon. You should also avoid any confrontation in front of other employees.

When you address the employee, state immediately, in as few words as possible, just what it is that is causing you concern.

(b) Predictable

The employee should be well aware that the behavior was in violation of some company rule or inconsistent with direction or instruction. It should be very clear that anyone exhibiting the behavior would be disciplined.

(c) Impersonal

Employees sometimes feel as though their supervisors are out to get them. It is important that your employees understand that when they are disciplined it is because of what they did — not who they are. You should be just as willing to approach one of your star performers with a performance issue as you would one of your problem employees.

When practicing positive discipline, it is important that you do not treat the employee as an adversary. Address the issue without lecturing, nagging, or losing your temper. Let the employee tell his or her side of the story. Ask questions only to obtain details. Listen with an open mind.

(d) Consistent

It is extremely important that you are consistent in your discipline of employees. Discipline must be consistent within a department as well as between departments. To determine the appropriate course of action, find out how other employees were treated in similar circumstances. Talk to other supervisors, review company policy, and make every possible effort to ensure that your disciplinary actions are consistent throughout the organization.

c. The Disciplinary Conference

When you meet with an employee who needs to be disciplined, there are several things you must keep in mind and several steps you should have already taken. As we have seen previously, you should gather as many facts as possible about the situation. You should review the employee's personnel file to determine if this behavior has occurred previously. You should make sure that the employee is well aware of the reason for the discussion. At the meeting you should —

➤ have notes and make use of them;

➤ explain the facts you have gathered as completely as possible;

➤ ask the employee to give his or her perspective. Allow the opportunity for some emotional venting;

➤ discuss the situation in depth with the employee and explore various ways the situation might have been handled differently;

➤ determine, in your own mind, whether discipline is justified;

➤ explain what you intend to do and why — refer to company policy and precedent. Try to obtain the employee's agreement that he or she has done something wrong and that disciplinary action is warranted;

➤ be specific about what the consequence will be for continued infractions; and

➤ provide a system for follow-up. Be specific about how future behavior will be monitored, what results you expect, and how you expect the employee (with your help) to achieve those results.

Here are some additional tips for providing constructive discipline:

➤ Give fair warning. Let the employee know that his or her behavior is not appropriate."

➤ Listen to the employee's side until you fully understand the motivation for the behavior.

➤ Deal with the objective issues and not your own subjective emotions and feelings. It is preferable to say "When you're late you create additional work for others in the department," and not "You're totally irresponsible and you make me look like a bad manager when you come in late every day."

➤ Discipline privately. Make every possible effort to avoid embarrassing the employee in front of others.

➤ Be sure to find out how the employee feels about the action you are taking. Does he or she feel that you are being fair?

➤ Obtain the employee's commitment to improve.

➤ Document the incident in writing and include it in the employee's personnel file.

Be as clear and specific as possible when communicating with employees about behavior or performance issues. A disciplinary letter can be a good way to outline the issue and serve as the basis for discussion.

Sample 19 shows a disciplinary warning notice, which can be a helpful form of documentation when addressing disciplinary issues. When completed, one copy of the form should be included in the employee's file and another copy given to the employee.

Depending on the infraction, and the policies of your company, you may also wish to send a letter to the employee that outlines the issue and addresses specific points about how you expect performance or behavior to change. The disciplinary warning letter in Sample 20 provides a good framework for developing such a letter. Again, it is always a good idea to have the employee read and sign the letter; place a copy of the letter in the employee's file and provide the employee with a copy.

SAMPLE 19
DISCIPLINARY WARNING NOTICE

Employee _____   Employee no. _____

Department _____   Position _____

Date of warning _____

Date of violation _____   Time of violation _____

Nature of violation

- ○ Lateness   ○ Safety
- ○ Conduct   ○ Substandard work
- ○ Absence   ○ Housekeeping
- ○ Disobedience ○ Others _____
- ○ Carelessness ○ Safety

This is your ○ first ○ second warning.
Subsequent violations may lead to immediate dismissal.

Remarks

_____
_____
_____

Action taken

_____
_____

Warned by _____   Supervisor _____

I have read and understood the nature of this warning. I have made my comments on the back of this form.

Employee's signature _____   Date _____

SAMPLE 20
DISCIPLINARY WARNING LETTER

Dear Paul Harris:

Re: Job performance

This letter is to draw your attention to certain unsatisfactory aspects of your current job performance, namely your three unexcused absences during the past month.

In order to improve your performance, I suggest that you call in no later than one-half hour after your scheduled start time and have no more than one non-medically related absences during the next 30-day period.

I will assist you in any reasonable way to meet the comany's requirements. However, further violations may result in immediate dismissal. If your job performance does not significally improve by 4/30/-, I will have no alternative but to terminate your employment for cause.

Yours truly,

I have read and understood the nature of this warning. I have made my comments on the back of this letter.

Employee's signature _____   Date _____

d. Disciplinary Procedures

The section of the employee handbook that covers company rules and the violations that might lead to disciplinary action or termination is a tricky area. While you want to let employees know what actions will not be tolerated, you can't possibly hope to cover all of the various infractions that might be cause for discipline or dismissal. You might find yourself in legal trouble unless you clearly state the purpose of your regulations in a manner similar to the following:

> *While it is impossible to list all of the rules employees are expected to follow, some of the more serious infractions that will subject you to discipline (up to and including termination) are outlined here. This list is not meant to be all-inclusive. Management reserves the right to terminate employees for any reason, at any time.*

As well, many companies outline in their handbooks the steps they will take when dealing with rule infractions or other disciplinary issues. This is another area where caution should be exercised. By no means do you want to give the impression that you will follow a strict path from verbal warning through written warning to dismissal in every situation. You want to reserve the right to begin disciplinary action at any step you deem applicable (consistent, of course, with company practice and past action). Including the following statement in your handbook can help you avoid problems:

> *It is impossible to outline every situation in which disciplinary measures or termination of the employment relationship will be appropriate. However, if disciplinary action is taken, it is the company's intent that the discipline will serve to correct employee behavior rather than to serve solely as a penalty for a past offense. At the company's sole discretion, various types of employee discipline may be imposed that include, but are not limited to, the following: informal warning, counseling, verbal reprimand, written warning, or suspension. None of these disciplinary measures is required to be used before termination from employment occurs, nor are the listed actions required to be used in any specific order.*

e. Separation Anxiety

You hired "Employee X" with great expectations. The resume was impressive, the interview went extremely well, the employee seemed eager to join your team. It wasn't long after hiring Employee X, though, that problems began to develop, and now you find yourself with a difficult decision to make.

Today many employers are extremely wary about terminating an employee. Horror stories of wrongful termination lawsuits can make you reluctant to move forward with termination. But as difficult as it may seem to dismiss an employee, it is not impossible. You do have the right to staff your company with employees who are good performers, and you should not feel obligated to retain someone who is a poor performer out of fear of retribution.

On the other hand, the decision to terminate should be, and can be, a last resort. Following are some guidelines to help you identify, monitor, and, if necessary, take steps to deal with a poor performer.

1. What you should know about employment-at-will

In the United States, most states govern employment relationships by what is known as "employment-at-will." What this means is that both employer and employee are free to end the employment relationship at any time and for any reason — with three important exceptions that affect the employer. These exceptions have developed over time based on decisions by the federal and state governments and the outcome of various court cases. These exceptions are important because they are the issues around which wrongful termination lawsuits revolve. They are:

(a) *Implied contract.* An example of an implied contract might be a personnel policy that says that all employees will be issued a written warning before a termination decision is made. This type of statement might limit your ability to fire an employee for gross insubordination, for instance, without first issuing a written warning. Another example of an implied contract is statements referring to "permanent" employment status. These statements have proven to be troublesome in some court cases and should be avoided in hiring, communication with employees, and certainly in any policy manuals or documents.

(b) *Public policy.* A termination may violate the public policy limitation if it infringes on the rights of the employee as granted by federal or state law, or if it is considered morally or ethically wrong. For instance, firing an employee for threatening to report wrongful activities by your company, or firing an employee because his or her religious beliefs are inconsistent those of with other employees.

(c) *Bad faith.* A bad faith termination could involve a situation where an employee is terminated shortly before becoming eligible for retirement benefits. Or it could be a situation where one employee was fired for a certain behavior or action, while other employees who had done the same thing were not disciplined or dismissed.

These exceptions are considered illegal cause for dismissal. To avoid potential legal liability, you should carefully consider any termination decision to ensure that it does not violate one of these limitations.

Employment-at-will is not a legal concept in Canada. However, all Canadian jurisdictions have legislation requiring an employer to give notice to the individual worker whose employment is to be terminated. In addition, the Parliament of Canada, British Columbia, Manitoba, New Brunswick, Newfoundland, Nova Scotia, Ontario, Quebec, the Yukon, and the Northwest Territories require an employer to give advance notice of a projected large-scale layoff to a group of employees.

2. Nip it in the bud!

Suppose you happen to be walking by one day and notice your telephone operator letting the phone ring while he is speaking with another employee. "It's the first time I've noticed this," you think. "I'll just let it go for now."

Bad move! The reason that small, correctable problems become big ones is that many employers avoid addressing the little things before they become big ones. What you should do in a situation like this is nip it in the bud — privately, firmly, and effectively. In this case, ask to speak to the employee privately and say, "I just heard the phone ring several times while you were talking to a coworker. That is unacceptable. As we've discussed, I expect the phone to be answered within two rings."

3. Document, document, document!

One of the most pervasive problems that employers have with termination decisions is that they can point to no evidence of documented performance problems. Hesitant to address these issues, they too often provide employees with glowing performance appraisals and document only positive performance outcomes. As you might imagine, this can lead to major problems when an employee (and his or her lawyer!) questions the decision and you are unable to point to any objective, documented evidence supporting it.

Be meticulous in your documentation. When a performance-related incident occurs, record the date it happened, what specifically occurred that was in violation of expected performance outcomes or company policy, and the interaction you had with the employee. This last part is critical. It is not enough simply to document these behaviors. You must also make sure that you inform the employee that an infraction has occurred and clearly indicate what will happen if future occurrences take place.

It can be difficult to admit that you have "failed" with an employee and it is time to terminate the relationship. But acting sooner, rather than later, can be best for all concerned.

Documentation is an important step when handling any employee infraction. Always document the incident in the employee's file and provide a copy to the employee.

4.   Coaching and follow-up

Your goal in dealing with negative employee performance is not to speed quickly toward a termination decision. Your goal is to maintain a productive and effective employee. In providing the employee with information about behaviors or actions that are inconsistent with policy or expectations, you should also provide coaching and assistance in improving employee behavior. Perhaps more training is required. Perhaps the tools available to the employee are insufficient to perform the job effectively. Remember, your goal is to develop positive performers — not to sever the relationship. A termination decision should only be made after all other avenues have been carefully explored.

5.   When the inevitable is unavoidable

Nobody wants to be placed in the position of having to terminate an employee; both because it is unpleasant to have such a negative effect on an individual's life and because of the fear of legal reprisal. How do you protect yourself from a wrongful discharge suit? There are three important steps you can take to limit your liability:

(a) Don't make any implied guarantees of employment. Even a reference to a probationary period can create problems for you later if an employee's performance does not meet expectations. Similarly, references to "permanent employee" can be troublesome and may imply an employment contract.

(b) Be clear about your expectations and performance requirements. When you hire a new employee, be specific about the requirements of the position.

(c) Provide specific, timely feedback — and document it!

Far too many employers run into problems simply because they have avoided dealing with sticky situations. Sugarcoated employee evaluations, designed to avoid conflict, can create problems for you later. If an employee is not meeting expectations, provide feedback immediately, along with information on how the employee can improve performance and what will happen if performance does not improve. Document all of these interactions.

If a termination decision becomes necessary, clearly explain your reason for termination, relating back to the performance expectations and the requirements you have previously communicated. Follow these steps:

(a) Within the first few minutes of the interview, tell the person that the decision to terminate has been made.

(b) Present the facts. Don't gloss over the real problem or give a phony excuse for termination.

(c) Empathize with the employee, but remain firm.

(d) Allow the person an opportunity to vent.

(e) Try to make the situation as painless as possible for the employee — focus on performance not personality.

And, as when hiring, remember that your decisions should always be based on the knowledge, skills, and abilities necessary to perform the job. Those are the only defensible considerations.

Sometimes termination is inevitable. You know it, and if you have been doing your job in addressing performance issues directly with the employee, the employee knows it too. When the inevitable is unavoidable, don't delay. If you have issued a final warning, let it be the final warning. Don't vacillate. Don't change your mind. Don't be inconsistent with actions you have taken with other employees.

Do, however, allow the employee to maintain his or her dignity. Focus on objective work behaviors that you can clearly tie to stated expectations and policy. Meet privately with the employee in a place that allows that employee to leave, after your meeting, with the least amount of potential for interaction with others. Be direct. Be firm. Refer back to prior, documented discussions.

Listen to what the employee may have to say, but avoid getting into a debate. The decision has been made. It is based on documented performance problems that you and the employee have discussed.

Finally, be clear about what will happen next. When will the dismissal be effective? Is there a severance package? What about insurance benefits? Will you provide a reference? How can the employee receive his or her final paycheck? When will the employee be able to remove his or her personal belongings from the office?

Employees have certain rights that you need to be aware of. But employers have rights too — you have the right to employ individuals who meet your performance requirements and effectively represent your company. To preserve that right be certain that you—

(a) understand the implications of exceptions to employment-at-will,

(b) clearly convey the requirements of the job,

(c) immediately address poor performance issues,

(d) document all performance-related discussions, and

(e) when a termination is inevitable, treat each employee fairly and respectfully.

You can use the dismissal letter in Sample 21 as a framework for preparing a formal notice of termination. This is the final step in your process of documenting the performance issues that have led to this point. The letter confirms the termination of employment and outlines severance and benefit issues.

SAMPLE 21
DISMISSAL LETTER

Dear Paul Harris:

Re: Termination of employment

I regret to inform you that your employment with XYZ Company will be terminated effective _____ for the following reason(s): multiple unexcused absences from work.

Your severance package will be administered according to company policy, and you will receive a statement detailing accrued benefits. Please also refer to the policies outlined in the company personnel manual covering applicable insurance benefits.

Jan Black is available to discuss with you these details as well as any other questions or concerns you may have. Please contact him/her at your earliest convenience, and he/she will arrange termination matters with you.

I sincerely regret that his action is necessary, and wish you success in your future employment endeavors.

Yours truly,

cc: _____[person named above as liaison]

_____Personnel Department

Since terminations are, hopefully, not something you will need to deal with on a regular basis, it may be helpful to use a checklist to ensure that you have dealt appropriately with key issues. Checklist 4, the Termination Action Checklist, covers pre-termination concerns, notification issues, the discussion with the employee, and the termination itself. It serves as a handy reminder — and documentation — for the termination process.

f. When You Don't Want Them to Go

Losing your best people can be devastating — to productivity, to morale, and to your own peace of mind. Even losing your marginal employees disrupts the operations of your business and means you must spend hours searching for and training a replacement.

Face it. In today's tight job market, nobody likes to hear an employee say, "I'm giving my two weeks' notice." And while many managers look upon those last two weeks as a challenge and a potentially negative experience, others find that an employee's notice presents just another opportunity to build those all-important relationships that serve to strengthen the business over time.

If your relationship with the employee is a good one, and he or she has agreed to stay on for a period of time (usually two weeks), you should make the most of the time you have available. First, work on an exit plan. Go over any unfinished projects with the employee. Ask the employee to develop or update procedures on important job tasks. Identify another employee who can take over some of the job responsibilities on a temporary basis until a replacement can be found.

It is also important for you to communicate with the remaining staff members. This should be done as soon as possible. Allow the departing employee an opportunity to share the news first, but then make sure that you update other employees at appropriate times — i.e., staff meetings. Be positive about the transition. Talk about the opportunity the employee is moving into and indicate that the employee will be missed.

Of course, how you handle the departure of an employee depends a lot on the reason for leaving. If the employee has taken another job because he or she felt mistreated or because he or she did not get a promotion or raise, you may not be able to expect high performance during the two-week notice period. If, on the other hand, this is simply an opportunity that was unavailable at your company, it is probably reasonable to expect high performance.

Ultimately, you want the transition to be as smooth and stress-free as possible — for everyone involved. Here are some strategies for making the last two weeks of an employee's tenure with your company a positive experience:

Make the last days of an employee's relationship with your company as positive as possible. You never know when your paths may cross again!

CHECKLIST 4
TERMINATION ACTION CHECKLIST

Pre-termination concerns

- ○ Issue appropriate warning notices
- ○ Apply progressive discipline
- ○ Allow employee the opportunity to correct performance
- ○ Consider mitigating factors
- ○ Consider overall record (length and quality of service)
- ○ Conduct an objective review

Notification

- ○ Obtain management approval
- ○ Send termination letter
- ○ Inform personnel department
- ○ Inform payroll
- ○ Include copies of all termination documents in employee's personal life

Discussion with employee

Ensure that the employee understands each of these areas of concerns and how it applies to him or her.

- ○ Severance package
- ○ Benefits package(s)
- ○ Trade secrets and patents
- ○ Confidentiality
- ○ Renewal of company documents
- ○ Employment with competitors
- ○ Reference policy

Termination

- ○ Inform other staff
- ○ Recover company property
  - ○ Office keys
  - ○ ID card
  - ○ Uniform
  - ○ Company documents and all copies
  - ○ Computer disks
  - ○ Computer books
  - ○ Safety equipment
  - ○ Tools
  - ○ Company vehicle
  - ○ Company vehicle keys
  - ○ Company credit card
- ○ Deliver Record of Employment form (available at government offices)
- ○ Deliver final paycheck
- ○ Conduct exit review

➤ Find out why the employee is leaving. Is there anything you might have done to retain him or her?

➤ Find out where he or she is going. First for administrative reasons — you may need to send information to the employee after he or she has left your company. But there is another good reason for asking this question: you may find that the employee is going to work for one of your competitors.

➤ Find out what the employee is currently working on and the status of those projects.

➤ Find out if the employee's job description is up-to-date.

➤ Get the employee's commitment to work at a high performance level for the next two weeks.

➤ Assign somebody to serve as the departing employee's buddy during this time period to make sure that any undone work doesn't fall through the cracks.

➤ Communicate with any customers — internal or external — who may need to know about the employee's departure.

➤ During the last few days, make sure all expense reports are filled out and any company property like credit cards or keys have been turned in.

Not every situation is a positive one, of course. In these cases there is nothing wrong with asking an employee to leave immediately upon giving notice, or to ask an employee to leave during the two-week notice period if necessary. Be watchful for signs of increased gossiping or spreading pessimism around. If you see an increase in these behaviors, pull the employee aside and have a conversation. If necessary, terminate the relationship immediately.

If the employee represents a potential security risk, you may want to take additional steps like cutting off passwords and access to funds, reducing access to computer files, and so on. Again, either for reasons of security or productivity, you may decide that you do not want this employee to remain on the job for the two-week notice period.

However, you never know when or how you may interact with a departing employee in the future — as a customer, as someone who influences other potential customers or employees, or as a future employee. If it is possible, maintaining a positive relationship can benefit everyone.

An exit interview can be a great way to end the employment relationship on a positive note and to gather valuable information from the departing employee.

g. Exit Interviews

The exit interview is one tool that many companies use to monitor turnover. Whether an employee is leaving voluntarily or involuntarily, the exit interview is a wonderful way to determine how you can do things differently with your current and your new employees. There are two functions to an exit interview:

(a) To process the terminated employee in an orderly way. You will need to take care of such housekeeping duties as severance pay, insurance premiums, pensions, and references.

(b) To understand the employee's reasons for leaving in the case of a voluntary termination.

1. Interviewing the involuntarily terminated employee

Even if you are the one who is doing the terminating, it is a good idea to conduct an exit interview. You will be able to explore the employee's perceptions of why he or she is being let go — sometimes these differ radically from your actual reasons.

The exit interview can help you determine how you may have contributed to the dismissal through any number of means, including poor communication, lack of proper training, or inaccessibility.

An exit interview with an involuntarily terminated employee can also offer you the opportunity to clarify the employee's rights of appeal, and to head off or gauge the potential for a future wrongful discharge action. You also have the opportunity to allay any strong negative feelings that the terminated employee may pass along to employees who remain with your company.

Your role with the involuntarily terminated employee is not to condemn or approve of any specific actions on the part of that employee. Rather you should be listening with an open mind and expressing empathy and understanding. While employee termination can never become a pleasant experience, it can be a constructive event — if handled properly (See section **e.5.**). Some of the questions you may want to explore include:

➤ What is your perception of the termination decision?

➤ In what ways do you feel that the company and I may have let you down during your course of employment?

➤ What do you think we could do differently in the future to avoid the problems you had?

Be aware that some employees may not be totally forthcoming with you in the exit interview — others may have an axe to grind.

It is possible that the employee will not want to answer any of your questions. It is also possible that the employee's state of mind during this type of interview may not be conducive to carrying on a mature discussion. This is why many companies provide employees with a written questionnaire that they are asked to take with them and return in a week or so after they have had time to think about the decision. Even then, you may never receive a response.

2. Conducting the exit interview

The primary steps you will take with both voluntary and involuntary terminations are:

(a) Put the employee at ease

(b) Explain the purpose of the meeting

(c) Question the employee

(d) Close the interview

As you can see, these are the same steps you would follow during a meeting with job applicants. To ask effective questions during the exit interview, it is important to keep the following points in mind:

(a) *Know what you want to know.* Don't go into an exit interview without preparing. Before meeting with the employee, you should know the direction you want to take and the information you would like to receive.

(b) *Have a plan of action.* If you haphazardly jump from one area of questioning to another, you will not only confuse and irritate the employee you are interviewing, but you are likely to confuse yourself as well. Follow a natural progression of data gathering. The important thing is that the interview proceeds smoothly from one area to another.

(c) *Don't ask unnecessary questions.* Whether an employee or the company has made the termination decision, it is important that the interview be brief. In both instances the employee may be uncomfortable and will want to finish the interview as quickly as possible. That is why it is important that you ask only those questions which are pertinent to you and the company.

(d) *Maintain control.* You don't have to be rude or abrupt to keep the interview on track. You are in the position of controlling the interview, and employees will expect you to provide them with some indication of when they have answered a question to your satisfaction. Don't be too timid to interrupt when an employee strays off on a tangent.

(e) *Ask open-ended questions.* Some types of questions will allow you to gather more information than others. You will want to ask a lot of open-ended questions to get the particular information you need.

(f) *Anticipate sensitive areas.* Establish a climate of trust and mutual respect so you will be able to effectively ask any necessary sensitive questions. Such questions often begin with a qualifying statement. For example, "It is not uncommon for employees to have things that they dislike about their jobs. What are some of the things you didn't like about your position here?" It is important that you let employees know that they can talk freely about sensitive areas. This is the only way you will get the level of information you need.

(g) *Close by tying up loose ends.* After you gather the information you need, it is time to close the interview. At this time you will want to tie up any loose ends, allow for questions from the employee, and establish a system for follow-up, if necessary. The exit interview is a stress-filled process — for both the employee and the manager — and it is possible that you neglected to obtain some important information. Now is the time to get that information. Review your notes and take a few moments to recap the interview with the employee to make sure you have covered all the pertinent information and gathered the responses you need. This is also the appropriate time to allow the employee an opportunity to ask any questions he or she might have. Some things the employee feels are relevant may not have been covered. By allowing the employee to ask questions, you may receive important additional information.

3. The interview from the employee's perspective

It is unfortunate, but true, that you seldom get the information you need during the exit interview. When dealing with an involuntarily terminated employee you will be hearing a great deal of emotional and probably bitter feedback that is colored, quite naturally, by the fact that the employee has been terminated against his or her will. Negative information about you and the company may be overemphasized. This may not be a good measure of how other employees feel, but at the same time it is important that you listen to this information to try to weed out the facts. Don't dismiss the negative information you hear as being sour grapes. Even an overly emotional, bitter employee can provide you with a few grains of knowledge that can help in your future employee relations. But don't accept everything that is said as truth either. When dealing with the involuntarily terminated employee, you will need to do a lot of reading between the lines.

Unfortunately, when dealing with a voluntarily terminated employee you may also find that the truth is somewhat colored. Employees who make a decision to leave a company on their own are often hesitant to deliver any negative information. They don't want to harm their chances of obtaining a good reference and they may want to keep one foot in the door in case the new position doesn't work out.

As an interviewer, you need to be aware of the potential for being "snowed" by employees — for whatever reasons. Don't expect a lot from the employee. Whether voluntary or involuntary, a termination is a traumatic experience and the employee will not be thinking clearly.

The exit interview form in Sample 22 can be useful for gathering information from departing employees. By documenting answers to these questions you may be able to spot trends or discover issues that can be corrected to minimize departures in the future.

Turnover is a factor for any company, and it is never easy to deal with — whether the termination decision is yours or the employee's. By following the steps outlined above you should be able to gather the information you need to keep your best people, to help your marginal people, and to make the inevitable involuntary terminations as painless as possible.

SAMPLE 22
EXIT INTERVIEW

The exit interview is useful for monitoring employee turnover and morale. It allows you to discuss the employee's perceptions of the company, address and reduce negative feelings, and gather information to help you adjust your management practices and company policies. Try to establish a climate of mutual trust and respect. Invite the employees to speak frankly amd honestly, even about sensitive issues (e.g., criticizing management style).

Employee name _____   Employee no. _____

Department _____   Position _____

Date _____

Reasons for termination   ○ Voluntary   ○ Involuntary

1. What did you enjoy the most while working here?

2. What did you find most frustrating?

3. Did you feel that management supported you?

4. Where you given appropriate training? Did you receive adequate supervision?

5. Were you treated fairly? Were your accomplishments acknowledged?

6. Was your salary reasonable and appropriate?

7. Were your working conditions satisfactory?

8. What are the company's strengths?

9. What are the company's weaknesses?

10. What would you have liked to see change at the company?

11. Are there any other areas you'd like to discuss?

Interview _____

Supervisor _____

17

Maintaining a Fully Functioning Work Force

Employee needs are changing, and to be effective, businesses need to change too. Motivating employees in the next millennium will be decidedly different than it was in the 1950s, 60s, 70s, 80s, and 90s. Today's employees are demanding more flexibility, more autonomy, and more recognition of individual differences.

As we move into the 21st century we will continue to see dramatic changes in the work force and its makeup. The baby boomers are aging, but they will continue to have a major impact on many aspects of society — including the workplace. Younger people entering into the workplace are different than those that have gone before them. Greater diversity in terms of race, religion, values, and ethics makes the job of managing a work force increasingly complex.

No two people are the same. No two of your employees are the same. Consequently, no single motivator is going to work with all of your employees. To motivate effectively you need to know your employees. No longer can employers tell their staff to leave their personal lives at home. Today we recognize that an employee's life outside the workplace has an undeniable impact on that person's life at work.

a. Individuals Have Individual Needs

Many aspects of good human resources management may seem basic, and they are. The best way to find out what employees want is to ask them. Their answers will give you the starting point you need to develop some effective ways of improving morale and productivity. Find out what they do in their spare time — both at work and at home. Be aware of what they do during break periods and lunch hours. Do they spend their time relaxing? Socializing? Reading? Working?

In today's diverse workplace climate, it's not enough to develop programs and policies for employees "at large." Consideration of individual employee needs is becoming increasingly important.

Take into account your past experiences with your employees. What have individual employees responded favorably to in the past? What types of projects or assignments really create a high level of productivity? What types of assignments create apathy?

It is a mistake to project your own likes, dislikes, and desires onto employees. To motivate them you need to tailor incentives to their individual needs.

Why do people work? There are many different answers, and chances are you will never get the same one twice. Unfortunately, the expectations that people bring to their jobs rarely equal the job's ability to meet these expectations.

Toni is 18 and saving money for college. Her motivation for working is strictly monetary and she expects little from her job as a shipping clerk.

Kevin, at 35, has worked hard to achieve his position as vice-president of marketing for a large firm. The aspect of his position that gives him the most enjoyment is his ability to network with fellow executives, to speak at various conventions, and to build a name for himself in his field of expertise. Kevin's motivation for working is prestige.

Kari has a job as secretary with a new company where the other 15 employees are all in her age range — mid- to late twenties. She plays on the company softball team, helps to organize various employee get-togethers, and spends most of her off-duty hours socializing with coworkers. The motivating factor for Kari is socialization.

The reasons people give for working parallel Maslow's hierarchy of needs: physiological comfort (i.e., good wages), safety (job security), social fulfillment (getting along with coworkers), satisfaction of the ego (receiving praise for work well done), and self-actualization (enjoying the job). But don't be misled into thinking that these reasons are limited to the five elements of this hierarchy. The number of reasons that employees have for working can be as varied as the number of companies there are to work for!

b. The Power of Communication

Whether you employ three people or three thousand, communication between them is the most critical factor in ensuring organizational success. Not new product development. Not financial systems. Not customer service. Communication — internal communication — is the most important factor. Employers are most successful in meeting their business objectives when they can get employees to understand what they are trying to achieve as a company — and when they can get each employee to understand his or her own personal role in the process.

Think of your employees as your front-line contact between the company and its customers. The more your employees know, the better your company grows. Companies cannot always give employees the response that will make them feel better, but they can be forthright and fair. What it takes is aggressive and ongoing communication that is happening in multiple ways. It's not just the employee newsletter. It's not just departmental meetings. It's not just e-mail. It is a combination of these and all of the other myriad ways that organizations have for communicating within and between groups.

How can communication work most effectively? Here are some critical truisms that can help you use communication as a driving force in management:

1. Communication must be tied to organizational objectives

Meaningful corporate communication should be tied to corporate goals. A direct tie to organizational objectives ensures consistent messages and direction throughout the organization and can simplify the communication process.

Effective communication will encourage employees to contribute more to goals based on their improved understanding of them and what they mean to employee well-being. Better communication will help secure wider support for the organization's stand on important national and local issues. Employees will be better prepared to explain the organization's position when in contact with friends, neighbors, and government officials.

2. Communication must address the "why" as well as the "what"

The organization has an opportunity to cultivate employee understanding and support of key organizational initiatives. Even employee reaction to negative changes can be successfully managed if communication extends beyond *what* is being done to include *why* changes are being made and how those changes tie back to organizational objectives.

It is not enough to tell employees what you are doing; they need to understand why. Even the most negative information can be more readily accepted if the reasons behind the decision or change are made clear.

3. Communication is the responsibility of each individual

While there are official communicators in any organization, each individual employee also plays a role and must accept responsibility for effective communication. The responsibility for communication always rests with the individual or group conveying the message.

4. Communication happens

Communication goes on continually, and on a variety of levels, at any organization. Communication happens. It is ongoing and influenced not only by what is said, or by whatever official information is released in printed form, but by what is done and by countless nonverbal cues that employees pick up on every day.

5. Communication is two way

Communication involves listening as well as talking. Feedback mechanisms should be available throughout the organization to ensure that the corporate communicators are receiving input from the audiences they serve.

6. Communication cannot be regulated

Because of the fluid nature of communication, it can be affected but not regulated. Efforts to stem the flow of information will ultimately fail. What can be controlled, however, is the accuracy and timeliness of that information. The goal for an organization is to position its official communicators — generally upper management and the communication department — as reliable sources of timely information. When these players fill this role effectively, there will be a marked reduction in unproductive communication — speculation, gossip, and second guessing.

7. The impact of communication can be measured

When communication is successfully tied to organizational objectives, its effectiveness can be measured both in terms of employee perspectives on how well the organization is communicating and in terms of employee awareness of key corporate issues and objectives.

Providing employees with the opportunity to share feedback and ideas can have a positive impact on your bottom line — and can help to encourage involvement while boosting morale.

c. Harvesting the Gold: How to Get Good Ideas From Your Employees

Companies are saving hundreds of thousands of dollars each year by reaping the value of employee suggestions. Through suggestion systems ranging from the simple to the complex, they are providing employees with the opportunity to come forward with ideas on how to increase opportunities, save money, improve safety, and so on.

More than this, they are devising ways to encourage employees to put their ideas on the line. Could your company benefit from a suggestion system? What are the important elements of such programs? If you have a program, how can you help it work more effectively? If you don't, what are the important elements of such a program?

Companies with suggestion systems have been surprised at how many suggestions they actually receive from employees. They wonder why they didn't receive these ideas before. The answer to that is simple: many people simply need to have an avenue available to them for submitting ideas. Left to their own devices they may keep the ideas to themselves. But given an opportunity, watch out! The ideas are out there. The challenge lies in harvesting those ideas and putting them to use.

1. Elements of a suggestion program

There are a number of elements that are critical to an effectively functioning suggestion system:

(a) Clear guidelines

Employees need guidance to help them channel their ideas productively, and an effective program will establish clear guidelines so employees can do just that. It is particularly important that supervisors understand these guidelines so they can clearly communicate them; they should be able to help employees fine-tune ideas so they meet the guidelines. Here are a few of the issues that need to be addressed in a suggestion system:

➤ What is a valid suggestion? Can employees only submit ideas relative to their specific job or work area? Are suggestions related to known technologies (e.g., a new computer software program) eligible?

➤ Who is eligible to submit a suggestion? All employees may not be eligible for the suggestion program. Should exempt employees be eligible? Upper management? Retirees? Part-time workers? New employees? Union members? Members of the human resources department or suggestion committee?

➤ Is there a form that should be used for submitting ideas? Is the form readily available? What should employees do with it once it is filled out? Are there certain requirements for completion of the form? Spell these conditions out clearly and make sure that all employees understand the guidelines.

(b) Ease of use

Make it as easy as possible for employees to submit suggestions. While you will want each idea to be complete, don't make requirements so stringent that employees are put off by the effort involved. A simple format for submitting suggestions might be the following:

➤ Describe the current situation.

➤ Describe your idea and how it improves the situation.

➤ Briefly outline the resources necessary to implement your idea.

In addition to making the form easy to use, consider how to distribute the form and how the employee should submit it. Employees should have ready access to forms and should be able to easily submit them. Supervisors should also have ready access to these forms to make them available to employees. Supervisors should be well versed in completing the forms and available to help employees who may need some assistance. The supervisor can act as a facilitator in helping employees take advantage of the program.

(c) Quick response

Once an employee makes a suggestion, the response to that suggestion should be timely — regardless of how it is perceived.

Many companies whose suggestion systems have fizzled out point to poor response as the reason. Don't let those ideas sit idle. Get back to the people presenting the ideas as soon as possible. Let them know that you have received the idea and what to expect next. Keep in touch with your employees once they have submitted an idea. Have they received a response? If not, can you intervene to speed up the process? Were they unhappy with the response? Can you, through your knowledge of the program, help to explain why an idea may have been rejected? Or can you arrange a meeting between the employee and the suggestion administrator or committee?"

(d) Fair disposition of each suggestion

Employees want to be treated fairly in all aspects of their work, and suggestions are no exception. If there is a perception that the system is rigged or unfair, it will not work. How do you avoid that perception? Again, it is critical that guidelines are clear — and that those guidelines be followed consistently. Communication is also important. Face-to-face communication can be especially helpful when turning down a suggestion. Make sure that the person submitting the idea understands why it was rejected and leaves willing to try again.

(e) Meaningful rewards

While employees benefit intrinsically when their suggestion is chosen for implementation, they also like to receive more tangible benefits while helping your program grow. Such rewards, however, need to be meaningful. A $10 cash bonus, after taxes, leaves a sour taste in the mouth of an employee who has worked hard to develop and submit an idea.

(f) Promotion

Obviously if employees don't know about the program, they won't be able to use it. Don't just set a system up, generate a memo, and forget about it. Communicating continually is a key to developing a successful system.

Use your internal newsletters as a means to solicit ideas. Encourage your employees to submit ideas to the program, and consider the use of posters and contests to help promote the program.

Even employees whose suggestions are not implemented will feel valued if you make an effort to respond to their ideas quickly and explain why the suggestion is not feasible.

And, most importantly, take advantage of every opportunity to publicize the successes. When an idea is implemented, make sure that everybody knows what that idea was and how it will benefit the company. Often one idea will trigger another, and soon you will see your responses increasing exponentially as employees learn that the system really works.

2. Some problems to watch out for

Suggestion systems often seem deceptively simple to implement. But aside from the inevitable differences of opinion over what constitutes a worthwhile suggestion, who should be eligible for the program, and how much to award for what types of suggestions, there are some additional areas that can cause problems. Here are a few things to watch out for.

(a) We tried it before, and it didn't work

Give equal consideration to all suggestions, even if something has been tried in the past. The business environment is constantly changing. An idea that didn't work yesterday may well work tomorrow.

(b) Give credit where credit is due

Because the business environment changes, one employee may submit an idea that is rejected and then watch a different employee cash in on that same idea six months later. To guard against this problem, many companies keep rejected ideas active for a certain period of time or allow employees to resubmit the idea after a certain amount of elapsed time. Beyond this, however, the best defense may simply be a good offense — take the time to consider each idea and realistically assess it when it is submitted to ensure that an idea won't be tossed aside and then later implemented.

(c) Outrageous ideas

"Give every employee a $10,000 Christmas bonus." "Fire management." "Let employees bring their children to work." Whenever a company solicits employee suggestions, it is bound to get a few suggestions like these. While some are simply submitted to be funny, others are signs of frustration and disillusionment, and supervisors may want to address them individually with the employee.

(d) Financial concerns

We already know that meaningful rewards are important. Therefore, the method for determining awards needs to be clear to employees. If awards are based on a percentage of savings to the company, clearly outline how these savings will be determined. And, again, consistency is critical. Many ideas have intangible rewards — their benefits cannot be easily measured. To address this issue, most companies establish a minimum award for these ideas ranging from $50 to $100. Whatever your system, make sure it is clear to employees.

d. Involvement in Decision Making

Employee involvement was a strategy to keep employees happy. As workers became more demanding, management felt a strong push to provide better working conditions, better benefits, and involve staff more in decision making.

How surprising that once these employees became involved, strange things began to happen. Motivation increased. Productivity increased. There were more new ideas. Innovative techniques, processes, and products were introduced. And, ultimately, the bottom line was fattened.

Managers are realizing that employees are more likely to participate in activities to which they are committed. They are more likely to commit if they are involved in the decision making behind the activity.

There are two important reasons to include employees in decision making:

(a) Reduced resentment over taking orders. Employees don't like being given orders and being allowed no input. The result is reduced morale, poor attitude, and increased turnover.

(b) They know more than you do. When it comes to the day-to-day operation of your business, nobody knows better what will work than the person on the front line.

Is it necessary to involve employees in all decision making? Certainly not. But it can be extremely helpful to involve employees in decisions that will affect them. You may not use every suggestion or respond to every request for change that an employee makes. However, by listening to and involving your employees, you will find that you make better decisions — and have a positive effect on morale and productivity as well.

Could you be doing more to involve employees in decisions? Ask yourself the following questions:

➤ Can we give employees more responsibility for setting schedules, deciding on work methods, and helping to train less experienced employees?

➤ Can we give workers more control over their time — when to stop work, start work, and take breaks?

➤ Can we encourage workers to come up with solutions on their own rather than relying on their supervisors for the answers?

➤ Can we provide employees with more information on the financial implications of their jobs and how they impact the bottom line?

➤ Can we place quality control closer to the employees so they get frequent and immediate feedback on performance?

➤ Can we provide employees with information about their performance and the performance of the company?

➤ Can we allow employees to detect and correct their own mistakes?

e. Maintaining High Employee Morale

Unfortunately, even though employee satisfaction is so important, many companies suffer from low company morale. There are a number of reasons:

➤ Lack of employee involvement in decisions.

➤ Lack of clear direction, adequate goal-setting, and follow-up.

➤ Perceived (or actual) lack of concern about employee well-being.

➤ Lack of adequate employee feedback and reward.

This list goes on and on. What can you do? You can learn to avoid the mistakes that lead to low morale, become adept at spotting warning signs, and develop some positive strategies for keeping morale at an adequate level.

1. The signs of a developing problem

It is easy to tell when morale is bad. But how can you tell when a problem is first developing? There are a number of subtle warning signs that the astute manager can pick up on. "I can usually tell something is wrong when my employees stop talking," says one manager. "Instead of saying 'hello' in the morning, they'll just walk by with their heads down. It's the old silent treatment. Or they'll be short with me when I ask them to do something."

Other signs? Tardiness, long breaks, absenteeism. "When an employee has had a couple of bad days on the job and then calls in sick, I can tell something's up. That's my signal to make sure I catch them as soon as they're back at work for a chat."

It is important that one employee's low morale is arrested before the problem spreads. Low morale can be like the flu. Employees pass it on quickly, and soon the entire department, or company, is affected. If it reaches that point, it can often be difficult to identity the precipitating factor. If morale is low, productivity will be too. You can't afford to have employees on your payroll whose work is lackluster due to bad attitudes.

There is no easy answer to boosting employee morale. It involves constant attention and a lot of simple actions like listening to employees and being available to respond to their needs.

2. Fifteen strategies for boosting employee morale

(a) Listen to what your employees have to say

Employees don't really expect to get what they want all the time. They just need to feel that they are respected and heard. Make sure that you really listen to your employees and their questions, concerns, and ideas. Active listening involves providing nonverbal cues to your employees to show that you are following (e.g., nodding your head, making eye contact); it involves questioning for understanding and clarification, and it involves follow up.

(b) Be available

It may seem like simple advice, but it is key to helping employees feel good about the work they do. Too few managers spend enough time with their employees. Many companies claim they have an open-door policy where employees can feel free at any time to speak with their managers about whatever is on their mind. Unfortunately, the doors are often open only literally — figurative barriers may exist that keep employees from stepping over that threshold. If you profess to have an open-door policy, make sure it is truly open and that employees feel comfortable coming to you. Circulate among your employees frequently to let them know that you are there and that you care about what is going on.

(c) Share information with employees

Employees need to feel in the know. When you share information with employees, you help them feel involved in the company. When they feel involved, morale improves and everyone benefits. Sharing information can be as simple as letting them know when a coworker is leaving the company or when a new hire is coming on board. Or it can be as involved as having regular meetings to discuss the financial status of the company and how individual and group contributions affect that status. Secretiveness can be dangerous to morale. More and more companies are recognizing the benefits of sharing even confidential information with employees.

(d) Give ample recognition for a job well done

Employees like their work better if they derive personal satisfaction from it. That satisfaction can decline if supervisors don't recognize achievements. Let them know about their accomplishments, always keeping in mind that recognition needs to be specific. Specific praise is more effective than a simple "Good job." There are numerous forms of providing recognition. Individual praise, of course, is a primary means of showing that you recognize and appreciate your employees' contributions. But there are other means as well — staff meetings, company newsletters, even news releases sent to local papers and trade journals in your industry. All of these means are at your disposal and are extremely effective in maintaining a high level of morale among your employees.

(e) Provide opportunities for personal growth

Today's employees want more from a job than a paycheck. They want to grow professionally and personally in their jobs. What are your employees interested in? What are their goals? If you don't know, find out. Then consider options that can help them meet their goals. There are a number of ways you can help, including the following:

➤ Allow employees to join professional organizations related to their current job or a job they are interested in.

➤ Send employees to courses to enhance their skills or help them develop additional skills.

➤ Work with employees on career advancement within the company.

➤ Recommend that employees be included on task forces and committees for projects they are interested in.

All these things can help employees personally and professionally and will give them a greater sense of achievement and involvement in their jobs.

(f) Treat employees as individuals

You will rarely find two employees with the same skills or personal objectives. One employee may react favorably to the opportunity to chair a committee, while another may balk at what he or she views as an unnecessary added responsibility. One may consider extra time off as a great way to be recognized for a job well done; another may feel that time off is a punishment. Again, it is important to take the time to know your employees and to understand their goals and objectives. You can't choose one means of motivating employees and think it will work with everyone. It won't.

(g) Give constructive criticism

Some managers avoid criticizing employees, particularly when morale is already low, because they don't want to make things worse. Surprisingly enough, most employees value criticism — if it is constructive. Employees want to do a good job. If their managers fail to tell them when things are not quite right, however, they will continue to perform as they have been doing, completely unaware that they are not doing good work. Constructive criticism focuses on the task. When you feel that an employee is not doing something well, approach that person immediately. First give them feedback on what you like about their work, then share with them your thoughts on how they can improve in the future. Never ignore problems in the hope that they will go away. They won't. They will simply get worse.

(h) Take a break occasionally

All work and no play can make all of us dull. When employees have been working nonstop for a period of time, they need and appreciate a little time off. Gather your staff together for a special breakfast or lunch to recognize their achievements. Suggest a brief get-together after work, or simply spend some time shooting the breeze. These are all wonderful ways to show your appreciation and maintain a high level of productivity at the same time. The next time a major project comes up, employees will be even more willing to give their all because they will know how much it is appreciated.

(i) Allow opportunities for increased responsibility

Employees can burn out doing the same things day after day. Particularly for your best employees, added responsibility can serve as a prime motivator and morale booster. By giving employees additional responsibility, you are not only providing them with what is probably a much-needed challenge, you are also demonstrating your confidence in their abilities.

(j) Involve employees in goal setting

Everybody wants to feel they have control over their lives. By involving employees in setting their own goals you enlist their support and commitment. You are happy because goals are more likely to be met. They are happy because they are shaping their future on the job. When organizational or departmental goals are unclear, motivation decreases. It is important for you to work with your employees and your superiors to set goals. Once goals are set, you can work together to meet those goals.

(k) Be open to new ideas

Employee input is critical to a company's success. Never jump on an employee's idea, however ludicrous it may seem. An employee will never come to you with an idea again if you react this way. Instead, listen carefully to the idea, thank the employee for his or her input, promise to consider the idea, and then report back to the employee about what you have decided. And if you do decide to use the idea, always give credit to the employee who made the suggestion.

(l) Don't play favorites

Employees quickly detect when a manager favors one of their peers. And once detected, that favoritism can create all kinds of bad feelings — between you

> Take time to celebrate successes and to make the workplace an enjoyable place to be. Employees that play together, stay together.

and your employees and between your employees and the favorite. Be cautious in all of your dealings with employees and treat everyone equally.

(m) Be honest

Don't make promises you can't keep, whether the promise is as simple as agreeing to give a day off or something much more important like agreeing to a bigger raise.

(n) Be motivated yourself

Nothing can bring down a work group faster than a manager or business owner whose attitude is bad. If you are having trouble maintaining your level of motivation on the job, do your best to keep your feelings from employees while you get yourself back on track.

(o) Never become comfortable with the status quo

Even if you have never had morale problems, don't become complacent once you have developed a smoothly operating work force. You need to pay constant attention to the mood of your staff and anticipate problems. A highly motivated work group can turn into a grumbling group of frustrated staffers quickly.

Gone are the days — if they ever existed — when employees were a dime a dozen and an eager new employee was always waiting in the wings to take over for someone who was departing. A tight labor market has made it painfully obvious to most employers that a good employee is hard to find — and even harder to keep. Taking the time to make a careful selection decision is, of course, critical to building a productive work force. But that is just the beginning.

Every day you are presented with opportunities to strengthen and reinforce the bond between your business and your human resources. Choose well. Train well. Motivate well. Give the same careful consideration to your human resources decisions and actions as you do to any other aspect of operating your business. The people you employ have a dramatic impact on your product, your customers and, inevitably, on your bottom line.

OTHER TITLES IN THE SELF-COUNSEL SERIES

Human Resources Forms and Disks
$7.95 each

Whether your business has one or 100 employees, it is essential that, as an employer, you take a positive and active approach to maintaining an effective and workable human resources plan.

Available in separate packages to address individual needs, the new Human Resources Forms and Disks Series provides a complete set of forms that can be copied and adapted for use in every business, large or small. In addition to the forms, the material is also included on a 3 ½" computer disk that is compatible with any PC word-processing program.

- Employee Selection Package
- Employee Hiring Package
- Ongoing Reports Package
- Performance Appraisal Package
- Employee Termination Package

Ready-to-Use Business Forms
$10.95 USA / $13.95 CDA

This handy book of tear-out forms is just what your small business needs to help you keep up with daily record-keeping and routine tasks, giving you more time to do business. It includes dozens of basic forms that every small business needs for its day-to-day operations, plus special poster forms and artwork for announcements and publicity purposes.

The book contains personnel, sales and marketing, bookkeeping, budget, memo, telephone, credit, message, inventory, and requisition forms.

Financial Freedom on $5 A Day

Chuck Chakrapani

$12.95

Even if you know nothing about investing, this book will show you how to achieve financial freedom starting with very little money, explaining investment strategies that most people think are only for the rich. Not a get-rich-quick manual for the dreamer, this step-by-step guide provides a comprehensive plan for long-term rewards. An excellent starting point for the novice investor, it includes hints on:

- Saving money painlessly

- Dealing with stocks

- International investing

- Keeping yourself informed about current developments

- Building a balanced portfolio

ORDER FORM

All prices are subject to change without notice. Books are available in book, department, and stationery stores. If you cannot buy the book through a store, please use this order form.

(Please print)

Name_____

Address _____

Charge to: ❏ Visa   ❏ MasterCard

Account number_____

Validation date _____

Expiry date _____

Signature_____

Shipping and handling charges will apply.
In Canada, 7% GST will be added.
In Washington, 7.8% sales tax will be added.

YES, please send me:

_____ *Human Resources Forms and Disks*

_____ *Ready-to-Use Business Forms*

_____ *Financial Freedom on $5 A Day*

❏ Check here for a free catalogue

IN THE USA
Please send your order to:
Self-Counsel Press Inc.
1704 N. State Street
Bellingham, WA 98225

IN CANADA
Please send your order to the nearest location:
Self-Counsel Press
1481 Charlotte Road
North Vancouver, BC V7J 1H1

Self-Counsel Press
4 Bram Court
Brampton, ON L6W 3R6

Visit our Web site at: www.self-counsel.com